Prairie Schooner
DETOURS

BY

IRENE D. PADEN

917.8
P

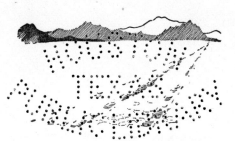

THE MACMILLAN COMPANY

New York

1949

First Printing

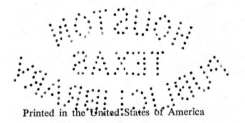

To the memory of my mother and father,
Rene and Wilbur Dakin, whose enthusiasm
for our trail work and practical
help with research never
faltered as long as
they lived.

Introduction

THIS is a firsthand description of two so-called "short cuts" traveled by the prairie schooners of our pioneer grandfathers on their way to the gold mines of California. They are Lassen's Cutoff and Hastings' Cutoff, the latter made famous by the venturesome Donner Party. Both of them took longer to travel and were more productive of thrills and adventure than the regular Overland Trail from the Missouri River across the plains to the diggings. The volume tells what happened on the cutoffs, how they appeared to the Forty-niners, what they look like today, and how they may be found.

The centennial year of the gold rush is an appropriate time to present these little-known facts to the public, for both short cuts carried hordes of gold seekers. Lassen's Road in particular was credited with dumping a large proportion of the Overland Forty-niners, shivering and down to their last ship's biscuit, into the Sacramento Valley more than one hundred miles above Sacramento, the customary supply base.

The research, both "armchair" and in the field, of which this book is the result, has taken my husband and myself over fifteen years. We have, we think, studied every available journal of travel written by the aforementioned gold seekers and examined every map of that period to which we have had access. We actually have found and traveled the old roads, carrying photostatic copies of both diaries and maps for comparison.

Every few years another journal is found in someone's attic, and then we quickly read to see if one of our pet theories has been exploded. At first this happened now and then, but it has not for some time now. We feel reasonably sure that the erratic stories of what happened on those romantic old roads have at long last been shaken down into facts. Not much else has survived the test of the years. Every person, gold seeker or only fact seeker, mentioned in this volume is real; every incident occurred. William G. Paden, who plans

William G. Paden, who plans and carries through our expeditions, is my more or less patient husband. We live in Alameda, California. Dr. Clarence W. Neff and Charles R. Bromley, who accompany us on most of our field-work, are of the same city, Dr. Neff having recently returned from long residence in San Diego.

Together we have followed the course of the old Oregon-California Trail, tracking down and mapping the forgotten portions in an attempt to bring them back to the consciousness of the neighboring farmers and the public in general. None too soon, as it happens, for the rapid changes of this decade are gradually obliterating miles of the faint trace left by the columns of covered wagons that carried to the West the greatest migration in the known history of the world— the greatest, that is, except the westward movement in the midst of which we are now living, just a century later.

In recording our trail findings, I have changed their time sequence sometimes in order to present a continuous line of travel from east to west. In fact, the geographic sequence is the only one which it is possible to maintain in such a travelogue. Any required section of either short cut may be found by comparing the text with the maps.

My husband's interest in our project is entirely geographical. He finds the lost portion of trail in question and that is all he cares about. My interest is exceedingly fuddy-duddy. I run along with a notebook and camera and record the findings. Dr. Neff keeps us in order and says: "Are you sure? What makes you think so?" every so often. He wants not only his facts but his suppositions steel-ribbed, copper-bottomed, and doubly reinforced. Mr. Bromley likes the inaccessible places where we so often find ourselves and where he can obtain out-of-the-ordinary colored pictures and rock specimens.

Between trips I do library research at home. "At home" is a euphemism. The libraries are actually in Sacramento, San Francisco, Berkeley, San Marino, and other cities. Of course most of these pleasant places are in California, but that doesn't mean that I can dash home for dinner. I read the daily diaries of pioneers who wrote them in jouncing wagons or beside the boiling bean pot; journals that show the smudge of wind-blown sand or a little soiled spot where the writer poked another jagged branch of sage into the fire and brought back a telltale fleck of soot; little notebooks whose plain-spoken writers never dreamed that someday they would be kept in fireproof vaults.

I also read letters written on the trail and given to some returning fur trader to mail when he should reach the Missouri River, which then marked the beginning of civilization. I read reminiscences written by these same pioneers when they became older and had more time to write. From all this invaluable source material I doggedly take reams of notes. When I get home (really at home, this time), all these accounts are screened for each new fact to be added to my growing mass of data.

At the end of the first nine years so much had accumulated that it was only occasionally I could bob up for air, and so I got rid of the bulk of it by writing a book, *The Wake of the Prairie Schooner*, that deals with the main Overland Trail traveled by the emigrants in crossing the plains, tells how to find it, and what were the outstanding happenings at each prominent landmark.

But a book necessarily has limitations. Although mine gave practically a blow-by-blow account of the Indian fights and kept what amounted to a fever chart of the cholera epidemics, the reader's interest remained centered (or I hope it did) upon the main trail to Oregon and to California. This concentration was not true of the gold rushers of 1849 and 1850. Main trails were to be endured if nothing better offered, but what each wagon master prayed for was a miraculous piece of road—grassy, level, and shorter than the one by which everyone else was plodding along; something that would cut distance from the two thousand miles of difficult, zigzag trail and bring him in ahead of the hundreds of teams that burned all the fuel and ate all the grass just ahead of him. By a process of wishful thinking, hundreds of the Forty-niners hoped to find truth in any optimistic misinformation which came by grapevine along the moving column of wagons and pack animals; and they turned away from the safety of a known route to travel with earnest pertinacity upon any set of wheel tracks rumored to be shorter or easier or more prolific of grass. These ill advised variants, miscalled "short cuts," were of the utmost importance in the history of the emigrant trail and of California; Lassen's and Hastings' cutoffs were of far more interest than most of the regular trail. The fact that lack of space prohibited their inclusion in *The Wake of the Prairie Schooner* is the *raison d'être* of this book. Although they might well have taken their place in that volume, they equally well can stand alone, for they are more extreme in every way; they are much stronger fare.

CONTENTS

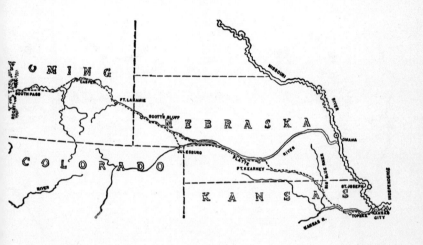

CHAPTER 1

At Both Ends of a Century

WE had been riding since early morning and were getting tired. I gave an absent-minded hitch back into my corner and dislodged a camera from the slick plastic seat cover where it had lain unnoticed between Dr. Neff and me. It ricocheted from his shoe and he retrieved it with mild displeasure.

"It didn't hurt the *camera* any," he reassured me with properly placed emphasis, putting it firmly in the box where it should have been. "But my feet are too cold for such treatment."

"It seems to me that it usually is cold when we cross Green River Desert," observed my husband from the driver's seat; "but that's because we go east about the first of July. It will be hot enough in August."

"Well, we won't be here to see it this year," I remarked with selfish satisfaction. "I like my Wyoming sagebrush cool, while Dr. Neff likes it hot."

The fourth passenger in the big car spoke impartially. "It's all fun for me. I've never made this run south to Fort Bridger." He crossed one long leg over the other and looked with interest at the high-slung plateau peopled by fat prairie dogs sitting bolt upright by their holes.

We were scudding southward, paralleling Green River on the right bank. The great sluicelike stream was not in flood; it was cold, and apparently the snows were holding well in the Rockies. We had our course charted, complete with soundings, and intended to start our field study of Hastings' Cutoff at its logical beginning, Fort Bridger, and to work west from there. But, to get into the spirit of the thing and to obtain the proper background, we were traveling to the fort, as did the first prairie schooner pioneers along the old Oregon Trail, by coming down from South Pass of the Rocky Mountains and crossing Green River Desert.

1

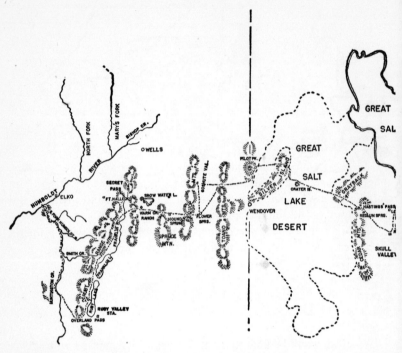

This high, treeless country of crisp distances was an old story to Dr. Neff, my husband, and myself, but new in most of its phases to Mr. Bromley, who had traveled only the better known highways to the Atlantic Coast and had never before been with us on an emigrant trail field trip east of Nevada.

The car purred along comfortably. All our equipment was ready. Extracts from diaries written by the pioneers while traveling this same route were in order so that, as we rode, we couldn't fail to recognize the landmarks they described. Every map of the section we had ever owned was palpably present between the back of my head and the rear window and rattled pleasantly against my ear.

There was nothing more for me to do until we should reach Fort Bridger. Nothing but to remember those first travelers whose steady, slow-stepping oxen had preceded us by just one hundred years, moving ahead in a day the distance we put behind us easily in twenty minutes, but heading inexorably for the same destination. With them, as with us, everything but the actual routine of living was held in

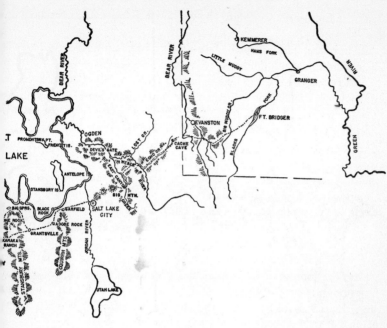

abeyance until the fort should be reached—the fort where each company captain was to settle the vital question (truly a matter of life and death) as to whether his wagons would remain with the known and reasonably safe Oregon-California Trail, or respond to the urging of an unknown man, Lansford Hastings, who had sent an open letter along the line of wagons asking that they allow him to guide them toward California by a new and shorter route.

Nothing to do but to visualize the prairie schooner pioneers of 1846 as they moved west across the Great Divide—on to their momentous decision.

And this is the way it all happened.

    *   *   *

It was storming in the South Pass.

The migration of 1846, which had curved rainbow-like over the Rockies for days, containing some two thousand people and extending three hundred miles, had almost completed the arc. The last wagons were slipping over the summit.

At the foot of the westward slope stood a little indomitable woman. She was angry.

On her right hand, near the free-flowing Big Sandy River, a sprawling encampment of mud-covered prairie schooners made ready to take the nearest road to California and Oregon—the one later to be known as Sublette's (or sometimes Greenwood's) Cutoff. She wanted to continue with those wagons and with her neighbors of the road. She felt deeply that safety lay in remaining together.

On her left hand, her own menfolk "catched up" the oxen and turned the noses of the patient beasts southwest toward Fort Bridger, where, if present symptoms continued, they would allow themselves to be persuaded to venture upon Hastings' new short cut to California. It was the common gossip of the camps. For a week they had talked of little else. The open letter that had come to the captains of the various wagon trains was carried by a lone rider, Bonney, traveling east, and stated that the California government was preparing to oppose the ingress of the American emigrants. It also suggested that those bound for California should concentrate their numbers and strength and travel by a new and shorter route explored and recommended by the aforementioned Mr. Hastings.

The Donner Party was not the only company on its way to the fort to talk over the proposition. A wagon train captained by George Harlan; Samuel C. Young, with his wagons; and a pack-mule train jointly led by Edwin Bryant and William Russell were all willing to try the new road.

These completed their preparations and broke camp, the pack train in the lead; but it was small comfort to Tamsen. Too many already had left them. More would leave them at the fort.

Steadfastly the Donners said their good-bys to J. Quinn Thornton who, three years later, was to be their posthumous biographer, and the two companies started off on the arms of an acute angle. Tamsen Donner, still a little angry and greatly heartsick, went with her husband. As long as life lasted, she would never do anything else.

For a while the diverging caravans lay tweezer-like across the sage spread plateau of Green River Desert. Then they lost their contact. The companies that intended to cross this difficult portion of the trail today were all on the road and moving slowly apart.

The plateau through which Green River cuts its way is the normal dry highland of Wyoming, which thinks nothing of being seven thou

sand feet in elevation and makes one glad that the Creator thought
to include it in the scheme of things, because otherwise what would
He have done with all the sage? The air is heady. It seems only proper
that the lambs should skip about with their wool-covered, woodeny
hind legs cast recklessly to the winds of heaven and their noses
between their front feet. Most of this expanse is treeless and bushless,
covered only with a nubbly broadloom of desert growth. There is
absolutely no impediment to communing, not with nature alone, but
with the infinite scheme of creation.

There is also no impediment to the winds which howl in from the
north and sweep magnificently across the upland. Snow fences and
refuge cabins now call attention to the fact that distances are great
and winter storms implacable.

Tamsen Donner and her family, descending only slightly from the
South Pass to the high sage desert, found it raining; and rain—if one
may be permitted the Irish bull—seems to be solidly fluid at this
elevation, poured out, as it were, and not yet sprayed into drops.
The men who walked by the oxen were soaked, and they shivered
in a blustering wind that flapped and snapped the white schooner
tops, flinging tiny drops back into the family wagon where the children rode with their mother. It was summer by the calendar, but a
summer hardly worthy of the name. Icy teeth of driving hail combed
the plateau, as it stormed and cleared and stormed again. A cold wet
dawn might change to a noon like the glance of a blue-eyed angel,
only to slip cheerlessly into a slate-colored twilight while the traveling
families slopped along the muddy trail and camped at night without
the comfort of a fire.

For the several days it took to cross the plateau to Fort Bridger,
Tamsen rode. The Donners were well to do, with plenty of stock and
comfortable wagons; she wouldn't need to walk, ever, unless it pleased
her. But Tamsen was a vital person with many interests. She liked to
pick and catalogue the small but vivid wild flowers that bloomed
below the scrubby sage growth. She watched the stout, fussy prairie
dogs and the small gopherlike creatures that zipped across the trail
ahead of the lead wagon. She was a comparatively young woman,
with three daughters of her own below the age of six and two older
stepdaughters. To acquire time for personal interests took stamina
and determination, and Tamsen had her full quota of those qualities—
as much perhaps as any person on Green River Desert that day. But

there was nothing she could do about her main problem, not at present anyway. Perhaps at Fort Bridger she would be able to influence her husband, and they could still turn north, toward Fort Hall, on a known road.

But George Donner, sturdy, genial, and sixty-three years old, was not easy to turn from the venture—not by her, at any rate, so much younger and a woman. Being confined to the wagon, she sat clinging to the pitching seat, absently smelling the pungent wet sage as the oxen, pulling at tender shoots, dragged whole branches from the shrubs and broke them underfoot; absently watching her young children playing upon the bedding so that they might not be hurt by a sudden lurch; absently dispensing cold Dutch-oven bread spread with the sweet butter which churned in a tight bucket beneath the wagon every day; absently doing all duties, small or large, required from an emigrant mother. And always thinking of Lansford Hastings.

Why should he—"an adventurer," she called him—persuade them to risk so much in order to get to California a month earlier? Why should he, projecting his unwelcome personality across the Continental Divide itself, advise them to take the new route which he would show them? Some plan for the furtherance of his own interests she thought contemptuously.

Then her mind wandered off at a tangent. Why did they succumb to his arguments? Others did not. Others had gone on their planned way undisturbed. And here were she and her husband and their young family contemplating such a foolish thing.

She had expressed herself forcefully to Mr. Thornton before they parted, but there was no one who wanted to listen to her now.

Another small comfort was gone since leaving the Big Sandy. A train of nineteen or twenty wagons had been on the road behind them—Mormons bound for Oregon. They would take the short road to Fort Hall, following Thornton, she just knew. Now the Donners were the last.

The flat plateau broke irregularly. The clumsy vehicles rumbled and jolted over the edge, down into the bottom land of Ham's Fork and then to Black's Fork, up which they traveled to the fort.

If only it had not been so cold! If only they had not suffered from damp clothing and blankets, while all their rheumatic joints protested, they might have made wiser decisions in the days just ahead. The bleakness of Green River Desert in this unusual summer was n

doubt largely responsible for such men as James Reed and the Donners and the Harlan Party considering seriously the proposition of
crossing a salt desert with their wagons. Heat and thirst seemed very
unreal as they trundled along Black's Fork toward Fort Bridger.

*   *   *

It was, of course, Bryant with his comrades of the pack train who
came first to Fort Bridger, riding wearily through a long rainy evening.
And Bryant is probably the most reliable informant we have as to
trail happenings of that year, his diary being full, well expressed, and
apparently unbiased. It is from his journal that we learn of the disagreements and petty bickerings that took place throughout the first
quarter of the journey. "The perpetual vexations and hardships," he
wrote, "are well calculated to keep the nerves in a state of great
irritability."

It is impossible to tell why this particular migration should have
had so many altercations; there are so few comments preserved to us
which were written at the time. Tamsen and two or three others
wrote letters home which have been preserved. There were a few
diaries: those by Thornton, Lienhard, Bryant, W. E. Taylor, the
Miller-Reed journal, and others, but no one advances an adequate
theory for the tremendous amount of quarreling. Probably there were
a few inordinately difficult persons on the road that year, but it seems
to me that the swarming, gnatlike irritations which beset the beginning
of the trip might have blown away with any truly "ill wind." If the
wagon trains had met with any real danger, the minor difficulties
would have subsided into their proper subordinate position; but they
met no danger. The Pawnee did not molest. Cholera was not in
evidence. Nothing bulked any larger in the daily scheme of things
than that the officers of the companies were not running them as
well as certain others thought they should, and who were they to be
running them anyway?

No doubt it was as much the desire to be rid of dissensions as
the desire for more speed that caused Bryant and Russell (erstwhile
captain of the large company containing the Donners) to trade their
ox team for pack mules. It was their small, apparently well agreed
party of nine horsemen who gladly glimpsed the lights of Fort Bridger
through the rain. And Hastings' campfire was the one they reached

first. He was camped where all who came from the east must pass him.

As Mr. Bryant had the inestimable advantage of a firsthand knowledge of events, let him tell what happened: "We determined," he wrote, "to encamp here two or three days, for the purpose of recruiting our animals, which, being heavily packed, manifest strong signs of fatigue. We pitched our tent, for the first time since we left Fort Laramie, near the camp of Messrs. Hastings and Hudspeth. These gentlemen left the settlements of California the last of April, travelling over the snows of the Sierra, and swimming the swollen water-courses on either side, reached this vicinity some two weeks since, having explored a new route, via the south end of the great Salt Lake, by which they suppose the distance to California is shortened from one hundred and fifty to two hundred miles. My impressions are unfavorable to the route, especially for wagons and families; but a number of the emigrant parties now encamped here have determined to adopt it, with Messrs. Hastings and Hudspeth as their guides; and are now waiting for some of the rear parties to come up and join them.

" 'Fort Bridger,' as it is called, is a small trading-post, established and now occupied by Messrs. Bridger and Vasquez. The buildings are two or three miserable log-cabins, rudely constructed, and bearing but a faint resemblance to habitable houses. Its position is in a handsome and fertile bottom of the small stream on which we are encamped, about two miles south of the point where the old wagon trail, via Fort Hall, makes an angle, and takes a northwesterly course. The bottom produces the finest qualities of grass, and in great abundance. The water of the stream is cold and pure, and abounds in spotted mountain trout, and a variety of other small fish. Clumps of cotton-wood trees are scattered through the valley, and along the banks of the stream. Fort Bridger is distant from the Pacific Spring by our estimate, 133 miles.

"About five hundred Snake Indians were encamped near the trading-post this morning, but on hearing the news respecting the movements of the Sioux [preparations for war], which we communicated to them, most of them left immediately, for the purpose, I suppose, of organizing elsewhere a war-party to resist the threatened invasion. There are a number of traders here from the neighborhood of Taos, and the head-waters of the Arkansas, who have brought with them dressed buckskins, buckskin shirts, pantaloons, and moccasins, to trade with the emigrants. The emigrant trade is a very important one to the mountain merchants and trappers. The countenances and bearing of these men, who have made the wilderness their home, are generally expressive of a cool, cautious, but determined intrepidity. In a trade, they have no consciences, taking all the 'advantages'; but in a matter of hospitality or generosity they are open-handed—ready, many of them, to divide with the needy what they possess.

"I was introduced to-day to Captain Walker, of Jackson county, Missouri, who is much celebrated for his explorations and knowledge of the North American continent, between the frontier settlements of the United States and the Pacific. Captain W. is now on his return from the settlements of California, having been out with Captain Frémont in the capacity of guide or pilot. He is driving some four or five hundred Californian horses, which he intends to dispose of in the United States. They appear to be high-spirited animals, of medium size, handsome figures, and in good condition. It is possible that the trade in horses, and even cattle, between California and the United States may, at no distant day, become of considerable importance. Captain W. communicated to me some facts in reference to recent occurrences in California, of considerable interest. He spoke discouragingly of the new route via the south end of the Salt Lake.

"Several emigrant parties have arrived here during the day, and others have left, taking the old route, via Fort Hall.

"We determined, this morning, to take the new route, via the south end of the great Salt Lake. Mr. Hudspeth—who with a small party, on Monday, will start in advance of the emigrant companies which intend travelling by this route, for the purpose of making some further explorations—has volunteered to guide us as far as the Salt Plain, a day's journey west of the Lake. Although such was my own determination, I wrote several letters to my friends among the emigrant parties in the rear, advising them not to take this route, but to keep on the old trail, via Fort Hall. Our situation was different from theirs. We were mounted on mules, had no families, and could afford to hazard experiments, and make explorations. They could not."

The wagon trains stayed several days at Fort Bridger. Their leaders went into conference and afterward Hastings called all of the emigrants together and made a speech. He argued persuasively and with discreet inaccuracy. He appealed both to their natural wish for safety and to their patriotism.

A great deal has been said and written about Lansford Hastings' ambition and selfishness. Much of it is no doubt true. He was young—only twenty-three; he was a lawyer and had the most unbounded confidence in himself, never hesitating to dominate a situation because of the justifiable fear that most people have that they might possibly be wrong. He first went west in 1842 with the Oregon-bound party recruited by Dr. Elijah White, supplanting Dr. White as captain quite easily by a popular vote of the company. The next year he traveled south to California accompanied by three dozen people whom he had talked into making the journey. Once there he cast a sapient look about him at the situation. The loyal population were too few, he thought, too unworldly and, in many cases, too indifferent, for Mexico to maintain control much longer. England had a calculating eye on the crisis, but a few more American emigrants might overset the delicate balance and win this beautiful country for the United States. Why should he not go back to the States, recruit a party and, by arriving at their head, assume a position of real importance in the new scheme of things? Not a reason on earth. With a ready facility for making momentous decisions and an amazing capacity for action, he started by boat for Mexico, crossed it overland to Texas, and there found more material to stir his nascent ambitions. Texas was a republic with a president at its head. California might, with a little judicious pushing, become a republic. He might, with luck and adroit manipulations, become its president. Legend tells us that he began actually to plot that audacious course. We know that July of 1846 found him busy at the crossroads of the Overland Trail. He wanted to lead as many emigrants as possible to California by his new short road. In fact he proposed to do so. Of course God disposed, but Mr. Hastings was always willing to lend Him a hand.

Immediately the companies were torn with dissensions. Ex-Governor Boggs of Missouri and Judge Moran (erstwhile captain of the Harlan train) were for going by way of Fort Hall, where Boggs was going to take the road to Oregon. On the contrary, Samuel C. Young, George W. Harlan, John Hargrave, George McKinstry and others voted for the cutoff. Bryant and Russell decided in favor of the cutoff for themselves but felt that it was not safe for the slow moving oxen. Bryant, as before mentioned, wrote letters to those whom he knew "among the emigrant parties in the rear," advising them to have nothing to do with it. This probably meant the Donner Party, who did not arrive until July 25th.

It was rumored among the travelers that Bridger and his partner, Vasquez, were greatly pleased with the idea of the new road, and even that they had hired Hastings to persuade the wagon trains to try it. In later years this was held against the two men. I think they did throw their influence toward sending travel on the cutoff. They would have been more than human had they not. They had never seen it and could only take Hastings' word for conditions. What they *did* know was that trade at Fort Bridger was at low ebb. Sublette's Cutoff had stolen their customers. Their trading post looked like a lost venture unless the new road could pull business their way.

Jim Bridger has come down through history as a rough old trapper and trader, a squaw man and a teller of tall tales. But the emigrants who partook of his hospitality recorded other qualities. Mrs. B. G. Ferris, wife of the United States Secretary for Utah in 1852, stopped at Fort Bridger on her way out to her husband's post in Salt Lake City. "This man strongly attracted my attention," she wrote home, "there was more than civility about him—there was a native politeness." There is no evidence in the writings of the many persons who met him to lead one to believe that Jim Bridger deliberately would have turned women and children into a country which he knew to be dangerous.

*   *   *

We have been at Fort Bridger many times. On this particular occasion we set up a camp and stayed three days.

On the third day, early, I walked through the knee-high, dewy grass to the entrance of the fenced enclosure of the fort and passed inside. It was, I suppose, seven o'clock.

The door of the museum was open, to my surprise, and Mr. Thomas, the curator, was sitting at his desk.

"How in the world do you happen to be here at this time of day?" I asked him.

"This isn't early," he replied pleasantly. "I've been here since six o'clock."

"That's hardly within museum hours."

"Well, now," and he squinted at me in amusement, "give me three good reasons why I shouldn't be here at six. I live right there" (pointing to a near-by cottage), "I like to get up early, and the people on this highway travel all night. They're really disappointed when they pass an important historical monument like this after daylight and can't get in."

"Yes, I suppose they are. Anyway, your being here is nice for me. You said that you would take me to the trail crossing of the next creek sometime. Perhaps we can go now?"

And so we sauntered out into air so fresh and chilled and through grass so succulent and crisp that I expected it to break with a snap when stepped on, like a stalk of celery. Under lovely aspen trees we walked, and among old historic buildings, and soon came to a little stream dashing itself lightheartedly here and there into the brush that lined its banks. It was Carter's Creek, the only one of Black's Fork's local branches to own a separate name.

We talked about the fort as we walked. It was really a trading post at first, built in 1842 by Bridger. He hand-picked the site as an advantageous spot to sell supplies to the Oregon-bound travelers; but in 1844 Caleb Greenwood spoiled his prospects by opening the route across Green River Desert.

Hastings and his cutoff helped a little, and in 1847 the Mormons really saved the situation by founding Salt Lake City. Immediately, much of the California-bound migration went that way. Jim Bridger found his fort populous again, a desirable condition that lasted through the first years of the gold rush. In 1853 he and the Mormons had a quarrel so serious that they preempted his property, for which, some years later, they paid (at least in part). Bridger fled, but returned again with Albert Sidney Johnston's troops in 1857, during the so-called Mormon War, only to find that the Mormons had burned the buildings and retreated through Echo Canyon of the Wasatch Range into the Salt Lake Valley. The "war" was settled amicably, but Fort Bridger, the trading post, soon was rebuilt into a real fort, with parade ground, officers' quarters, barracks, and all the necessary accessories.

"The soldiers dug a well here," Mr. Thomas told me as we passed the spot, "just in case of siege by Indians; but it was never needed."

Through the years more adjuncts of peace were added—a little old schoolhouse, a dairy. He pointed as we walked by them. "Those buildings are old," he said, "built in the fifties."

"Did the trail pass them?"

"Yes, it went back of them—no trace now, of course."

"How many branches has Black's Fork through this valley?" I asked.

"Well, it begins to spread apart up at the beginning of the flatland, and separates into different little streams. I don't know just how many. In a wet year there may be about seven. Other years there aren't so many, and some of those run dry on account of irrigation taking out the water."

"And they all run together again?"

"Yes, in just a few miles. Here we are. Here's Carter's Creek. I think we'll have to walk a hundred yards or so downstream before we find the place where the crossing was. The trail came right along from the pony-express stables back of the museum and through that field where you can see they've been cutting hay. The wagons crossed the creek just where they happened to strike it. In later years there was a bridge there."

While he talked he was reconnoitering along the bank, shoving aside the heavy bushes, and peering into the edge of the water.

"I hope the last few logs haven't been torn loose since I was here," he commented. "It wouldn't take much, and the water's high."

Well, I sincerely hoped so too, but we hunted up and down the bank ten minutes before we located the supports to which the ends of the logs had been spiked. One remaining log was lodged against the bank beneath the water. I think another winter will finish the old bridge completely.

Back at the museum we found the rest of the party. Their occupations were characteristic. My husband, who is the most gregarious man I know, was reading the register to see if any of his wide acquaintance had passed during the last week. Mr. Bromley had found a rock. Almost any rock pleases him, but this was a slab of limestone, or what not, and had been brought over from the other side of Green River, where the trail came through the hot sagebrush to the ferry leading to Fort Bridger. The name Simpson Hollow was carved on it rather shallowly; but it had remained surprisingly well, for over three-quarters of a century, to denote the place where the ragged but game Mormon militia (startled into belligerence by the news of the approach of Johnston's army) had attacked and burned part of a U.S. Army supply train without shedding any more important blood than that of a mule.

Dr. Neff was standing silently watching an unimportant but amusing comedy staged by a group of the sense-of-duty sightseers which an American highway can spawn at any hour.

Preeminent among these was a large man, evidently there by his wife's desire, the wife just mentioned, and two small tourists made on the same pattern. At the first removal of the wifely gaze, the large man rounded the glass cases in the center of the room with long strides and withdrew, pulling a well blackened pipe out of his side pocket as he neared the door. I was reminded of my husband on the few occasions when he has been inveigled into art exhibits and felt a certain sense of acquaintanceship.

Remaining with their mother was Sister, aged about nine, and little Junior, who was leaving greasy facsimiles of his fat hands on the glass display cases, accurately spaced with smudgy imprints of his not over-immaculate nose.

Sister, chocolate-coated and stolid, gazed at me with bovine attention, the constant motion of her jaws adding to the illusion.

"Sister, take that gum out of your mouth," admonished her mother genteelly.

This was done regretfully, under the watchful maternal eye, and stuck beneath the rim of the case, whence it was immediately salvaged for personal use by Junior.

A howl from Sister acclaimed her knowledge of this injustice and she promptly landed a haymaker on his little fat nose.

The mother hastily handed him her handkerchief, escorted Sister to the door, and shoved her at the large man. "See that you shake her good, too," she admonished as if she had presented him with a dose of medicine.

Junior blew his nose and looked at the result with pride. "See, I bleeded," he informed me as he trotted after them.

"They'll be perfectly happy now," said Mr. Thomas. "They've gone through the motions. But if the museum hadn't been open, they would have been honestly disappointed."

"I guess we'd better follow them," my husband said. "We're all packed and ready to start."

Outside the door was Sister, still sunk in chocolate deposits, receiving a recuperative cup of water from her secretly sympathetic father. She was a gifted drinker and each swallow was hitting bottom with a loud *ug* from somewhere in her inmost vitals.

We moved slowly to where our car and trailer were parked back of the pony-express stables. "Did they ask any questions about the place?" I asked Mr. Thomas.

"No, some people don't. They come in and look at the pictures and the bear trap and after a while they leave. A few during the day will have some idea of the history of the place, and they certainly ask plenty of questions and find plenty to look at."

"You should have a short movie that you could run through," suggested my husband, "just to show interested groups what actually has happened here."

"I wish we did have one," Mr. Thomas replied. "Fort Bridger saw plenty in its day, if people only knew it."

From the time that the first settlers commenced to use the Oregon Trail, clear through the Mormon migration, the gold rush, stage-coaching days, and the exciting period of the pony express, the men living at Fort Bridger kept perceptive fingers on the heartbeat of the nation as it pulsed through the great artery of the Overland Road.

"Yes," agreed my husband, "Fort Bridger was always important, from its founding until the withdrawal of the troops in the nineties, and then it just didn't have anything more to contribute."

Said Mr. Thomas, "I guess you're right."

And, to myself, I thought that the most quietly and unwittingly dramatic incident of its long career was the morning of July 31st, 1846, when, ignoring Bryant's warning letter, the Donner-Reed Party yoked its oxen and started out on the broad trail left by the Harlan wagons eleven days before. Thornton's best guess as to the date was July 28th but the date given by the Miller-Reed diary should be correct. Thornton wrote that they were "buoyant with hope, and filled with pleasing expectations," but we may safely say that whoever was buoyant and filled with pleasing expectations, it wasn't Tamsen Donner. To her judgment, Hastings was still a man of whom they knew nothing, one who thought only of himself and not of them. Time proved her right, to this extent, at least, that while he may have thought of his country as much as of himself, he didn't think of them at all.

Time proved her right and, in the proving, she was scorched and dehydrated by the waterless salt deserts, fagged by the long mountain miles, chilled almost to death by blizzards while she lived in a hole like a wolf den under twenty-odd feet of Sierra snow, starved and emaciated from a diet of boiled oxhides, and was still strong and purposeful enough to send her children to safety and return to her husband, who, she knew, would die within hours. Then, her duty done, she herself died from exposure and probably from the fact that there was nothing left to protect—no one who needed her.

Tamsen Donner, whether from premonition or from native good sense, started out on the cutoff with a protest.

CHAPTER II

West Through the Wasatch

O N the morning of July 20th, Bryant's companions saddled their animals and left the fort and security behind. James Hudspeth and three young emigrants also were setting out that day, in advance of the ox trains, to find the best route for wagons through the mountains that lay between Fort Bridger and the valley of the Great Salt Lake. He was persuaded to guide Bryant's party and to take them as far.as the edge of the salt desert. The pack train covered ground quickly and was soon miles away.

Many times, as the later migrations covered this same mileage, the oxen, plagiarizing the fable of the tortoise and the hare, eventually passed the horse and mule companies; but Bryant's efficiently handled outfit was cumbered by no wagons; it was steady and fast, and the wagons never caught up with it. As the mules started over the wide rolling upland that leads past Bridger's Butte, Bryant looked back and saw the corralled wagon companies scattered like children's toys around the fort. He would not see them again until California was reached. The Donners he would not see until after.their snow-buried winter in the Sierra, nor until, in the next late spring, he watched General Kearny's soldiers bury unrecognizable bones of half the company.

Bridger's Butte was the landscape's salient feature, a large eroded section of the original plateau of the type usually termed a table mountain.

The Harlan wagons, starting the same day, left the first wheel marks on what was to be a portion of the most important stage line to the West by passing below it and to the left. It was a well marked trail for the Donners to trace when, on July 31st, they should get around to leaving the fort, but by the next summer, the grass having grown up, their spoor was so exceedingly faint that the pioneers of the Mormon migration had difficulty in finding it. Elder Orson Pratt wrote, as they left Fort Bridger: "We again resumed our journey, taking Mr. Hastings' new route to the Bay of San Francisco; this route is but dimly seen, as only a few wagons passed over it last season."

The westbound traveler on the modern highway will pass to the right of, and above, Bridger's Butte and will find himself unexpectedly close to the clouds, for he has been climbing steadily and is well on his way to the Wasatch Mountains. Before reaching the main spur, however, he has a nearer ridge to cross—the Bear River Divide, which splits from the Wasatch mountain chain south of the pass where the wagons crossed. The divide is not as high nor as rugged here as it is farther north, where Sublette's Cutoff winds up and up among the aspen and fir groves on its stupendous headlands, but it is the first obstacle for a follower of Hastings' route, either now or one hundred years ago.

Sage and occasional clumps of aspen formed the principal growth as Bryant's pack train spearheaded the companies up the mountain. To the south intermittent sun-slants glinted coldly on the snow-draped summits of the Uinta Range, sheeted freshly almost every night by the laden clouds. Ahead curved the Little Muddy, where, at the end of fifteen miles, they camped. It is a common, friendly creek of clear water, but running over a soft bottom. As they struggled through the deep adhesive mud, they discovered that its name was not a misnomer.

Suddenly the foremost mules pricked their long ears forward and snorted. They were always better than any watchdog when Indians were around, and the men moved ahead cautiously. After all, some of the Shoshone tribes were reported in bad humor with the whites. It was not too safe in the Bear River Divide.

A peculiar trail lay across their own. The mules objected, but crossed it. Probably it was Hudspeth who interpreted the signs of the dragging teepee poles which had left a broad swath across the rain-softened mountainside. The "travois" was what the French trappers called such an arrangement of long saplings tied to the sides of a pony and heavily piled with the household effects of an Indian family. Scattered poles had loosened, pulled away, and lay here and there in the bruised grass of their passage. Many families—probably a whole village—had gone by. Evidently they had packed in great haste. Even the hard-gotten furs, which constituted their trading power with the whites, were slipping out of the hasty bundles, and Bryant's men retrieved a few to tuck in their own packs for use if their boot soles should give out before the end of the journey.

The hurrying red men were Snakes, said Hudspeth. He was glad to observe both that they were going in the other direction and that they were going fast. Possibly he was even grateful to the Sioux whose war-dance in preparation for an attack on the Snake Nation had been described by Bryant. Both tribes would be much too busy to bother with the migration.

The clouds broke for a while, and sunshine painted the placid prettiness of the Little Muddy; its grassy banks were splashed with the bright pink and purple of wild geranium where, in the 1860's, old Mose Burns ran a ferry at $1 a wagon. Those who paid it did so more because of deep mud than the depth of the water.

From the ford (or ferry, depending upon the year in which one traveled) the emigrants climbed the rough slopes of the divide accompanied by a battalion of junipers. Four miles from the river were the copperas springs, and, in one and a half miles more, the top of the first ridge. Then, going down a long hill and up a short one, they came to the summit of Bear River Divide, which separates the waters of the Colorado River from those which run into the Great Basin and have no outlet to the ocean.

Here, as well as on the slopes of South Pass of the Rockies, the emigrants were apt to suffer from what they termed "mountain fever." After many years of uncertainty, due to lack of opportunity for research, scientists seem inclined to acknowledge a definite malady which they call by that name, not nearly as deadly as the Rocky Mountain spotted fever, although also caused by tick bite. The emigrants also suffered a minor indisposition while crossing the high ranges, probably because of the effect of the unaccustomed elevation upon malarial victims.

Affairs in the pack train, therefore, were complicated at this juncture by illness. "McClary has been quite sick," wrote Bryant, "with a fever which has prevailed among the emigrants, and frequently terminated fatally. This afternoon he was scarcely able to sit upon his mule, from weakness and giddiness." It did not, however, prevent the party from traveling steadily on their way, and McClary fortunately recovered.

Since leaving the Rocky Mountains, the emigrants had been dependent upon the waters of the Green River and its tributaries, which, in turn, swell the tremendous flood of the Colorado. Now they looked eagerly for the water flowing west, water which was eventually to die a salty death in the Great Salt Lake. Apparently La Chappelle Creek was the first. I am not prepared to defend the spelling. It is not on any map to which we have access, and of those whom I asked, no one had ever felt it necessary to write it. So I have simply followed the precedent of many of the pioneer journal writers and put down sufficient letters to show I mean well. At any rate it soon fades into Sulphur Creek, and the trail continues down the latter, through the Lester Ranch, where large charcoal kilns now serve as bedding places for sheep.

The trail here was not easy, but it had no staggering difficulties. After going two miles along Sulphur Creek, the obvious course was to leave it and cut across to where the infant Bear River is cradled between the full bosom of its mother range and the more rugged breast of the Wasatch. On a still day the precocious baby river may be quiet, but it is never safe to depend upon it. If it has stormed the night before, it will be found threshing in the arms of the parent mountains. At such times many an emigrant company has been forced to await the pleasure of the small despot.

I say "many a company" advisedly, for the portion of Hastings' Cutoff lying between Fort Bridger and the City of the Great Salt Lake became the commonly used thoroughfare to that Mormon metropolis and was, after the city was founded in 1847, not considered as part of the cutoff. The gold seekers of 1849 spoke of Hastings' Cutoff as beginning at Salt Lake City.

The trail is still perfectly visible as it drops from the sagy highland into the Bear River bottoms, and it is marked for the information of such persons as may pass that way. The Bear flows northward from a canyon into the open on the Fred Myers Ranch, about eight miles upstream from Evanston, Wyoming. The old ford was where the bridge now is, near the ranch house. William Kelly, a Forty-niner, had cause to remember this crossing. The Bear was high, almost in flood; but Kelly raised his wagon bed a little higher with blocks of wood (a tried and established custom of the emigrants) and urged his team out into the surging water. A rope had been tied to the lead mules and then carried across the river by a horseman so that men on the opposite bank could prevent them from turning downstream with the current. The snorting animals drew the wagon safely to the deepest part of the current, where the force of the water began to sweep them off their feet. Oxen probably could have negotiated the same channel with imperturbability. Their immense weight stood them in good stead, and their large cloven hoofs usually stayed where they placed them. But the compact hoof of the mule was often its undoing and, in this case, a small mule lost her footing completely on the rolling rocks, went under, and was trampled and drowned. The men, working to their armpits in the millrace current, were helpless to loose her. Other men, pulling on the taut rope, saved the situation, and the almost unmanageable team finally reached the far shore, dragging her body with them.

In the sixties the picture was quite different. A small stage station stood well above the highwater mark and tempted travelers with the smell of baked bread, roasting mountain sheep, and the pungent sage hens which actually seasoned themselves with sage, almost to the point of bitterness, so the emigrants complained, before cooking.

The stages stopped, of course, and so did the emigrant wagons which still were rumbling along the old trail each season. In one of the wagons was Ada Millington, all of thirteen, and keeping a very good diary in which she recorded daily events and philosophized, poor child, on hardships and sorrows which she was not too young to know. Arrival at a stage station was exciting. They stopped and "Pa" went in. When he came back, he had a guidebook from Salt Lake City to Carson City, for which he had paid fifty cents. This in itself would tell us that the station was probably run by Mormons, who were never averse to turning "an honest penny" and who had, since the gold rush, sold road directions, hand-written on loose leaves at first and later printed. Bruff, Sawyer, and Moorman all purchased guidebooks of this sort, paying more for them than Millington, as presumably they were not so plentiful in 1849 and 1850. Probably "Pa" bought vegetables too, but Ada was too excited to mention it after their experience in crossing the toll bridge.

The river was high, sluicing along through the willows that lined the banks. Turgid water covered the slanted approaches and made the narrow little bridge look as if it stood far out in the middle of the stream. It was, however, their one chance to get across, and "Pa" drove into the water, heading for the near end of the bridge. This, in the heavy current, took a little doing; but they managed to make a landing on the logs of the bridge floor and started across.

It was strictly a one-way affair, with scarcely room to stand beside the wagon as they carefully felt their way along just above the roaring river. Their cattle were under the care of the hired man. When he saw the wagon safely on the bridge, he fiercely drove his horse into the huddled herd, shoving and pushing them out into the water. They yielded to his impetuous attack and started wading toward the main current, but, as it deepened, they became frightened and one after another made a landing on the end of the bridge, crowding for a footing. Ahead of them was the familiar wagon. They were mighty glad to see it and hurried to catch up and pass. They did—and almost disastrously. Like two cows stuck in a barn door who will tug until they pull their own hips out of joint rather than back up, they pushed past the wagon. Only the weight of the load saved the occupants; but it tipped dangerously, and the child saw the dark stormy waters rushing below her before the wheels crashed back into position on the logs.

The Millingtons had no choice but to pay the toll but, even at low water, prosperous emigrants were glad to pay to avoid the chances involved in fording. It was cheap insurance and saved discomfort and work. Ada did not give the toll rate, but during the next year, 1863, Silas Hopper paid $1.50 per wagon. Those who could not afford the toll objected bitterly to the fact that many of the bridges seemed to be placed over the best places to ford, whether or not it might be the best place for the bridge, thus forcing all comers to use them. The road to California was becoming too expensive to travel, they said.

The Myerses' present-day ranch house and barn are of hewn logs with a second story of frame on each, and they stand under heavy trees. The valley runs downstream from the buildings, toward the north. A low gap to the east shows where the trail comes along the course of Sulphur Creek, but the hills to the west are steep. Instead of climbing them at once, the trail went along the low grassy bank on the west side of Bear River for a distance that varied through the years. Its travelers were entertained by looking across the stream at palisades of an undistinguished, dirty white; and by the end of the third mile, the trail had left the river, curved west, and had completed the climb to the summit of the first ridge.

Velvety white sage, limp and flexible, blows silver in the constant wind. Bunch grass is raw-green and shiny. Wild flowers are all brilliant. There is nothing wishy-washy about Wyoming plant life. It may have to grow under sagebrush, but it is bright enough to catch the eye: scarlet, magenta, eggy-yellow, and the you-can't-miss-me blue of an enamel saucepan. Three miles down from the summit, the emigrants struck the first waters of Yellow Creek. In three and a half more they crossed it at the foot of the Needles, so called at least since the sixties, when the journal of Silas Hopper mentions them by name.

Elder Orson Pratt describes the country quite well in his journal entry for July 12th, 1847: "Plenty of grass of an excellent quality," he wrote, "is found in almost every direction. The country is very broken, with high hills and valleys, with no timber excepting scrubby cedar upon their sides. Antelope again appear in great abundance, but rather wild; ten or twelve were brought in by our hunters in the course of the day. The road is exceedingly difficult to find excepting in places where the grass has not completely obscured it. We halted for noon a little east of a pudding-stone formation. This ledge is on the right of the road, which passes along at its base. The rocks are from one to two hundred feet in height, and rise up in a perpendicular and shelving form, being broken or worked out into many curious forms by the rains. Some quite large boulders were cemented in this rock. President Young, being sick, concluded to stop a few hours and rest; several wagons stopped with him for company, the rest being requested to move on."

So it chanced that the Mormon pioneer company was divided here at the Needles. Brigham Young was forced to wait a couple of days for partial recovery from the fever that had so suddenly sickened him, and eight wagons remained with him. The main body of pioneers traveled on to the head of Echo Creek, while Orson Pratt was placed in charge of forty-two men and twenty-three wagons to travel ahead and spy out the route which had been opened in 1846 by James Reed of the Reed-Donner Party over the summit of the Wasatch Range just ahead.

In order to see the Needles as they are today, we left our car in front of a ranch house just below them. The ranchers were away for the annual sheep shearing, but the lady of the premises gave us permission to go through their corral in order to climb the slope behind the buildings. They are a strange, rocky formation and protrude on a slant from the top of the little ridge like spines along the backbone of some antediluvian monster. Dr. Bradway called it "a ledge of conglomerate terminating in turrets." In the corral we were joined by two gentle fat gray horses, and we all went in procession to the top of the hill behind the house, where the high ground flattens into a meadow in which Yellow Creek is flung softly in regular scallops edged on both sides with tiny bush willows. Here are forget-me-nots but an eighth of an inch across and a skimming of dandelion bubbles. A small unrailed bridge spans the narrow waterway, which looks decidedly too ditchlike for comfortable fording. Kelly found it purling along slowly at the bottom of eight-foot banks, and his company made a bridge of two cottonwood logs, over which they carried their goods by hand; floated the wagons, and repacked on the other side. The meadow spread below the Needles is as sweetly pretty as one could wish, "springy with thick herbage," wrote Kelly, "like a Turkey carpet, and piebald from the beds of flowers and the wild flax, with its soft blue blossom."

A flurry of cold rain sent us running back down the hill toward the car, with the slow-stepping horses now and then breaking into a lumbering, stiff-legged trot to keep up. The one who honored me with her company had, unfortunately, no initiative. She wanted to go just where I went, and hoofs the size of soup plates thudding at my heels added materially to my speed. I thought for a minute she would try to get in the car with me.

Another mile—a precarious mile, too, in the mud—brought us to the shearing camp. Hundreds of blatting sheep were beginning to move slowly before the storm, tail to wind, with the intelligent dogs circling in front to detain them. A covered wagon cookhouse stood authoritatively on the horizon, proud possessor of its own front steps, which utilized the recumbent tongue as first in the series. Fragrant wood smoke curled downward from its chimney and swept past us as we climbed the rutted fragment of road. The leaky beanbag of a cloud which was walloping over our heads, changing shape from one minute to the next, commenced to scatter its contents in the shape of hail.

Dr. Neff gave voice to an opinion. "It would be a good idea to get out of here," he said.

Mr. Bromley endorsed the proposition. "This is one time we have an advantage over the emigrants." He climbed in behind the wheel and eased off the hand brake. "We don't have to stay and get wet.

At least," he added anxiously as the wheels began to spin, "I hope we don't."

He twisted the car to safer territory and skillfully straddled the wheels over the right-hand rut. "We had better not discount the advantages of good able-bodied oxen," he advised. "We may wish we had a pair before we get through."

On the next day we found the five and three-quarter miles of so-called "road" between Yellow Creek and Cache Cave too feeble and muddy to use, so we circled on the highway to the west end of the stretch and drove in as far eastward as we could. The country is all mountainous, with now and then a draw that might be considered level. For much of the way we dared drive only because Mr. Bromley walked ahead of the car. When we were forced to stop driving, we all walked and, in this way, saw most of the stretch.

This portion ends by coming down a typical draw filled with bunch grass and sage. Then, quite suddenly, a valley opens up ahead—a lateral from Echo Canyon. The shortest course would be straight across, but against the hillside to the right a spring seeps out and forms a pond, one of the beginnings of Echo Creek. Above it, and quite a steep, short climb, too, is Cache Cave. The spring and the extended grassy valley made it a good camp site.

Unfortunately, we don't know just where Hastings took the Harlan wagons. We do know that Hudspeth and Bryant missed Cache Cave altogether, by going six miles down Bear River instead of three. But, by the next year, the Mormons had permanently established this route past the Needles and Cache Cave. It was used throughout staging days.

Caroline Richardson, camping here in 1852, visited the cave after supper by lantern light. She called it the greatest curiosity she had yet seen, and really it *is* an odd object that looks as if it might have been at one time a bubble in thick mud and then solidified in its form of a smooth, hollow half-dome. In some manner a perfectly oval door, wider than high, has been broken through the front wall. A man may stand upright in the cave toward the front but must stoop to approach the rear.

We left the car by the pond and climbed to reach the cave. The rain had stopped, but water was widespread here and there on the flat below. Mr. Bromley and my husband arrived first, circled the queer structure, and climbed to the roof from some vantage point in the rear. Dr. Neff and I approached the oval door, hesitated a moment, and then stepped inside.

When just under the shelter of the curving roof, we stopped.

Again he expressed an opinion unrequested. "It's better outside."

"I think so too," I agreed emphatically. He went out, but I kept going. What if sheep had bedded there, apparently for decades? I wanted a picture that showed the trail winding off through the rolling valley, with the black, framing walls of Cache Cave on either side, and I got it.

Names are carved within the cave—many of them. Unfortunately, it has appealed to the sense of humor of persons unknown to fake these names here and there. Then, when ten years or so have passed, it is hard to tell the real from the synthetic. I should have liked a roster of the names that had been authenticated to add to my list of similar pioneer records, but I was unfortunate in not meeting anyone who possessed a list.

All of this day's exploration had been near the Wyoming-Utah line. The farmhouse at the Needles must have been very close indeed.

The old trail does not go out to Echo Canyon by the shortest route, but angles across the little valley from Cache Cave, coming into the great modern highway, which runs through the canyon, almost one and a half miles west of Faucet Road, which goes straight from the cave to the highway. The point where the trail emerges into the highway is marked with a historical monument.

Near the point where the Faucet Road joins the highway is a reddish knoll, north of the latter. There is a story told about this unimpressive bulge, which I do not personally guarantee, but which comes to one's ears, sooner or later, if one stays long in the neighborhood. It happened during that tense period while Johnston's army was advancing to Fort Bridger with the intention of finding out what the ten-year-old Mormon colony was up to and why it was up to it. There was trouble, real trouble, between a tactless parent government and her recalcitrant child. It had originated in false reports and had been fostered by the complete lack of communication during the winter. It is ridiculous to term it the Mormon "War" when no blood was shed, but it made a great deal of discomfort for brave men on both sides.

The incident is told somewhat as follows: The advance scouts of Johnston's army had been sighted by the Mormons; its columns were expected to march straight through Echo Canyon to the Salt Lake Valley. In reality the Mormon militia could not have halted the main files of the detachment, but they intended to try, and they piled great rocks on top of the cliffs in the canyon which might be rolled down to stop progress for a while if it became necessary. If only, they thought, Johnston could be made to think the militia stronger than it was, he might wait for reinforcements, which, with winter coming on, would take weeks to arrive.

While affairs were at this indefinite state, ten or twelve Mormon horsemen were out reconnoitering in the canyon and again glimpsed the army scouts a long way off.

Where the idea originated is not clear to me, but the horsemen appeared in single file out of a canyon into the line of vision of the scouts, rode their horses slowly around the historic knoll, and disappeared behind it into a gully. Once out of sight, each man galloped as fast as his horse could go to encircle the knoll in the rear and again take his place in line. A great many horsemen had apparently ridden past in single file when Johnston's scouts decided to go back and report, which was just as well, because there was no end to the performance—the men being nobly willing to ride all night if necessary. The narrator of this incident believes that it saved a good deal of trouble, for it is a fact that Johnston's army remained near Fort Bridger all winter, without proceeding through Echo Canyon, and by the next spring the affair had been settled peaceably through the simple means of a go-between—a man of honor whom both sides trusted.

So well did the ruse succeed that after the settlement of the difficulty in the spring of 1858, when Mr. Cummings, the new governor, was being escorted to Salt Lake City, the Mormons used almost the same plan. He was taken through Echo Canyon at night, and around every campfire was a fine group of the militia—about 150 men. It is doubtful if Mr. Cummings ever knew that the same 150 men did duty at every fire.

Echo Canyon itself was an object of awe to the emigrants, many of whom had never seen such a thing. When half of the distance to California had been covered and they were on the east slope of the Rocky Mountains, they passed through a small canyon, several miles long, called Three Crossings because they forded the Sweetwater River three times within the gorge. It was a great wonder to them, but it was short and small. The rest of the ascent of the Rockies was gradual and smooth, and no other tight-fitting canyon had appeared in their road until now. The endless crowd streaming to the goldfields in 1849 and 1850 had heard of, and were watching for, Echo Canyon, and they were impressed or depressed according to their condition of mind at the time.

Some, like Henry Bloom, accented the good things to be found in its rocky confines. Here were elderberries, hops, wild wheat, and scores of speckled trout. Above all, here were wild roses enough to perfume the breeze as it passed through.

Some were awed. Tompkins described it as "an awful defile between two sky-proping mountains." Littleton said firmly that it was decidedly the worst road yet, while John Wood (always in trouble, poor fellow, and about whom we will hear more later) was upset over the fact that he had crossed Echo Creek thirty times in eight miles. There was no need for this, for eighteen crossings in the twenty-one or twenty-two miles was about average. However, things never seemed to work out right for John; he usually did have bad roads; but this, said he, "is so much worse that it baffles all description."

In 1853, after the first flurry of the gold rush was past, Thomas Flint and his party came down Echo Canyon very slowly, with a band of sheep for California. "The report of a pistol shot," said he, "would reverberate from crag to crag until it would seem to die away in the distance." Flint's main interest was in bear, with which the canyon abounded: first, a big one which had designs on the sheep for dining purposes; next a small one on which he cast an eye with the same intention. Both bear and man were frustrated, and we gather that the sheep were the only ones who really ate well that evening.

One woman who had become reconciled to the wolves howling every night in the shadows beyond the campfire, became quite over-wrought because they now howled overhead, the echoes, of course, making it triply hard to bear.

By 1862 a little roadwork had been done, but, instead of being in the bottom of the canyon, it had been simpler to grade it along the side of the cliff. Little Ada Millington wrote uncomplainingly, but as a simple description of the nature of cows, that they *would* push between the rocky walls of the canyon side and the wagon, thrusting the wagon sideways, much too close to the edge of the bank for comfort. Harriet Sherrill Ward became so emotional over this stretch of shelf road that she was impelled to run ahead for fear that she might see some wagon "precipitated over the precipice." The new trail soon came down again to the floor of the canyon, where it re-engaged in a game of hop, skip, and jump over Echo Creek.

The current of the little rivulet was so narrow in places that the women jumped it easily; but it was so deeply cut that the wagons plunged, wallowed, and tugged out again, straining and wrenching the load and wearying the patient teams.

At night, though, they camped comfortably enough with wood, water, and grass and the luxuries of berries and game added. Mrs. Ward borrowed a book and sat by a spring to read it. It was entitled *First Love, or a Tale of a Woman's Heart*. Having finished it from cover to cover, she remarked virtuously to her diary: "I am sure, it is a work which I would not wish to put into the hands of the young." Then, gazing at the towering cliffs, she gave herself up to admiration. On the right, she said, they were craggy and fantastic; on the left were huge masses of green velvet in wavy grandeur.

Anyone who has ever glimpsed Echo Canyon with its high cliffs of red rock on the north and its soft rolling mountains of green, tufted here and there with aspen groves, on the south, can visualize exactly what she saw as she wrote in her journal.

James Hudspeth led the Bryant pack train quite easily among the great rocks that jammed the floor of the canyon, but he was always mindful of the ox trains so patiently tracking behind him. He made several sorties to one side or another in an effort to pick a better route for the wagons, but, on July 24th, the party came to the canyon of

Weber River, where small Echo Creek disappears into its embroiled waters. As they crossed the river, someone's quick eye discovered an Indian trail high on the mountain, "winding under and over the project-ing and impending cliffs." It would permit the passage of pack animals and they took it, but described it as "a path so narrow that a slight jostle would have cast us over a precipice to the bottom of a gulf a thousand feet in depth." Hudspeth's conscience hurt him in taking a ready-made path which would be of no possible use to the wagons, and he determined to return and find a better way as soon as he had the pack train safely off the hair-raising trail and down into the canyon.

While on this alpine detour, they by-passed the famous Devil's Slide and came down to the Weber River below it. We are sure that this is true, for no one as fluent on slight provocation as Edwin Bryant would omit to mention such an unbelievable monstrosity if he had seen it. They followed the course of a small stream on the west side of the river for five miles, coming, at last, to its junction with the river, after having traveled that day (partly on the Indian path) some twenty-four miles. The valley to which they descended was estimated to be fifteen miles long and from one to three wide, and it is probably the one that surrounds the town of Morgan.

Hudspeth left the men encamped in what to them was an earthly paradise of grass for the mules, ripe currants for themselves, flowers to see if they cast their eyes down, and snowy summits cleaving the sky if they looked upward. First, he went alone downstream through the next canyon; then, returning, he took two of the young emigrants and went up the river, probably by-passing the Devil's Slide on the east side, and met Hastings, guiding about forty wagons, six miles above. The Harlan-Young Party had covered the distance from Fort Bridger.

Hudspeth gave as his opinion that the canyon of Weber River could be traveled. Certainly it had difficulties beyond any that they had yet dreamed of, but they could get through. We cannot know what advice he gave Hastings, but it was probably detailed. Then he plodded back to catch up with Bryant's group, who, while he was gone, wormed their way through the lower canyon, now called Devil's Gate, by climbing "along the side of the precipitous moun-tains." He found them peacefully fishing for five-pound trout, which were so plentiful that they could not eat them all.

This was the end, for Bryant's party, of any real difficulty with

cold, swift water, or ledge trails. Their troubles from now on were
of a different ilk.

But the Harlan wagons were still to come.

It is unfortunate that no one in the company kept a daily journal.
Jacob Harlan wrote recollections which give us a blurred picture
of what happened. The *California Gold Book,* by Allen and Avery,
has a compilation of incidents and descriptions, taken from various
sources available in 1893, but only Orson Pratt gives us an inkling of
what the procedure of the party must have been, although he did
not wish to follow their route. "We had been informed," he wrote,
"that it would be impracticable to pass through the canyon on account
of the depth and rapidity of the water." Probably the information
was given at Fort Bridger, for when Pratt's advance company of
Mormon pioneers arrived in the vicinity of modern Henefer, he left
them there and, taking one companion, rode along Harlan's year-old
tracks to see the terrain for himself. "The road," he wrote, "crossing
the river to the right bank, makes a circuit of about two miles, and
enters the canyon at the junction of a stream [Lost Creek] putting
in from the right bank, about one-third as large as Weber's Fork.
I rode on horseback, in company with John Brown, about five miles
down from our encampment, and being convinced that this was the
ten-mile canyon which had been spoken of, we returned to camp."

So we are indebted to Orson Pratt for the knowledge that the
Harlan wagons made no attempt to go through the canyon of Devil's
Slide, but by-passed it on the east side and followed down the course
of Lost Creek to its mouth, where they entered Weber Canyon about
one mile below the slide.

*   *   *

Following the route of the prairie schooners we left Faucet Road
and moved slowly down the great canyon of tiny Echo Creek, stopping
to read the marker where the trail from Cache Cave comes into the
highway and driving on again, dutifully craning our necks to see the
top of the red cliffs where mountain sheep used to lead the hunters on
fruitless quests.

A marker showed where to look for the "Pioneer Fortifications."
These are the rock piles prepared at the top of the cliff by the
Mormon militia as a gesture of preparedness if Johnston's army kept
coming. No one has ever needed to know whether the fortification

would have been used, and, if so, for what purpose. The army didn't keep coming. And when, after the misunderstanding had been settled the next spring and Johnston *did* take his men through Salt Lake City to Camp Floyd (west of Utah Lake in Cedar Valley), his promise was given and kept that his men would keep marching straight through the city and out the other side.

About twenty-three miles from Cache Cave, Echo Canyon ends. The modern excursionist finds here the waters of Echo Dam but is not prevented from turning to the right down the course of the Weber, just as the earliest wagons did. Trappers knew that horsemen might turn to the left (or south) and move up the river, and, by 1850, the Mormons had a toll road going there, but I, personally, do not know when the first wagons went that way.

Traveling down the Weber from where we entered its canyon, we passed the old fording place and moved on to the small town of Henefer. It is about three miles above the constricted "upper canyon" dominated by Devil's Slide and is located near the mouth of Little East Canyon Creek, otherwise termed Henefer Creek, up which the Donner Party began their struggle over the summit of the Wasatch Mountains instead of following the Harlan Party down the Weber River.

Here we set up a permanent camp.

"What shall we do first?" my husband asked next morning while we still sat consuming pancakes.

"Finish breakfast," suggested Dr. Neff succinctly.

"No, I mean which way shall we go today. We can start west over the rest of the Wasatch—Big and Little Mountains, you know, and East Canyon Creek. That's the road the Donners opened. Or we can go the way the Harlans went, down the Weber."

"Well, the Harlans were ahead of the Donners. Let's do first things first," I suggested. "Besides, it will be clearing something off the books that can be done in a day or two. There is no way to tell how long it will take to get over the mountains."

"Going down the river suits me," Mr. Bromley agreed cheerfully. "More rocks and more pictures than the other way." He flipped a pancake expertly and came back to the table with it balanced on the turner. Finding that everyone else had had enough, he added butter and syrup and ate it himself—still cheerfully. This was all quite in character. He is always ready to do anything that the rest want to attempt and never is let down when (as sometimes happens) the project turns out to be a dud. Still, he is probably happiest when there are more rocks, more pictures, and more to eat.

We had set up a very comfortable camp in a lot belonging to Mr. Deardon. The sun had not yet come over the peaks and we were wearing heavy sweaters, but the day would be clear. Just beyond the fence a drove of fat cows, driven by a small boy on a wabbling bicycle, walked slowly down the lane to their daily pasture. The one nonconformist cow, without which no drove of cattle is complete, rested her chin on the fence and looked at us until the small boy, leaving the rest uncomfortably close to the highway, came back to get her.

My husband, remembering his own experiences of cattle herding at a tender age, went out to help. Dishwashing is usually his job, but, in such a worthwhile cause, we divided it between us and were through when he returned.

Our daily routine while on a field trip is remarkably uniform for a project where the most trivial circumstance may change our plans for a week. Leaving out such efforts as photography and field notes and only noting our contributions to actual progress and comfort, we each do about the same things every day. My husband and Mr. Bromley drive alternately, spelling each other every fifty miles. Dr. Neff sets up the camp with casual help from all of us. He and Mr. Bromley get wood and water and keep the gasoline lanterns filled. My husband washes dishes and I shop and cook. I think we have settled into this because of Dr. Neff, who likes to know where he stands and what's to come next at all times.

We left the camp tidy but without any effort to hide our spare coats and so forth, or to take them with us. It is unthinkable that anything untoward should happen in Henefer. It just isn't that kind of a place.

Three miles down the Weber and we were at the foot of Devil's Slide, a natural landmark that takes no special aptitude to appreciate. It doesn't stagger the imagination. It knocks it flat. Two parallel, unbroken walls of rock extend from the mountaintop to the edge of the river. Their vertical measurement is uneven but they come straight as rulers at a uniform distance apart of possibly one-third their height. It is a tremendous affair, as impossible to overlook as one of the

Pyramids. Our much appreciated but voluble Bryant never saw it, we can be perfectly sure, or he would have told of it in detail.

Below the slide the canyon narrows. A freight train, which was rolling easily along the grade of the river, disappeared into a tunnel. The geography of Weber Canyon might be likened to a string of beads, some large and some small, with several places where there is nothing but the string. The valley of Devil's Slide is a tiny bead and it constricts immediately into the particularly tight string of the river.

The highway goes along on its unobstructed way. The engineers used dynamite to take it through, so that the several hundred yards that were impassable to the Harlan wagons meant nothing to us. We skimmed between the towering cliffs on a perfect roadbed.

"This is one of the two bad canyons," I explained unnecessarily, "the upper one, that Hudspeth came back to find a way around."

"I don't see how he ever had the nerve to attempt any part of Weber Canyon," said Mr. Bromley flatly.

"Well, there they were," said my husband, "camped in the valley above Henefer. They couldn't stay forever."

As our car flowed through the funnel provided by dynamite and smoothly laid concrete, it was easy to forget the incongruous highway. Like a well trained servant, it was so perfect as to be inconspicuous. We passed Morgan in its beautiful long valley and came to the beginnings of the lower canyon.

Dr. Neff was first to see the dim scarlike line across the river and part way up the sloping walls of the cliff. Rocks had been cleared away years ago, but the natural growth of a century had hidden much of it from view.

Here Hastings led the Harlan-Young wagons. High on the cliffside they went, over boulders as big as henhouses, through snagging sage and crowding juniper. This was the worst type of going, horribly rough, slanting, and insecure. When a wagon got beyond control on a sidling stretch such as this, it was usually impossible to salvage much. Team and all were sacrificed, rolling to the bottom of the canyon.

The story of the struggle made by the first wagon caravan down the Weber is told in the *California Gold Book*: "The sides of the mountains were covered with a dense growth of willows, never penetrated by white man. Three times spurs of the mountains had to be crossed by rigging the windlass on top, and lifting the wagons almost bodily. The banks were very steep and covered with loose stones, so that a mountain sheep would have been troubled to keep its feet, much more an ox team drawing a heavily loaded wagon. On the 11th of August, while hoisting a yoke of oxen and a wagon up Weber mountain, the rope broke near the windlass. As many men as could surround the wagon were helping all they could by lifting at the wheels and sides. The footing was untenable, and before the rope could be tied to anything, the men found they must abandon the wagon and oxen to destruction, or be dragged to death themselves. The faithful beasts seemed to comprehend the danger, and held their ground for a few seconds, and were then hurled over a precipice at least 75 feet high, and crushed in a tangled mass with the wagon on the rocks at the bottom of the canyon."

It cannot be said with certainty just where this incident took place, but it fits very well the sidling course and steep descent of the detour around Devil's Gate. Almost superhuman efforts were made to clear a pathway, and, at this point, it may still be seen. One day was not enough for the tedious passage of the cliffside trail; the wagons had to be left, when darkness fell, perched precariously in the rocks above the angry torrent.

Into the gate itself we went, the highway flowing along with the river, which was constricted by concrete walls and protesting passionately. The almost invisible scarlike line goes outside the knob that forms the left side of the gate and comes into the canyon proper just below the narrowest portion. The cliffs are quite perpendicular until a hundred feet or so above the foaming water, where the accumulated erosion of the centuries fans out into a projecting base, steep and incredibly rocky. Along the ragged slopes of this base the same almost imperceptible mark may be seen, amounting simply to a course where the biggest rocks have been avoided and the smaller ones moved. Pines and juniper and scrubby growth encroach upon this least used of all the roadways to the west. When at the level of the river again, a narrow flat hardly wide enough for a wagon took the caravan between the Weber and the cliffs, and the ordeal was over. The rest of the way to the Great Salt Lake was easy.

If Hastings had permitted the Donner Party to follow in the footsteps of the Harlans, the canyon road might have become an accepted portion of Hastings' Cutoff and of the gold-rush trail through Salt Lake City. The Harlans, starting from scratch, made the trek along the river in about a week; the Donners, utilizing the roadwork already done, could have negotiated it in less. But Hastings took it upon himself to make their decision for them, and when they arrived at the ford of Weber River a note was waiting for them, wedged into a cleft stick by the side of the trail. Don't attempt the canyon, it said in effect, go over the mountains to the west. And so, with incredible labor, they cleared the shorter, safer, and better way to the valley of the Great Salt Lake. The Mormons, coming the next year to establish their new city, found the route ready at hand. They used it, and the mountain trail became firmly fixed.

Posterity had been served, but at the expense of many lives later sacrificed in the Sierra snows because of the time lost now. And again it was Lansford Hastings' propensity to decide the destiny of others that was the determining factor.

And this time we can say with certainty that he meant well.

≈

CHAPTER III

The Big and the Little Mountains

IN the soft, history-haunted valley where Henefer now stands, the Donners and their company camped five days. It was a small group, since the large companies had broken up at Fort Bridger and had gone their various ways. It was under the captaincy of bighearted George Donner but bore the hyphenated name Donner-Reed Party, acknowledging the co-leadership of James Frazier Reed. They stayed from August 6th through August 10th.

From this point on we are indebted solely to the Miller-Reed journal for all dates having to do with their activities. It is a dual diary, begun by Hiram Miller of the Boggs company and continued until, on July 2nd near La Prele Creek, Edwin Bryant rode back and persuaded Miller to join his pack train, which had been weakened by the defection of one member. The notation for July 3rd appears in its proper place without comment, but it is in Reed's handwriting (a fact duly attested by experts). The little diary was kept daily by him until, on October 4th, it ends abruptly with an unfinished sentence at about the time that Reed, in an uncontrollable fit of anger, killed John Snyder and was banished from the party. The book remained in the possession of his family and was secured and brought from its century of oblivion by Carroll Hall, curator of Sutter's Fort, in 1946. Contact between Miller and Reed on the required date (July 3rd) is established by Bryant, who mentions that the Boggs company arrived in camp on that evening and that all and sundry resolved to celebrate the glorious Fourth of July fittingly. Hundreds of guns were fired and each family feasted as best it could. Mr. Reed had saved some liquors especially for the occasion, said Bryant, and they were used. Whether or not the entire Donner-Reed company had arrived, James Reed was certainly there. Miller had kept merely a chronicle of geography and mileage. Reed carried it on in the same way, maintaining the style and always speaking of himself in the third person; but he could not keep it impersonal; he himself was too impetuous and human. All sorts of sidelights creep into the few lines he set down for each twenty-four hours.

After the frustrating experience of finding Hastings' note by the side of the trail, the Donner-Reed Party came on in great indecision and, if we may judge by other crises, in a decidedly uncertain temper. The note said that if the Donners sent after Hastings, he would return and pilot them through a new and direct route to the Salt Lake. Immediately they sent out Reed, Stanton, and Pike with instructions to bring him back.

Reed wrote in his journal with (it seems to me) sarcasm about the impassability of a canyon through which a large wagon train already had made its way, but he started out with the others, soon became separated from them, and went on alone. If the route was feasible, he could find out as well as the next man. Moreover, he intended to see that Hastings came back and fulfilled the promise so lightly made on paper.

James Frazier Reed had many of the qualities of leadership marred by an angry and violent temper. He was of noble Polish stock which had migrated to Ireland rather than submit to Russian power. The name originally was Reednoski, and he did not come to the United States until he was a youth. He married a widow with one child, Virginia, and both were with him, together with three children of their own marriage.

We can imagine Reed impatiently refusing to be held back by the caution of the other two men and guiding his horse competently over the rolling contours of the tree-clad mountains. Now and then he caught glimpses of the great shining lake and knew that he must pass to the south of it. Once on the valley floor he had no trouble in picking up the wheel tracks of the Harlan-Young Party and went after them as fast as was practical. Finding Hastings in the unknown country ahead was not nearly as difficult as it sounds, but it took courage of a high type to breast the heat, the possibility of hostile Indians, and the long waterless stretches where he was dependent upon the endurance of his mount.

In Tooele Valley he caught up with the wagon party in which Lienhard was traveling and found Hastings with them. There is unrecorded drama in the situation which will never be known. Reed's demands were far from agreeable to Hastings; but, with righteous indignation and an irrefutable justice in his demand for the rights of the party which Hastings had persuaded from the safe pathway to their future home, Reed took that gentleman back.

It would seem that Hastings was supposed to accompany Reed over the mountains to the Donner camp; but, when actually on the way, he balked and would not go through the Wasatch. Instead, he took Reed to some point from which he was supposed to be able to work out the entire route, probably the summit of Little Mountain. Then, in spite of persuasion, which we can imagine was forceful, he went back to the Harlans. Reed, self-reliant and capable, returned in the manner suggested—becoming rather pleased with the route on the way—and rode alone into the camp in Weber Canyon Meadows. Another shock awaited him. Stanton and Pike had not come back.

A search party was sent out that eventually proved successful, and the rest of the company started the next morning over the mountains toward the Great Salt Lake.

*   *   *

It was evening. The sun had long since disappeared behind the summits, but a pleasant warmth remained behind. Instead of hot cakes, a thick and tender steak, which sizzled ecstatically and shot red-hot, fragrant particles of fat all over my hands and apron, was cooking in the pan.

"You dripped water in it," my husband admonished me. "You shouldn't have stirred the coffee with the fork handle."

"I suppose not," I agreed absent-mindedly, "but it was boiling over." I filled the cups with steaming coffee while Dr. Neff cut the steak and Mr. Bromley dished the fried potatoes and scraped the pan for the last bits, thick with browned onions, which had stuck to the bottom and sides.

"You know what?" I began tentatively.

Nobody knew or cared at this stage of the meal, and so I went on: "While I was shopping at the grocery, Mr. and Mrs. Richins—that's the proprietor and his wife—said that they can tell us how to get almost to the top of Big Mountain on the trail the Donners opened. Do you want to go into town, see the new Pioneer Cabin, and talk to them?"

Apparently we all did, so when we had finished dinner we strolled out into the lane on which our tents faced. The cows were returning from pasture fatter, if possible, than they had gone out in the morning. All animals are fat in the Wasatch. They develop double chins and an air of solid benevolence that is very pleasing.

The cabin proved to be a model of its kind, a place such as each small town needs for community affairs. Around the large gathering room were relics of the pioneer days, so many that I have forgotten them; but I shall never forget the pictures of the pioneers themselves. Framed portraits were ranged on the walls. Men with steely eyes and grim, thin-lipped mouths. Remarkably, I thought to myself, like the Pilgrim Fathers, but with a slight variation in hats. Just the type to walk out of organized society and found a religious colony of their own, and not expect any nonsense about it either. The women were no less unbending and were reinforced at every vulnerable spot with buckram and whalebone. Stalwart men and women they were, determined to conquer the new frontier, and whose unrelenting gaze, directed at the unoffending daguerreotypist, would cause any marauding Ute to think twice. When we had seen everything and collected a few ideas for similar projects at home, we commenced to gather data on our rather harebrained project for the next day.

"You can't get to the top of Big Mountain with a car," Mr. Richins told us. "Three weeks from now you might. They've got men and machinery up there trying to scratch out a road to the top so that cars can go over the mountains on the trail by July 24th. That's the centennial of the founding of Salt Lake City."

"Do you think they'll get it done?" Dr. Neff wanted to know.

"I don't see why not. Maybe the cars will be jeeps or trucks, but I think something will get over."

"Well, we can't wait for a road to be built," my husband decided. "What we do, we'll do tomorrow."

Roughly the directions resolved themselves into short phrases: up the canyon of Henefer Creek, to the top of the first ridge, over and down Dixie Creek, around the dam to East Canyon Creek, up East Canyon Creek to a spot called picturesquely Little Dutch Hol, up this creek to the top of Big Mountain.

With dozens of more or less conflicting admonitions in our several confused minds, we returned to camp, determined to start tomorrow morning at all costs and worry about completing the trip when the time came.

*   *   *

The canyon of Henefer Creek is wide, shallow, and open. For some reason it is sometimes called Little East Canyon Creek. It isn't, however, a branch of East Canyon Creek, but runs straight into Weber River from a different watershed. We continue to call it Henefer Creek because that was the name we first learned and because it is far less confusing.

The bottom of the canyon is green with willows, and the trail winds through them along the north bank of the creek. As we progressed, sudden knolls covered with pale gray sage broke through the bright foliage like islands from a placid green river. Sagebrush, oversized from the fertilization of the trail-driven cattle, marched up the hill beside us. One or two ranch houses, starred with the butter-yellow blossoms of climbing rosebushes, gave life to the picture. Dogs barked as we passed.

Gradually we left them behind and attained the first summit, 6,300 feet in elevation. The view to the west was another shallow, slightly sloping draw with a small stream zigzagging down the middle. Presently it resolved itself into a **V**-shaped gully filled with aspens and some rugged old cottonwoods that stretched themselves lustily to reach the sun and wind. Sage was stuffed like excelsior packing into the few yards that lay between the road and the creek at the bottom of the gully. Here, although it seemed unbelievable, was the site of Dixie Creek Pony Express Station. It was marked, or we certainly would have passed by without a glance. There didn't seem to be room enough in the little ravine for a building, however small, but there was water and wood in plenty, with some fair patches of grass into which a brood of tiny quail were scuttling in all directions. These essentials being much more important than space, the stock tenders had managed in some manner to insinuate a tiny log cabin and a shelter for the ponies into the gully. It may have been all one building; such things happened.

From here we came down to the irregular lake formed by the dam on East Canyon Creek, where for several miles the trail is under water and impossible to visualize. All we could do was to follow the road around the edge of the water line and admire the wild flowers: tile-red Indian paintbrush, big yellow daisies, bushes of the frail white tissue-paper poppies, and the sweetest of pink wild roses. Scattered groves of massed aspen trees on the shoulders of the hills made the rest of the short sage-covered slopes look as sheared as a poodle.

Our road was a laboriously constructed shelf high above the surface of the reservoir which contains the water supply for Ogden.

After a long circuitous drive we found that we had climbed high enough to meet East Canyon Creek on its course downward to lake level. It was not easy for us to guess how much water ran in its narrow, deep, brush-walled channel, but the current was very swift.

Orson Pratt wrote: "We followed the dimly traced wagon tracks up this stream for eight miles, crossing the same 13 times. The bottoms of this creek are thickly covered with willows, from five to fifteen rods wide, making an immense labor in cutting a road through for the emigrants [the Donners] last season. We still found the road almost impassable, and requiring much labor. The mountains upon each side rise abruptly from six hundred to three thousand feet above the bed of the stream."

We stopped the car on the rolling top of a subordinate knoll and looked down at the tumbling creek described by Elder Pratt. It was encased fluffily in greenery. Sleek-looking hilltops were iced with last year's shining grass; silvery white sage flattened its supple tops before the breeze; elderberries formed soft hedges topped with the pastel shades of its purple fruit, while under them grew pinky-lavender thistles. Out in the open, on the wind-swept slopes, beautiful cactus blossoms were poised on incredibly tiny plants. They were as big as peonies. With the sun low behind the mountaintop and shining directly through their melon-pink petals, they had the translucence of stained glass. For a few moments the scope and beauty of the prospect actually flattened us into a silence broken only by the crooning of two doves on an elderberry bush.

Presently Mr. Bromley said: "I know perfectly well that Jordan had nothing on East Canyon Creek for being a hard road to travel, but, compared with those cliffs in Weber Canyon, or even the rocks up Echo Creek, this country looks positively soft and downy."

"Yes," Dr. Neff agreed partially, "it looks that way from the top of any of the hills; but when you get down into the growth in the bottom of the draws, it's pretty tough to get through."

"Well, there never was a time when any lives were in danger coming this way, or any place where a wagon could have rolled over a cliff."

"No, I guess this route wasn't quite so hard on the nerves as Weber Canyon," my husband admitted; "but I'll bet the oxen weren't any more comfortable. Their legs were always gashed from stepping on the sharp stakes where the Donners hacked the willow bushes out of the way. Reed gives daily mileage along here, doesn't he?" He turned to me. "Let's hear what it was."

"The first day up from Weber River they made five miles." I found the reference and read sketchily aloud. "The next day, two; the third day, two, cutting willows to let the teams through; on the fourth day they made one more mile in East Canyon, which Reed seems to call Bosman Creek, then they turned off into a side canyon to climb up to Big Mountain and really got into a thicket. Things evidently kept getting worse as they went along, but they made one mile in the branch canyon."

"That small side canyon is what they now call Little Dutch Hol," said my husband, "and it's spelled 'Hol'—without any *e*. Don't ask me why," he admonished, as I opened my mouth, "because I don't know. That adds up to two miles the fourth day, doesn't it? Eleven all told?"

I added slowly in my mind and gave it up. Figures just won't stand still for me. "I guess so," I replied inconclusively. "There was a spring where they stopped in the branch canyon; they camped there three full days after the first night, cutting and clearing out the trees and brush ahead. Reed was beginning, in his odd third-person sort of way, to call the gap they were heading for, Reed's Gap. Probably that's what the rest of the company called it too."

"You don't know that they did," Dr. Neff reminded me perfunctorily.

"No, of course not; but they would be apt to. This route was his 'cup of tea,' as the English say, and nobody else's."

"If the Miller-Reed journal had been in circulation all these years —like Bryant's for instance," said my husband, "this pass might be called Reed's Gap."

"And he would have earned it," Mr. Bromley decided. "After all, he made a hard trip after Hastings and picked this way over the mountains as a solution to an impossible situation. And it's not so bad," he added, looking over the canyon we had come up, and then ahead. "Not nearly as bad as I've always pictured it. I don't see how they could have done any better from where they were camped near Henefer, unless they discounted Hastings' warning and followed the Harlan wagons."

"And that really would have been dangerous," I put in. "I can't imagine them getting to the foot of the canyon intact—not the unlucky Donner Party!"

"How long did it take them to get through this way?" asked my husband.

"From the time they left the Weber," I summed up from the journal in my hand, "they were eleven days traveling to Salt Lake Valley, but of course they had wasted an extra four full days before starting, in the Weber Canyon meadows, waiting for Reed to get back."

"And how long were the Harlans in the canyon?"

Again I thumbed through the index of my notebooks and found what I wanted: "Jacob Harlan wrote in his recollections that they reached the valley on the seventh day."

"Four days' difference in traveling time—both parties breaking trail. It doesn't sound like much in a trip lasting six months," Mr. Bromley summed up, "but if they had been four days earlier, they wouldn't have been caught by the storm in the Sierra Nevadas."

"It made the difference between life and death," said my husband, "for the thirty-six members of the Donner Party who died in the snow."

We drove on and presently saw among the trees the cookhouse of a construction camp. The cook emerged as we drove up. He was carrying garbage and took his time about dumping it in a recently dug pit. Then he strolled over to meet us. He was white-aproned and his stomach bulged like the sail of a racing yacht. He looked extremely knowing and competent.

The men, lighting cigarettes, lazily left the questioning to me.

"We want to go up Big Mountain," I began. "Oh, I know it's just ahead and we could walk up on the construction road; but we don't want to do that. We want to follow the emigrant trail."

As usual, I was inoffensively but unmistakably wrong. The cook frowned at me. His thick brown eyebrows moved toward his nose like humping caterpillars. "Up the construction road is just where you *do* want to walk," he informed me, "because up the construction road is just where the trail is. There's no place else for it to go."

And we found it to be true. Reed's Gap was a natural pass, and there is still no better way to get to it than the way Reed went.

At the turn of the canyon of Little Dutch Hol, the frantically working construction crew thoughtfully presented us with another mile of passable road. The steady, unhurried, immutable passing of time had completed a century since the first (and probably, until now, the last) time a road had been constructed here. I sat as adhesively as possible and tried to take notes, but it was out of the question and I finally devoted myself exclusively to keeping the cameras and the thermal jug unscrambled. My coiffure disjointed and fell down strand by strand; and, worst of all, from my point of view, it was impossible to take pictures out of the window without damaging the mechanism of the camera. We reached the construction equipment and passed it, heavy steam shovels, trucks, and tractors. At the last point where it was possible to turn the car around, we stopped, and I slid out at once to solid ground. The relief was that of leaving a pitching boat for the stability of the wharf.

"What's the matter with your stomach?" asked my husband with true husbandly frankness, turning quizzical eyes toward my midriff. "Did you eat too much lunch?"

I glanced down casually and then stared with horror at the region immediately south of my belt. There was undoubtedly a pronounced bulge.

"Why, no—why, for heaven's sake!" I gasped, clutching at the convex surface with both hands. It deflated flimsily and I discovered, with relief, that my skirt had made a half-revolution during the heavy weather just completed and that the bulge was merely the well stretched area in which I was accustomed to sit.

Little Dutch Hol is fundamentally stony but it is also solidly filled at the bottom with small, leafy trees. Wild roses and clover run down the steep hill slopes to meet them. This was probably the most thickly grown-over and the most resistant of any portion of the Donner-Reed Party's hard won roadway.

We walked to the top of the next small summit, and from it we could see Big Mountain painted in, a blob of grayish green against the clean biting blue of Utah's sky. On its slopes slender firs pointed dark fingers from among the soft rounded contours of willow and aspen. We didn't trouble to walk to the top. It was getting late, and we had formed a nebulous plan to arrive there, quite painlessly, from the west side.

*   *   *

Planning was quick and easy. Actually getting around the **mountain** and establishing camp took two days, at the end of which time we presented our inquiring selves, with apologies, to another construction crew. Its headquarters were on Little Mountain, to which there has been a good road for possibly ten years. (We saw it during the process of building but have forgotten the date.) The workmen were on the same project as the ones in Little Dutch Hol: digging, gouging, filling, everything but smoothing, a road to Big Mountain's broad top. We asked if we might ride in the workmen's truck, but instead were granted the privilege of traveling in the rough, tough car of the superintendent of construction, Mr. Cornell Clyde, who took us as far as the road was passable. Our car would not have been permitted on this stretch under construction, and therefore we were saved a five-mile walk uphill. Our only objective was the top of Big Mountain; we would gladly hike back; so, rather reluctantly, Mr. Clyde left us at the foot of the last steep pitch and went about his business.

The final five hundred yards was a workout. My own performance was a scramble, and the business of keeping the camera box and the field notebook with me was all too suggestive of a cat with two kittens. I arrived finally, hot and breathless, and dropped down on the spongy grass.

A gusty wind jumped at us through the gap and blew vigorously.

Dr. Neff produced a grimy handkerchief and wiped his face and hands. "There's the marker," he said pointing.

My husband turned to look at it. "Pratt's Pass," he read aloud. "Well, Orson Pratt came next after the Donners. As long as it's not named for Reed, Pratt is in line for the honor, I guess."

"What date did Pratt get here?" asked Dr. Neff.

"About the middle of July in 1847, a year after the Donners," my husband told him. "I remember it because of the date of the Mormon centennial celebration—July 24th. That was when Brigham Young and the last wagons arrived in the valley. The Mormons really opened up this route and kept it open for years."

The pitch down from Big Mountain was bad but soon became more reasonable. It still showed the ruts of the original trail. On either side the ferns and brakes were luxuriant, for the spring of 1947 had been the wettest in many years. Even the construction work had not covered the greenery with dust, and the canyons had a new-washed look. The thimbleberry bushes are always a particularly vivid green, and today one could fairly sense the sap threading through the bright broad leaves.

The trail is in the canyon of Pine Creek, an unpretentious mountain rivulet about three to five feet across. The modern road follows the course of the trail closely, but where the road crosses Pine Creek from right bank to left, close under the granite bluffs, the trail continues on the right bank for several hundred yards and crosses somewhere before its confluence with Dell Creek.

My husband and I walked the road, watching its relation to the creek and the trail. The two other men, being rather more interested in the construction work, left us and went off to see what had been done in that line.

Presently Dell Creek made a sharp bend to the right and the road forded it. The trail, diving through the brush, seemed to go around the bend; but it was easier, we thought, to stay with the road. There was no bridge, but two slender, sapling logs lay side by side, slung from bank to bank, about two feet above the water.

The creek was not very wide. We decided to walk the logs.

I am inclined to be dizzy on such occasions, therefore my husband went first and I after him, with one hand on his shoulder. He carried the camera.

The first step proved that the saplings were going to bend beneath our weight, so we stood poised for a moment and decided that he should proceed with the right foot on the right log and I with the left foot on the left log, moving in unison.

We got under way, and I go on record that changing horses in the middle of the stream has no terrors compared with changing step. The first plan didn't work at all, so I stood on my left foot until he could get his weight over on the left log, which promptly submerged. The right one snapped up knee high. At that elevation it was no use to me, and we decided to walk the slippery six-inch cylinder we were on.

After a few more steps I lost my balance and we made a run for it, during which I pulled my husband off center and regained my own equilibrium. He stood in front of me, about three feet from the bank, windmilling both arms. I couldn't save him or (what was more important) the camera from a complete sousing except by pushing with all my might.

He fell on the bank and I fell in the creek.

When we met Dell Creek returning from its short digression, and had to cross it again, we waded.

The trail continued with Dell Creek but crossed the line of the new roadfill at some easily recognizable giant cottonwoods and proceeded down into Mountain Dell. Never have I seen more or lovelier wild flowers than those covering the slopes of Mountain Dell, which housed, in its day, the next pony-express station west of Dixie Creek.

From there the trail proceeds up to Little Mountain, accessible by highway, and down Emigration Canyon, thick with brush, into the immense open valley of the Great Salt Lake.

To the emigrants of 1846, the valley had no points of interest except the hot springs near modern Salt Lake City, and the Jordan River, which they called Utah Outlet, as it carried the waters from Utah Lake to the Salt Lake and the Great Salt Lake itself. By the next summer the story was quite different, and from that time on the Mormon City of the Great Salt Lake was the chief attraction between the Missouri frontier and California for those who took the Overland Road leading that way.

The first two years of the gold rush found many travelers of Hastings' Road spending a pleasant day or two in the City of the Saints. It was reassuring, especially to the women of the migration, to see the neat houses in their ample grounds. They were built of sun-dried brick, "some looking," wrote James Blood in 1850, "very well. Upon the whole I think the town has a better appearance than Nauvoo" (the latter being the town in Illinois from which the Mormons had been driven). The gardens were watered systematically by ditches which tapped the rushing creeks from the Wasatch Mountains, and, almost at once, the people had vegetables; within an incredibly short time they had fruit and would sell or trade for tea, coffee, and things that they could not raise. The competent Mormon women kept boardinghouses during the season that the emigrants were in the city and thus brought a little hard cash into the coffers of the community, although we have Stansbury's statement to the effect that, in 1849, there was a mint in operation, making money of its own.

Polygamy, an acknowledged institution in 1849 and 1850, stimulated the interest and piqued the curiosity of the westbound visitors. A land where a man might have all the wives he was able to support interested the vital, warm-blooded men who had responded to the call of adventure. A land where no woman, no matter how unattractive, need go unmarried caused chatter among the women of the migration, who were not so slow themselves or they wouldn't have been there. De Wolf summed it up: "Their creed allows them a plurality of wives according to their means of supporting them & their Constitutional strength, hence a man of a strong Constitution & worth much property is allowed more wives than one of weak Constitution & not much of this world's goods."

It was seldom that any person traveling through Salt Lake City made derogatory remarks about anyone of the community; and the exceptions to this rule almost invariably objected, with the unconscious bigotry of the times, to the dignitaries of the Mormon church. Such comments, although sometimes scathing, are greatly in the minority compared to the grateful acknowledgments of invalids who were nursed back to health, women who received sisterly help with their small children, and men who simply remembered how good the home cooking had tasted. "Farewell," Darwin wrote as he left the desert city in 1849, "farewell to thy kind hospitality so stomach cheering & thought invigorating after the famine of the plains of sage & mountains of barrenness."

At first, of course, Hastings' Road was the accepted thoroughfare west from Salt Lake City, but its dangers were such that the Mormons soon commenced to use the old trappers' trails that led north and west. In 1848 Samuel Hensley opened the route to the City of the Rocks, thence to California; and by 1849 the migration was deflected that way so that it carried more than half of the gold seekers who had visited Salt Lake City. But Hastings' Cutoff had the prestige of having been longer in use by wagons, and few persons knew enough about it to speak logically of its dangers.

As late as 1850, many wagons turned into the older road south of the lake. Those who did so regretted it with every fiber of their being and almost every mile of the way, but they were the last. Before the next year its delayed bad reputation caught up with it and the section from Salt Lake City west (which was the portion commonly known as the cutoff) became utterly lonely and unused beyond the valley settlements of the Mormon people.

CHAPTER IV

Salt, Sand, and Sage

A T six o'clock in the morning we left Salt Lake City. We took our mileage at Pioneer Square, the place where the original fort was built in 1847, and headed for the Jordan River. We reached it before we had cleared the outskirts of the city. It is a full, silent stream, deep and undisturbed. Large bushes line the banks and squat upon the glossy surface, sitting squarely upon the reverse end of their own reflections. Bold rushes break the curved monotony. So many miles has the Jordan come through flatland that it is difficult to see which way it flows. The emigrants found it marsh bordered and wearied their teams and wore themselves out in the effort to put its seeping waters behind them.

There are few diaries to which one can turn for information of this section of the Overland Trail to California. The country didn't seem to lend itself to literary achievements. Men were too busy, too anxious, too tired to write at the end of the day; and many who did write lost their journals when their luggage was abandoned along the line. Much that was amusing and of great interest happened in the stretch of 250-odd miles between Salt Lake City and the place (just west of modern Elko, Nevada) where the cutoff rejoined the main Overland Road. Much that was discouraging and tragic took place also. But accounts of daily happenings are hard to find.

The only journals of Hastings' Cutoff that were in common use when we started our field work were those of Clyman, Bryant, and John Wood. To those I soon added Udell, Lienhard, Blackburn, Chalmers, Shinn and Bloom. Suddenly, in a two-year period, two more useful diaries appeared in print: first, in 1946, the Miller-Reed journal, the only day-by-day account of the journey of the Donner Party extant (but lacking the portion from the Big Blue River of Kansas to La Prele Creek in Wyoming and also the finale, as it ends at Gravelly Ford of the Humboldt River); and next, in 1948, the journal of Madison Moorman who traveled the cutoff in 1850 and maintained a coherent diary without interruption. Of these, Bryant is the most useful for the study of early days on the trail; Moorman, for the gold-rush period and ordinary field work.

I thought of Moorman as I looked at the Jordan River. He found a Mormon-built bridge there in 1850 and wrote: "We had a miserably bad bog to cross immediately after leaving the corporation, and about two miles on we had to encounter the river Jordan, about sixty-feet wide and very deep. We found an old bridge very much mutilated, upon which we crossed our wagon by man-power, having to use a broad plank which was carried from one end to the other, to roll the wheels upon from the land, where it was disconnected. Our packs were carried over on our shoulders, and the mules made to swim. As tedious as this may seem, all hands soon accomplished it."

By "the corporation" Moorman meant the Mormon settlement at Salt Lake City. The "bog" was the marshland, since drained and rendered habitable.

At the Jordan we connected with the trail eastward from California in 1827 of Jedediah Smith, the great pathfinder, with two comrades, Robert Evans and Silas Gobel. In 1826 Smith and his trappers were the first white men to travel overland from the States to California. Now, a year later, these three were the first to make their way back across the Nevada and Utah deserts, the country eventually to be traversed by stagecoach, pony express, and telegraph. They were almost dead from thirst when they finally won through to the east side of the salt flats and journeyed northward through Skull Valley, but found good water and had almost recuperated from their experience by the time they arrived at the Jordan. Smith called the river the Outlet from Utah Lake, and found it swollen and overflowing.

The three had no time to detour. They were headed joyfully for the trappers' rendezvous and wanted to get there before it broke up. "I determined to make a raft," wrote Smith in his journal, "and for this purpose cut a quantity of Cain Grass. . . . In the first place I swam and lead my horse over, the mule following. . . . I then returned and, attaching a cord to the raft and holding the end in my mouth, I swam before the raft while the two men swam behind. Unfortunately neither of my men were good swimmers, and the current being strong, we were swept down a considerable distance, and it was with great difficulty that I was enabled to reach the shore, as I was verry much strangled."

It is a country of extremes. Two days previous, this hazardous experience in a flooded river would have seemed a very paradise to his parched and dehydrated body.

From the west bank of the Jordan the wagon road sponsored by Hastings went as straight as was practical to the northern point of a short range of mountains, running south from the lake, where a

spring surrounded by fair pasturage made a natural camp. This is the Oquirrh Range, or, if you will, plain Mineral Mountains. Moorman wrote: "Our road lay in the direction of the point of a mountain that appeared to be not more than two or three miles, which we found to be fifteen. The sun was down when we reached it, and there being fine grass and plenty of water, though a little brackish, we stopped for the night."

The modern traveler looks past the spring and sees as the chief object of interest the tall chimneys and the heap of black slag that mark the big smelter at Garfield. This was the natural stopping place on the first day out from Salt Lake City, the next good water being too far away for wagon trains to reach that night. Bryant's pack train went on; but the Donner Party stayed here, and Reed made a notation on the margin of his journal that it had taken them eighteen days to come thirty miles. Chalmers and Bloom each stayed here in 1849 in a drenching rainstorm. Moorman and John Wood stayed at the point in 1850, and Wood made the remark that the water along this portion of the trail was, in general, brackish.

In late July of 1850, Moorman and his company traveled five miles around the north end of the Oquirrhs and were interested to note that someone had found use for Black Rock, a gigantic stone (too big for a boulder and too small for a hill) which now broods over a cluster of painted cottages for all the world like an old black hen over a hatching of white chicks. "Five miles," wrote Moorman, "brought us to the briny sea, at a point where an exploring party, under pay of the U.S., had erected an observatory, upon an isolated rock of immense magnitude, which had been surrounded by the waters of the lake but made accessible by filling up and making a road with volcanic stones."

I was insufferably proud of myself when, on a hunch one day, I read through Stansbury's report of his survey of the Great Salt Lake in 1849 and found that his men had erected the framework on Black Rock. He was surveying the vicinity of the Lake and caused stations to be erected at various points to enable him "to cover the whole surface with a series of triangles, which would verify the work." He put one up on Frémont Island, one on a small rocky island about a mile west of Antelope Island, one on Mud Island, and so on. Then he decided to put one on Black Rock. This was on April 20th, 1850. He said that the station "was framed from timbers which had been previously cut in the mountains and hauled to the spot for the purpose; but the force of the party was not sufficient to raise it. Orders were sent to the herdsmen in Tuilla [Tooele] Valley, near by, to bring a team in the morning—the station was raised on the following day, and," he continued, "we started for the city, leaving the boat's crew encamped on the shore of the lake."

An interesting side issue during their sojourn on the rock was the corned-beef episode. They had some good beef, more than they could eat at once, but they were not fond of beef after it had dried. There may have been a few people who liked jerky, but apparently they were not fluent writers, as one never reads of their appreciation.

One man related, with apparent sincerity, that, feeling the pangs of hunger while walking along the trail, he fished in his knapsack and drew out what he thought to be a piece of jerky. After he had chewed on it for some time without making much impression, he discovered it to be the sole of an old Pawnee moccasin which he had brought along, probably for repairing his own. He didn't feel any more pangs, at least not of the same order, and he threw it away.

That is not a necessary anecdote, but it certainly puts jerky in its place.

When Stansbury's men decided to corn their beef, they tied it to a long rope and simply dropped it off the rock into the salt waters of the lake. Of course it kept nicely for as long as they left it there, and it was an acceptable change in diet when eaten.

The Mormons had a primitive saltworks at Black Rock. Moorman wrote: "A man was also engaged in making salt here for the supply of the city. He told me that four measures of the water would yield one of salt, the purest, whitest and most delightful article I ever saw."

From this point one may have a good view of the islands of the lake, only three of which are large enough for ready identification. The one smallest and most distant from Black Rock lies southeast of Promontory Point and was the first to be visited by white men. On September 9, 1843, Frémont, with four of his company, made the trip in a tiny boat of rubberized linen stuck together with glue. Frémont's report to his chief of the topographical bureau is a miracle of understatement. "The insecurity of the boat," he wrote restrainedly, "was sensibly felt by us." Later he amplified it a bit: "So long as we could touch the bottom with our paddles, we were very gay; but gradually, as the water deepened, we became more still in our frail batteau of gum cloth distended with air, and with pasted seams." The five men were Frémont; his assistant Charles Preuss; his loyal friend and comrade, Kit Carson; and two French Canadian voyageurs, Baptiste Bernier and Basil Lajeunesse, of whom the latter was his favorite on several expeditions and an extremely skillful swimmer and canoeman. The boat was light and rode the increasingly rough swells like a bird, but she was slow to paddle and two of her airtight divisions had given way before they arrived at the temporary security of the island. They climbed to the summit to make observations and here Frémont accidentally left the brass cover to the object end of his spyglass, noting the incident in his journal. They spent the night on the island and a strong wind rose which caused waves to break heavily on the shore and the island to tremble. There was neither water nor timber on this rocky islet, which was about twelve or thirteen miles in circumference, and Frémont, in his first reaction from the discovery, called it Disappointment Island. In the morning they dared the waves, whose flung spray hardened into a crust of salt upon their clothes, and reached the shore in safety. Probably in the winter of 1849-1850 Captain Howard Stansbury hunted on this rocky summit for the brass end of the telescope, but without success. He renamed the island for Frémont with more lasting results, as it is still so marked on modern maps. Some ten or twelve years ago my husband had a young man in one of his extension classes at the University of California. He doesn't remember the man's name. He doesn't remember whether the class was in Oakland or in San Francisco. (This is a disgustingly indefinite incident.) He doesn't remember the year. All he knows certainly is that the young man lived, or possibly taught, in Tecoma, Nevada. Now Tecoma is close to the line of the Overland Trail, and the young chap became interested in the early history of the country. "Why don't you," my husband asked him at the close of the semester, "go out on Frémont Island and see if you can find the end of the telescope? It is brass and can't rust. If no one has found it, it must still be there." In a month or two he received a letter from the man stating (with moderate enthusiasm, considering how long the search had lasted) that he had found it, giving details, and saying that he would show it to us when he passed this way again. He has never passed this way. We have never seen the brass end of Frémont's spyglass; but we haven't the faintest doubt that he wrote the truth. This historic relic has been found and brought away from its long-time hiding place. If, by reason of this publication, anyone can send us word of it, we shall be glad.

The largest island is three-peaked Antelope, bare and brown, just north of the pseudo-Moorish domes and roller coaster of Saltair. It was also visited by Frémont, but two years later, in 1845. He called it a "peninsular island," and the Indians told him that at low water it might be reached on horseback. So, on October 18th of that year, he took Carson and a few others with him and rode to it through shallow water. The floor of the lake was a sheet of salt, so he said, like softening ice; and the horses sank to their fetlocks. On arrival they found water and rolling slopes of grass, over which bounded several bands of antelope—hence the name which Frémont promptly bestowed and recorded. They killed some for meat. Returning, they found awaiting them a serious and reproachful old Utah Indian who accosted them at once. They were *his* antelopes, *all* of them, and he must have payment. Frémont, equally serious, acknowledged the debt, had a bale unpacked, and gave him some red cloth, a knife, and some tobacco. Richer than he had ever been in his life, the old man was pleased and triumphant.

The most picturesque of the three large islands of the Salt Lake is Stansbury Island, northwest of Black Rock. It is sometimes peninsular and can then be reached by road from Bonneville Station, but it was completely surrounded by water the last time we saw it. A fine deposit of silica sand provides its only industry. It was named in commemoration of the work done by the Stansbury Expedition in 1849-1850.

Great Salt Lake with its islands can be very hideous, with spume-covered, rotten edges where one dare not walk for fear of sinking through the crust and would not walk if one could on account of the loathsome white worms, larvae of some insect, writhing in a nightmare tangle on the beach.

Or, if one will but take the longer view, Great Salt Lake can be charming beyond words. It is most beautiful when seen early or quite late, with the gracile, misty loveliness of its curved shores against the dawn-draped peaks; in amethystine sunsets; on black velvet nights when suddenly a glory shows above the Wasatch and the moon lays a long arm across the lake, pushing herself high enough to see the radiance she herself creates. I prefer the long view. Then, to me, the lake is lovely.

Some two miles beyond Black Rock we passed the most northerly projecting point of the Oquirrhs and then curved swiftly southward into fertile Tooele Valley. The modern name (pronounced Tuilla) is a somewhat painful spelling of the Spanish "tule," a plant which grew there luxuriantly. The valley, caught between two forbidding mountain ranges, the deadly waters of the lake, and an aloof, uninterested sky, is all the more relaxing because of its grim surroundings.

The first thing one sees in the valley is a large monolith, probably sandstone, projecting skyward on the left of the road. Its most inappropriate name has been, from earliest days, Adobe Rock. We asked many old-timers and students of Utah's romantic history why it was called by such a contradictory title, and no one ventured a guess. Finally, as Moorman mentioned a building at the eastern end of the valley and Chalmers saw it also and called it an "old mud house" near a spring, the idea commenced to take root in my mind that the house was adobe and the rock had been called so because of their proximity.

It was the historian of the Church of Latter Day Saints in Salt Lake City who, at my request, browsed through their early files and came forth with the statement that the adobe building in question had been built at Stansbury's order for the same "herdsmen in Tuilla Valley" who helped to raise the station on Black Rock. So, although the journalists spoke of it as "old," it was actually only rain soaked and dilapidated.

Bloom evidently referred to the same adobe hut when, after bathing near Black Rock at noon, he passed the "last habitation" in the evening.

From other sources I found that a prominent trailside spring, reached early in the trek through the valley and spoken of as one of the main water supplies, was a double affair called Twin Springs. Inquiries were unavailing. No one had ever heard of it, but still I reasoned that the old hut had been built near its necessary water.

"Never mind what they call it; I don't care about the name," I told the three men. "If I could just find a pair of springs near the rock, the whole proposition would click and I'd know that my hunch isn't impossible."

Mr. Bromley has a large and easy tolerance for my ideas. We climbed the rock and looked around the valley. "I don't see any patches of green grass that look as if they were around springs," he said. "Not two together, anyway; but there are two big ponds across the highway. Maybe you can make something out of that."

My husband joined me as I passed the car. Dr. Neff had already settled down with a newspaper in expectation of our departure; he now moved over, handed Mr. Bromley the editorials, and hung on to the sports sheet. The paper crackled and snapped in the breeze, and, as I stepped off the cement, I heard Mr. Bromley sucking at his pipe and the scratch of a match. They would be busy for a while.

We started toward the ranch house beyond the ponds and presently could see that the latter were actually one body of water divided by a fill or causeway used as an approach road. "Well, there goes my theory of two springs," I admitted, "but let's see what we can find out anyway."

A knock elicited Mrs. Castagno, who knows the valley like a beloved book. She was interested in my theory at once and came out to show us around. She never had heard, she said, of an adobe on the premises; but the place is full of little log cabins, one of which, standing in dignity under a tree, is the oldest house left in Tooele Valley. The adobe, she agreed, might have been anywhere near by, for this was the logical building spot; but if it had begun to look old and decrepit after only two years of existence, surely there would be nothing left after a century.

I said I really hadn't expected to find any trace of the mud hut and only wanted to know if she had ever heard anyone speak of it.

Across the easterly section of the pond, as we moved toward it, stood Brigham Young's old woolen mill, which was one of the starting points of Utah's wool industry. It did a brisk business in its day and hired women workers. The water of the reservoir glinted like green silk shot with metal threads as the fattest and most prosperous of goldfish swarmed toward us to be fed.

"You must raise goldfish for the market," I hazarded.

"Well, yes, we do. Not that we particularly want to sell them, but they thrive in the pond and we get too many."

"I'm disappointed in your pond," Mr. Paden told her. "We had hoped that it was two ponds until we saw that the road between them is a fill."

"And why," she asked with real curiosity, "do you care whether it's one or two?"

"We are looking for two springs close together that we hoped might be near here. No one seems to know anything about them. I guess we'll have to give them up."

"And why," she asked again, "do you care whether you find one spring or two?"

Her interest was real and unflagging, and so we told her the reason in detail. "All right," she said, "you can stop hunting. Your twin springs are right down there," pointing toward the more easterly body of water. "They feed the pond. It's really a dam, as you can see; and enough water flows out of the dam to run the smelter at Garfield. That's not a figure of speech, either," she hastily assured us. "It *does* run the smelter."

I have seldom been more delighted over a small fact. "What luck!" I exclaimed. "Now everything dovetails."

"You may well call it luck," she asserted. "If you had come here two years ago asking the same question, I don't suppose anyone could have answered it; but we drained the pond last year because the carp got so thick. We hated to do it, but we had to get rid of them in some way. So we sold or moved the goldfish and opened up the dam."

"And the springs were there?"

"The springs were there, all right, or rather one spring in two sections. You can see their output flowing over the spillway. Is that what you wanted to know?"

"Nothing, simply nothing, could be better. And the carp? Did you get rid of them?"

"No, the only thing we got rid of was the goldfish," she said indignantly. "We waited a month before we refilled the pond; and when we turned in the water, every carp that had ever been there wriggled out of the mud in perfect health and took up residence again."

The trail laid out by Hastings did not bend so far to the south as does the present highway. After the emigrants had passed the spring with its mud hut, they began to look for the jutting point of Stansbury Range, around which they must pass, and only stayed far enough south to keep out of the salt flat which rounds out from the lake shore toward Tooele Valley. Some camped on the nearest fork of Willow Creek, a pretty mountain stream stemming from the Stansbury Range. Others pitched their tents near some of the deep "wells" peculiar to the valley.

On the evening of the day he left the spring at Garfield, Moorman wrote: "Just before sundown we encamped on Willow Creek, a deep, clear and cold little stream of about four feet wide, having travelled for the day twenty-five miles."

And Willow Creek would be, for us as well, the next point of interest, for it flows through Grantsville, and Grantsville has grown up on the site of the Twenty Wells, named by the Donner Party; called also Hastings' Wells by Jefferson. We could see the town ahead, at the most southerly point on the highway as it curves around the incroaching salt flats. Its dominating feature is the wealth of spirelike Lombardy poplars that rise above the streets.

They are the largest I have ever seen, with swollen trunks and towering tops. One side road has a double row that demands attention, and its length stretched out before us like an unwrapped bolt of goods, satin-striped with sun and shadow between the pointing fingers of the trees.

Of course the poplars have no part in the picture as the emigrants saw it; but down this same lane are a few of the wells, and a densely shaded reservoir beside the road holds the overflow from four small units of the original group.

An even century, to the month, stretched back from the day of our visit to the time when the first wagon trains reached the twenty wells.

Reed's references are not very lucid, but they seem to indicate that a group of ten, called the Lower Wells, were found at a distance of about twenty miles from their last camp (near the spring at Garfield), and that the Upper Wells, numbering ten (one fresh and nine brackish), were found slightly south of the trail two or three miles farther west. It has seemed hard out of all reason for us to substantiate his statement, or to find out much about the groups of wells; for most of them are out in the fields, capped and overgrown, and we always arrive at the harvest season, when every farmer is busy.

Some one who is familiar with the country as it used to be should take the time and trouble to work out the geography. For, where the camp road to the Upper Wells left the main trail, a man is buried. Here the Donner Party left Luke Halloran beneath the friendly sod of Tooele Valley. Throughout the century we have known only that Halloran was buried not far from the grave of John Hargrave of the Harlan Party, and various reminiscences placed the latter near the Jordan River. It remained for the Miller-Reed journal to fix the place definitely. These two statements are in Reed's handwriting; the first on August 25th: "left Camp [near Garfield] early this morning intending if possible to make the Lower Wells being fair water 20 which we made and in the evening a Genntleman by name of Luke Halloran died of consumption having been brought from Bridgers Fort by George Donner as distance 151 miles We made him a coffin and Burried him at the upper wells at the forks of the road in a beautiful place"; the second, on August 26th reads: "left Camp late and proceeded to the upper wells One of them delightful water being entirely fresh the rest in no. about 10 in all Brackish this day Buried Mr. Luke

Halloran hauling him in his Coffin this distance 2 which we only made and buried him as above stated at the forks of the one [road] turning directly South to Camp   the other West or onward."

Reed's literary prowess is not in any manner comparable to his undoubted intelligence, and the lack may be attributed to the fact that English was not his mother tongue. The dating of his entries is confusing also, since it seems unlikely that they had two funerals; the explanation may be that he started to write the description of the interment at the end of the first day's statement about the death, then decided to date it properly.

Besides the interesting data as to Halloran's burial place, we gather from Reed's statement that the Upper Wells were on a branch, or camp, road and not on the main trail.

Henry Bloom, camped probably on Willow Creek, slept too soundly after his hard day's trip and let his horses stray. He lost a full day searching, but, toward evening, they were found eight miles back at Twin Springs. Starting from camp, he and his comrades then made seven miles to another stream of cold mountain water, a better one, where they spent the night. The camps were no doubt on the two forks of Willow Creek, although Bloom's wanderings make the mileage vary from the usual.

Bryant's pack train camped on Willow Creek. They had made a swift trip of forty miles during the day, from the foothills of the Wasatch, and in the evening three intelligent young Utah Indians came to visit. Friendly Indians usually *did* visit; they liked everything about a social call, but especially the food. These were the last word in what the well dressed Ute was wearing, and they appeared in buckskin shirts, gaiters, and moccasins. Trousers were omitted as unnecessary. They were armed with bows and arrows. One young man of about twenty-five years was so eager in his desire to learn English words that he kept Bryant up far into the night and finally had to be requested to go to bed, which he did with reluctance. Bryant's list of words from the Utah dialect, written by the flickering light of their campfire, is included in his journal.

In the morning Hudspeth and Bryant decided to cross over the Stansbury Range, instead of circling around it to the north, and laid their course due west toward a gap. When Hastings later arrived with the wagons, he did not attempt to imitate their course but chose the more circuitous route as being easier. Immeasurably the greater number of emigrants in the years to come followed Hastings, passing through what are now fields of clover.

Fertile Tooele Valley, slow and soft, is a law unto itself. The streamlets that cut its padded pastures are cool and placid; living springs well up from unknown depths below and lie motionless; the cattle graze quietly or stand replete and chew their cuds; nothing ever seems to hurry. It rests tranquilly at the heart of Utah.

The objective of both trail and highway, the craggy head of Stansbury Range, is blunt and broken nosed. The flattened north end is several miles across, with big recessed coves in its structure, which is solid rock covered with the merest skimming of earth. To the right, across the white salt flats, is equally rugged Stansbury Island, with its feet in the blue waters of the lake. It looks like a continuation of its namesake range. Once the rocky headland of the latter is passed, trail and highway part company. We ventured to the left on a small dirt road and, turning, saw the great cement thoroughfare leaving us with Olympian unconcern. Go ahead, I thought indignantly; I don't care about you either.

Our course was now southward into Skull Valley, the flatland that lies between the Stansbury Range and Cedar Mountains to the west. We were on the road to Iosepa; and it was kind enough to hug the western foot of the Stansbury, just as the trail was forced to do, so that we were enabled to see the path of the emigrants in comparative comfort. We had no sooner left the highway than we saw Big Spring, and smelled it, too, a queer salty whiff that just missed being offensive. Its flat waters shone against the bright green of its greasewood-covered banks. They are undrinkable.

The fact meant nothing to us, but to the emigrants and their thirsty animals, eyes and nostrils clogged with blown salt dust, it was unforgivable. The presence of Big Spring was always an insult. We questioned a tall gangling man who was doing something technical to a small truck on the road nearby. He had the blackish-brown complexion of overbaked bread and appeared to know the country. He said that Big Spring is almost as salt as the lake itself.

Extending south, a chain of brackish springs lies irregularly spaced, big salt tears wept by the lake for her misdeeds and appearing on the white face of the barren flat. The contour of Tooele Valley is repeated here in Skull Valley, but without so much fertile land. It lies between two mountain ranges and a curve of salt projects from the lakeshore southward into its heart. Both trail and modern dirt road move from one spring to the next down the eastern edge to avoid the salt. In different years the springs vary in degrees of undrinkableness, but the first one, Burnt Spring, seems to be the least offensive.

At the right, as the traveler moves south with the Stansbury Range on his left, is a dark, grotesque rock. It stands isolated on the floor of the flat and is so prominent that early emigrants called this Big Rock Valley. It is shaped somewhat like a wide-brimmed hat with a high crown.

Near the rock is the brackish pool called Burnt Spring, which is probably the place where Jedediah Smith spent the night of June 26th, after passing several salt springs and a lodge of Bannock Indians, who cheerfully divided their little store of antelope meat with the hungry white men.

As we came up to the spring, I called a halt to get a picture of the rock over the little brackish fount and rivulet that trickled from it for a few yards only to disappear into the sand.

"I wish one of the cameras had colored film in it," I complained. "Look at that pinky-purple flower around the spring. It's the prettiest color I have seen for days."

Dr. Neff surveyed it dispassionately. "Yes, it looks better than the dead cow that was lying in it the last time we passed here."

The head of the house, to whom the matter of whether I do or do not get colored pictures is completely unimportant, walked to the edge of the road and balanced up and down on his toes. "For a long while," he said, "those who knew most about it thought that this was where the Donner Party stocked up with water for the desert—even though it isn't very good."

"Yes, I've heard so," I agreed, "but more information popped up from somewhere. You know how it does. Somebody cleans out the attic or goes through his great-uncle's old trunk and comes up with a journal nobody ever heard of."

"And then," said Dr. Neff with complete disillusionment, "they either burn it up just before you get there and you are upset for weeks, or it contradicts all of your pet theories and you're upset anyway. You can't win."

"Well, we got something definite this time," my husband told him, "because the Miller-Reed journal settles it. He said that they went south till they came to a number of good fresh-water wells."

"That *does* settle it," said the doctor. "Burnt Spring doesn't fit that description. It has to be the Kanaka Ranch."

"Most of the people around here seem to think that this is the spring where Frémont saw an Indian drinking," my husband went on. "If that's the case, they must know that it is drinkable some of the time."

"There's no reason to stand here wondering," said Dr. Neff impatiently. "It's been a wet year, and the water will be good now, if ever. Give me a cup and I'll go through the fence and find out."

We watched him coming back up the slope, slopping a little from the cup now and then, and Mr. Bromley went to the fence to take it from him. "I don't know which would be more polite," the latter said, "to take a drink and test it or stick to 'ladies first.' "

"You can give it to her," said Dr. Neff. "The spring is pretty clean, considering, and it doesn't taste too bad. I tried it."

So we all had a swallow from Burnt Spring. In a wet year, early in the season, it would quench thirst. Made into a thin gruel, in true trail custom, to disguise a brackish taste, it would at least help to replace the body fluids which evaporated so quickly in this desert country. It wasn't too bad, but it certainly wasn't good.

In October of 1845, John C. Frémont completed his exploration of the Great Salt Lake and started for the Pacific Coast. It was his purpose to find out why it was necessary to detour around the salt deserts lying to the west which no white man had ever crossed, except Jedediah Smith and his two comrades. They were reckoned the most desolate and forbidding region between the oceans, but Frémont was not easily turned aside by hardships. Neither was his band of sixty carefully selected men, which included Joseph Walker and Christopher (Kit) Carson, both of whom already had been overland to California.

They did not go south to the Kanaka Ranch but began their trek into the salt by cutting across Skull Valley to the pass in Cedar Range, later to be named for Lansford Hastings.

The Stansbury Mountains look obstreperous, not to say unruly, and crowd together, pawing at each other, like excited horses. In some long-gone moment of irritation, they shoved out a quantity of boulders, quite uniform in appearance and often about the size of one's head, that lie along their western foot just to the left of our road. We passed them and came opposite Mushrat Springs. According to the people I happened to ask, these never have been, and never are intended to be, called Muskrat, so I give it as I got it. A long mile brought us to another spring, strikingly marked with a dark-green irregular border. We were told that this was Horseshoe Spring, and its shape suggests it. It also seeps out toward the salt. These springs receive no care, of course—why should they?—and are trampled by cattle. For this and other reasons we did not taste any more of the water but understand them usually to be quite unfit for use.

Most of the travelers who kept journals noted these salty springs, for they were a constant aggravation!

After a few more miles we came to a fine meadow where seepage collects in large pools. Buildings and gnarled old willows indicate that good water may be found here. It is the Kanaka Ranch, entitled on modern maps Iosepa. T. H. Jefferson, who traveled with the Harlan-Young Party and mapped the country as he went along, called this garden spot Hope Wells. In fact he gave names of his own choosing to many landmarks but, as his map was not given a wide circulation, they were not perpetuated. Very few travelers gave the place a name, however, and Hope Wells is most appropriate. It seems entitled to some recognition. A large irrigation ditch is bridged three times for convenience between the house and the outbuildings. A saddled bay horse beside the fence nickered as we drove past. He was a shiny, high-strung rascal and pawed impatiently.

This, we discovered upon interviewing the superintendent, Mr. Glenn Hess, was one of the Desert Livestock Company's ranches. We had left the white-and-green country of salt and greasewood, which indicates utter sterility as far as useful products go, and had entered an indeterminate gray-and-tan section of small sage and smaller wild oats which occupied a shelf between the desert flat below and the mountains above. A few potbellied junipers punctuated the landscape. Bunched willows huddled in lovely green meadows. Big old haystacks, brown and crusted on the outside, awaited the lean year that comes once in a while. On the dry foothills bronco grass grew thickly. Cattle and sheep were everywhere.

On June 25th, 1827, Jedediah Smith and Gobel, having left Evans exhausted three miles to the southwest, arrived at this abundance of good water and plunged into the spring, accompanied on equal terms by their horse and mule. Smith immediately carried five quarts of water to Evans, who drank it at one draft and recuperated at once. Smith then took time to record in his journal some pertinent facts about hunger and thirst, on which subjects no one will deny that he rated as an authority. "Hard as it is to bear for successive days the knawings of hunger," he wrote, "yet it is light in comparison to the agony of burning thirst and, on the other hand, I have observed that a man reduced by hunger is some days in recovering his strength. A man equally reduced by thirst seems renovated almost instantaneously. Hunger can be endured more than twice as long as thirst. To some it may appear surprising that a man who has been for several days without eating has a most incessant desire to drink, and although he can drink but little at a time, yet he wants it much oftener than in ordinary circumstances."

The comparatively recent release of a verbatim copy of Smith's journals called attention to the fresh water at the Kanaka Ranch as the most likely spring to have been encountered by these emaciated explorers. Corroboration is supplied by an old Goshute Indian, Moodywoc, who told Charles Kelly, author of *Salt Desert Trails,* that in his youth his grandmother liked to tell of the three starving white men—the first she had ever seen—who came from the western desert into what is now Skull Valley.

At Mr. Hess's suggestion we set our camp within a fence to defeat the curiosity of the whitefaced cattle, and had some dinner. Afterward we took Dr. Neff's powerful field glasses and went down to the bunkhouse, where we sat on the steps with the men, watching for wild horses in the Cedar Range until it was too dark to see.

I have been disgusted with myself ever since to think of the real thrill I missed that evening by being so sure that they were fooling me. I took my turn looking with the rest, but with my tongue so permanently in my cheek that it's a wonder I didn't bite it off. The next morning, in discussing it with Mrs. Hess, I found that a band of wild horses actually lives in Cedar Range, some fifteen miles away, and only comes out for water about every third day, at evening. They are so suspicious and apprehensive that they emerge from the hills at full gallop, leaving a plume of dust that is in full view from the ranch. The men were quite sincere in hoping to catch a glimpse of them. Once in a while someone catches a colt from the band, and the favorite and intelligent saddlehorse we had seen tied to the fence was born wild in the Cedar Range. While camped at the Kanaka Ranch

Spring, Jefferson wrote: "North-east of Hope-Wells, upon the mountain about two miles from the road, is situated Cedar Spring. It affords an abundant supply of delightful water, has cedar trees and some bunch grass near it; a horse trail leads to it from Hastings-Wells, over the mountain. If the Indians catch an unarmed man alone, they will rob him." Moorman's party and many others watered at this spring.

It must have been along this same route that Edwin Bryant's pack train, still guided by Hudspeth, dared the ill humor of the peaks and canyons and of the Indians that dwelt therein and crossed the mountain chain, the first emigrants to arrive at the Kanaka Ranch Spring. As they ascended the eastern slope, Colonel Russell discovered that he had left his rifle, a "nine-shooter" at camp on Willow Creek in Tooele Valley. Bryant, who apparently didn't think much of the weapon anyway, was satisfied that the young Utes who had visited them would have carried it away. Anything left in camp was fair spoil, according to their code. Russell and Hiram Miller went back to search, but fruitlessly. In the ordinary course of affairs, that would have been the last seen of the gun; but it happened that Hudspeth, camping soon afterward in Tooele Valley with the Harlan-Young Party, was visited by the indignant Utes and the "nine-shooter" was handed back to the white man with some ceremony. Its finder, displaying it with untrammeled pride in the Ute village, had shot himself painfully in the leg, and the Utes no longer wished to be responsible for such an eccentric weapon's proclivities. It was restored to Colonel Russell some weeks later, in California.

Bryant's party selected a camp on the western foot of the mountain slope on the Kanaka Ranch. The next morning, August 2, 1846, as the company were making preparations to start across Skull Valley, they had callers again. Bryant wrote: "We were visited early by three miserable Digger Indians." They were, he added, adorned artlessly about the loins with a few small and filthy skins—most impermanent and, so to speak, deciduous arrangements. The original purpose of the Indians in braving the white man's camp was to trade a delicacy composed of mashed grasshoppers and sunflower seed for "some articles" (Bryant is indefinite) that the white man possessed. Probably the articles were clothes, for, when it was evident that the grasshopper confection had no allure, one of them offered to guide the party to the next water, which he indicated was at the base of the slope of the Cedar Range on the farther side of the valley. For this he received a shirt and a pair of pantaloons somewhat more conformable to the requirements of politeness; but when the time came to fulfill his part of the agreement, he could not be found. Four years later Moorman and party, while camped at the same fresh-water spring, also were visited by three Indians. Thy claimed to be well acquainted with the desert and offered to guide the company across Skull Valley, but, when the start was made, the canny aborigines were not there. Their pay (a huge dinner for the three of them) they had consumed in advance. It was, in its season, a profitable racket. Moorman said that the three were quite well dressed, and I can think of no reason why they should not have been so by this time.

The emigrants, of whatever year, breaking their comfortable camp at the fresh-water spring were far from lighthearted about the forty-eight hours that lay just ahead. They were not half as carefree as they had been when, cool and at ease at Fort Bridger or in the valley of the Great Salt Lake, they had decided to come this way. Yesterday they had been hot and their animals had been thirsty on most of the long road from Twenty Wells to this spot which, in trail days, seemingly had no name. The trek past the line of brackish springs had shaken their inherent belief in the bounty of nature. It was plain that one could and would be most miserable in this strange, saline terrain. And so men who had lightly decided on Hastings' route, although possessing an insufficient number of water containers, filled their canteens and their coffeepots and then, hesitatingly, their boots; and then, frantically, their oilcloth pants, tied tightly at the ankles and started across Skull Valley. But some did not have boots nor waterproof trousers, and some had not even a coffeepot. Men have been known to leave this spring with only a pint of water for self and animal. The desert, if measured from here, is ninety miles—ninety miles from fresh water to fresh water! But, some fifteen miles ahead, in a ravine at the foot of the east slope of Cedar Range, is the tiny brackish waterhole (called Dell Spring by Jefferson but now known as Redlum Spring) that Bryant's defaulting Indian guide had indicated.

Redlum Spring makes its first claim on our attention in the diary of James Clyman, who camped there as he accompanied Hastings and Hudspeth on their trek east to meet the emigration. Caleb Greenwood, with two of his half-Indian sons, was in the party. None of these experienced men had wanted to take this unknown route, which at that time, was marked by no trail save that left by Frémont's sixty riders; but they had developed no sales resistance to a man who could argue like Hastings and consequently they arrived at Redlum Spring after thirty hours without water. It is an inconsequential, queer-tasting trickle, and, even at the time of melting snow, only runs a few rods before sinking into the thirsty earth. In July and August, when the emigrants were passing, it was pitifully inadequate and seldom furnished the animals enough to drink.

Skull Valley is only green along its extreme eastern edge. On the dingy crust of the white salt flat, traces of the old wagons are still visible through the desert growth, where dead rabbit brush rattles in skeleton dances to the piping of the wind. The day's trip from the fresh-water spring to the brackish mudhole in the Cedar Range lay in plain sight. It was only necessary for each man to decide whether to stay as long as possible with the strengthening green forage and good water, not depending on the tiny spring ahead which might be exhausted by the earlier comers; or to leave early and hope that his animals would be among the fortunate and get a drink at the end of their day's journey. This led to the first breaking up of companies into groups so noticeable during the crossing of the great desert.

The first five parties known to have crossed Skull Valley were under the direction of trained scouts and mountain men. First was Jedediah Smith, going northeast; then Frémont's sixty riflemen, who first found Redlum Spring, going west. Next, in the spring of 1846, were Clyman, Hudspeth, Hastings, and old Caleb Greenwood, with their party going east. Then, in the summer, back toward the west came Hudspeth with Bryant's party, followed by Hastings with the Harlan-Young company whom Hudspeth had meanwhile rejoined. It is evident, then, that the Donner Party, who were next in line, were the first to come this way without the adequate advice of someone who knew the ways of the desert. It is true that the wheels of the Harlan Party had marked their course. The danger of getting lost was minimized. But the extra two weeks that had elapsed before they arrived dried Redlum Spring. Ninety waterless miles confronted them—an ox-team outfit!

Fortunately (or possibly unfortunately) they did not know its exact extent. Survivors said that they found a note at the last fresh-water spring informing them that the desert was a longer journey than they had been led to expect. Hudspeth has sometimes been given credit for making a special trip back to the Kanaka Ranch Spring to leave the warning, but that would seem unnecessary. He had to go past them anyway on the return trip, as he left Bryant on the top of Cedar Range a few miles beyond Redlum Spring and went back to join Hastings and the Harlan-Young Party. Experienced woodsman that he was, he certainly knew that Redlum Spring was drying rapidly. What could be more natural, then, than to leave a note at the Kanaka Ranch Spring as he passed it on the westward trip for the last time?

Samuel C. Young's story (compiled by his family for his obituary) makes the bald statement that Hastings had told them the desert was but forty miles across. It is probable that we can discount that a bit. The story came at second hand after many years. Hastings may have said that there was not more than forty miles of salt, or may have made some other misleading remark. The family of James Reed remembered through the years that he had told them fifty miles from water to water. Memory, when swayed by indignation, is an uncertain quantity; but there is no shadow of doubt that Hastings had completely belittled the danger from heat and thirst.

The bird-picked note at the springs was a belated and inadequate gesture of warning supposed to mitigate the danger into which he had led them.

No special difficulty obstructed the travelers crossing the flat floor of Skull Valley except a few water-worn gullies as they approached the western side. Bryant described its physical characteristics: "The breadth of the valley at this point, from the base of one range of mountains to the other, is about twenty miles. Large portions of it are covered with a saline efflorescence of a snowy whiteness. The only vegetation is wild sage; and this is parched and shrivelled by the extreme drought."

After Bryant's party actually had commenced the ascent of Cedar Range, they struck Frémont's trail, which came more or less due west from the chain of salt springs. A party of mountain men, accustomed to privation, would not travel out of their line of march unnecessarily unless their horses needed recuperation, and it seems evident that Frémont omitted the swing south to the lush grasses of the Kanaka Ranch.

The two trails joined: Frémont's of 1845 and that of the Bryant-Russell Party led by Hudspeth approximately nine months later. Together they moved to the natural camping place at Redlum Spring. Bryant wrote: "There are a few dwarf cedars in our vicinity and scattered bunches of dead grass. In a ravine near us the sand is moist; and by making an excavation, we obtained a scant supply of water, impregnated with salt and sulphur. . . . We gathered the dead limbs of the cedars which had been cut down by Captain Frémont's party when encamped here last autumn, and igniting them, they gave us a good light." This can be taken as true, for Hudspeth could attest that they were not cut by himself and Clyman with their company, the only other party that had camped there to date.

Ideas of the best time of day (or night) to leave this camp were as varied as had been the times of departure from the Kanaka Ranch. Men plodding toward the desert during the gold rush usually started in the late afternoon, finished the crossing of the Cedar Range, and went down into the valley on the west about five or six o'clock. Leaving the last spot where the canteen might be filled was done with something of the same desperation that is shown in leaving the temporary security of a slowly sinking ship. It had to be left, for there was no permanent safety there; but the terror ahead was almost prohibitive. All ordinary ties of business or comradeship vanished. Companies hardly ever started as a unit; but, if it so happened that they did, every man went on as fast as his individual strength or equipment permitted, and soon they were widely separated. Families clung together—man to wife and children, brother to brother, or sometimes a man to his dearest friend—but in the main it was, as in shipwreck, every man to sink or swim for himself.

Long before daylight Bryant and Hudspeth were stirring. They watered the animals and made coffee with the brackish spring water. A small powder keg, holding three to four pints, was filled with this beverage and was supposed to suffice nine men with their animals for the distance still to be traveled. At dawn they started the unspectacular one-thousand-foot ascent to the top of the pass which is now called Hastings'. At the summit Hudspeth was to show them the symmetrical shape of Pilot Peak against the horizon, seventy-five miles distant, just a little north of west. At its foot was, he said, an abundance of water. It was to be their goal.

At the summit everyone stopped, for here they were to say good-by to Hudspeth and the one companion left of the three young emigrants who had started with him. The good-bys were said, but they looked in vain for Pilot Peak, for the plain was filled with a dense brownish smoke that blotted out all distant landmarks. As best he could, Hudspeth pointed their course and then, with deep misgiving, for he was a conscientious man, saw the little group start down the mountain. When a short distance separated them, he shouted; they turned and saw him standing with his long arm stretched out. "Now boys," he admonished them loudly, "put spurs to your mules and ride like hell!"

Two or three miles through scraggly juniper brought them to the western foot of Cedar Range. The trail coming down from the pass winds through shallow canyons of unbearable bronco grass full of stickers and past the buildings of the old aragonite mine where Mr. Du Valle, who runs it, courteously gave us what information he had at hand and something cold to drink. And still the trail winds on, down the gradual slope overgrown with horsebrush and tiny sage and pegged with juniper. It is an itchy mountain.

When we had completed about half of the descent, the view ahead disclosed the seventy-five miles that intervened between us and the living springs of stately Pilot Peak. From here it did not seem so far by half, nor did it look much more forbidding than the dry hillside where we stood. The old trail crossed the railroad just below us at a flag stop called Aragonite, and was barely visible snaking over the rolling country ahead eight or ten miles to the summit of a low ridge known as Grayback, where it disappeared on the horizon.

True, this portion of the trail was not pleasant and was (quoting Bryant) "thickly strewn with sharp fragments of basaltes and vitreous gravel resembling junk-bottle glass," but it was still mother earth and may be considered the last of the ordinary traveling before all precedents were cast aside and, prepared or not, they faced the expanse, white as sugar and lethal as so much arsenic, known as the Great Salt Desert.

CHAPTER V

White Hell

GRAYBACK doesn't look like much of a mountain, but the upward haul was stiff. Toward nightfall, the main body of wagons plodded over it. At the top they rested and, as a rule, the stragglers were able to overtake their comrades. The wait was not extended and, as far as my memory serves, I have never read of a man who, while crossing the Salt Desert, turned back in search of a laggard or to help anyone until he had obtained water and could take some along on the return trip.

The descent of the west slope of Grayback is gradual but rough, and it was obstructed with so many large rocks that necessity forced the travelers to roll some aside.

Charles Kelly, who traced the cutoff across the desert in 1929, wrote that he found this descent strewn with articles which had jolted out of the wagons. Among them was a heavy rifle whose barrel had been bent in two places. Probably some packer had tired of carrying it and, conscientiously intent on destroying its usefulness to hostile Indians, had selected a rocky spot and placed it ahead of the front wheel of a wagon. The front and back wheels, striking at slightly different places, might cause two distinct curves. This is a guess but a fair one, as abandoned guns were supposed, by the ethics of the trail, to be rendered harmless in that fashion.

Night usually overtook the travelers before they had cleared Grayback. The sun dropped and hung poised for a flaming moment, disappeared, and twilight came on. A sage flat—dry, dirty and disagreeable—had to be crossed, several miles of it; and then the large sand dunes commenced, high, rounded, and whiskered with greasewood. Between them the wagons lurched and groaned and the short-legged oxen sank to their knees in ashy sand. Their clogged plodding consumed priceless hours; the night was almost eaten away when they struck the knife edge of the salt flats. Sometimes these precious hours of cool darkness were moonless, and the wind held its breath. The distant stars could not light the whole width of the sky; blackness leaned over the moving caravans and friends imperceptibly drifted apart. Or again, more fortunate pilgrims experienced the mauve and dun and silver of a night when moonbeams pushed the clouds apart and, streaming through the rabbit brush, patterned the white edge of the desert floor with black-lace shadows. Sometimes the wind sang like struck glass or shrieked around the wagon tops and back across the desolation that was Grayback Mountain, scouring its rocks with salt and sand.

Night, of whatever sort, was welcome.

During these midnight hours of respite, the caravans took a short rest. Where was immaterial, for no one place was better than another. The wagon trains carried grass cut at the fresh-water springs and the prudent had casks of water. The well managed pack train had one out of every three animals loaded with grass, but it was the water problem that turned the hair of its captain white. Seemingly, the pack train *never* had water containers. This pause allowed most of the stragglers to catch up, so that there was again some semblance of unity. Those in the lead who had strong animals and were doing well would not be seen again until safety was reached. Each man must decide how long to rest, whether time spent now would result in added strength when strength was needed, or whether to push his animals to their limit while darkness lasted. They pulled out separately, acting either by considered resolution or simply at the behest of overstrained nerves.

And now, for a few hours, they made good progress. On a moonlit night the salt is a scrubbed marble floor, cold and hard. The Stansbury Expedition crossed from west to east in the fall of 1849, after the gold rushers had passed, and this report was sent to the chief of the Bureau of Topographical Engineers: "So firm and strong was this unique and snowy floor, that it sustained the weight of our entire train, without in the least giving way or cracking beneath the pressure. Our mules walked upon it as upon a sheet of solid ice." Miles and miles of it lay before the westbound emigrants. How much, very few could tell, as only the ones who had remained near a wagon equipped with a roadmeter knew how far they had come.

It seemed to the anxious emigrants that the night fled into eternity like air sucked into a vacuum. No death-chamber occupant could dread the dawn more; the human consciousness can hold only so much of trepidation. Very early of a summer morning the darkness shivered and broke; the sun flung itself from behind the horizon. At no time or place would humanity be more reluctant to see it. And the day brought something new to think about: ahead of them stretched a mountain chain running approximately north and south. It was low but rough and jagged, extending across their pathway and far beyond. Strangely enough, this range of rugged hills is now called Silver Island and has an isolated rock some miles to the east (which, of course, would be reached first by the travelers) called Crater Island.

When Pilot Peak is viewed from a distance, for instance from Cedar Range, it looms high and important with Silver Island appearing as incidental foothills, although actually they are separated from it by over twelve miles of flat salt bed. Now, as the wagons approached closer, Silver Island assumed startling proportions and hid the taller peak behind its jagged bulk. The person was rare who did not mistakenly think that water was to be found there and that the Island was their goal. Perhaps this fallacy was a blessing, for the hope spurred the weaklings to reach at least the shade of Crater Island.

Amazing phenomena astounded the eyes and the comprehension of those earlier parties who, starting at dawn, passed this widest portion of the glaring salt flat in the middle of the day. Edwin Bryant and party were moving ahead steadily with a minimum of difficulty when they all saw gigantic horsemen riding along at a distance apparently of six or eight miles. All sorts of conjectures were made, and the strange phenomena appeared every now and then for several hours. Finally, experiments proved them to be their own shadows, "produced and reproduced by the mirror-like composition impregnating the atmosphere and covering the plain."

It seems reasonable to suppose that it was from some such gigantic apparitions on the Arabian deserts that the stories of genii were born.

During the continuance of this mirage, Bryant's party crossed the lowest depression of the salt bed, the place where the sheet of water, which in winter covers the entire flat, remains the longest. In certain years the water dries during June and July; by August the footing is reasonably good. By the mercy of Providence it must have been so in 1849 and 1850, for, in the few records that we have, no mention is made of deep mud. In other years the water remains. I, myself, in 1945, having told a fellow traveler of the direful waterless characteristic of the Salt Desert, was compelled to show it on the first of July as a wind-riffled lake as far west as the Nevada line, with sea gulls wheeling over it. The year 1846 must have split the difference between these two extremes: the edges of the salt flat were hard, but the scarcely noticeable bottom of the depression was still soft underneath. Charles Kelly, following the cutoff in a car in 1929, was mired to the axle and forced to return again and to proceed on foot, and yet he may be considered lucky to have selected a year that approximated the conditions found by the Donner Party, in whose fortunes he was most interested. He wrote in *Salt Desert Trails* in the chapter "Trailing the Pioneers": "Walking became rapidly more difficult as we entered this imperceptible depression which constitutes the 'deep mud.' Our boots picked up enormous quantities of it, which was shaken off with difficulty, and it can easily be imagined what must have happened here to the wheels of the emigrant wagons. In attempting to remove this mud with a shovel, the shovel becomes burdened with the sticky mass, which clings to everything it touches. In their already thirsty, sleepless, exhausted and irritable state, the emigrants must have suffered the torments of hell when they found themselves mired in this bottomless glue."

It was in this difficult mud that the Donner Party left several of their wagons. Other wagons left by the gold seekers dotted the white plain, dismembered by passers-by in need of a wheel or a piece of iron, and also, no doubt, by Indians who prowled the flats when winter weather and snow solved the heat-and-thirst problem. And here the animals began to die. Whether impeded by mud or not, suffering and exertion were beginning to tell. Lips and nostrils were caked with salt; the refracted heat baked their eyes under the lids like potatoes in jackets; they reached the unbearable absolute somewhere around Crater Island. It was well termed the Rock of Misery. Where its isolated bulk formed the first shadow of their journey, men and animals lay down to die. For the beasts it was the end; for the men it brought succor, of some kind or another, from their fellow plodders. Some few succumbed, but not many of whom we have record. Although the Donner company lost thirty-six head of stock, dead or rendered unmanageable by thirst, no person died—not even the nursing babies, of which there were six or seven. And it is likely that this company consumed more time in crossing than any other. It seems to have been a full five days from the time when the wagons left the last water until Mrs. Reed and her children were brought off the salt to the spring at Pilot Peak. During this period they sat twenty-four hours in their wagon embedded in the deep mud, while Mr. Reed walked to Pilot Peak to see that his teamsters, who were driving his stock to water, brought the cattle back to get the wagons moving again. Those interested in this history-making story know that the drivers lost the thirst-crazed animals, who stampeded frantically into the darkness and were never found, leaving the Reeds with but two animals, an ox and a cow.

The mud ended somewhere east of Crater Island and the trail, stretching defenseless under a sky of steel and fire, turned slightly, as if headed for its shade. The desert was by now a great supernal furnace. The sights and sounds were almost beyond endurance. I shall let Henry Bloom tell the story of this zero hour of crossing and pass on presently to pleasanter aspects: "Got to the Rock of Misery, 65 miles," wrote Bloom, "our water all gone and our horses nearly famishing for water. Teams giving out, men lying by the side of the road in the hot sun speechless for the want of water. Some lying in the shade of the rocks nearly dying from thirst. Men offering one, ten, twenty and five hundred dollars for a single drink of water. It was a sad sight to see strong, healthy, robust men reduced to such an extremity in a few hours' time. Came on 8 or 9 miles and there learned it was 16 miles to the spring. It was rather a severe shock to us as we were suffering severely for water and our horses nearly gave out. We took the packs from the horses and concluded to rest a little and then try to reach the spring with the horses if possible. While sitting there a man came along and inquired how far it was to the spring. I replied: '16 miles.' He then exclaimed, 'Oh, my God, I can never reach there without water!' We still had some hopes of getting water where we were for there was a load of water sent out every day by the emigrants who had gotten across the day before. In about an hour from the time we stopped and just as we were preparing to start for the spring, the water wagon came and Oh, what a relief to ourselves and others. It seemed like an act of an angel of mercy at the eleventh hour."

Very little is known about this "water wagon." We don't know whether the emigrants of 1849 had as yet established the custom, but in 1850 diarists were deeply indebted to it for comfort and spoke of others who owed their lives to its ministrations. We do not know whether one of the abandoned wagons was fitted up with tanks and the emigrants who happened to be camped at the spring made up a purse each day to hire a driver, or whether the hired driver took his own wagon, outfitting it temporarily each time with borrowed water containers. I think it is more likely that an abandoned wagon was used, as no man would care to return into the desert with a vehicle on which he was forced to depend for the rest of his journey. The air was so dry that it was with difficulty one crossing was completed before the spokes loosened in the wheels. John Wood and Madison Moorman each mentioned the water wagon in 1850.

Wood had expected to find water at Crater Island or, as he termed it, "the bluff of rocks." On arrival he was told that it was twenty-five miles farther, which seems about right. I am not as sure of these distances as I like to be, for we have never made the crossing of the salt flat, but mileage given by several diaries of the journey, compared with the record of Charles Kelly, seems to indicate that the trail passed about one half-mile north of Crater Rock, with numerous sidetracks leading to the rock for shade or in desperate hope of water because of its deceptive green greasewood fringe. From there the trail went fairly straight to the nearest point of Silver Island, turned, and proceeded north along its foot to a low gap. From Crater Island to the eastern foot of this gap or pass was considered nine miles, of which probably five was the distance between Crater Island and Silver Island and four the distance northward to the gap. Near

Crater Island, Wood met an old lady with water in a coffeepot for her husband who had lain down to die. Someone had given it to her as it is inconceivable that she had walked a fifty-mile round trip, and the daily water wagon had not, as yet, arrived. Wood moved along, suffering by reason of the glare refracted from the salt, and passed a woman sitting with some teams, waiting for her husband to go ahead to Silver Island and bring back the water which he confidently expected to find there. By this time Wood knew that water was in a range of mountains temporarily invisible beyond Silver Island; realizing that she must suffer greatly before her husband's return, he divided his supply with her, then moved on again, and left her there. When he had reached the rocky fortress of Silver Island, he found the husband so stunned by the news that he still had forty miles of traveling to the spring and back that he had lain down, faint and weak, and could not even return to his wife. The name of this couple was Hall, and they were from Cincinnati.

Somewhere along the foot of Silver Island, Wood fed the last of his grass and used the last of his water. This item of information, which he includes in his journal, makes his gift of water to Mrs. Hall an act of pure heroism, for he still had about four miles through the low pass or gap and then twelve miles of salt flat before reaching Pilot Peak with its life-giving fountain. Shortly after this he met the water wagon on its way. It had already come sixteen miles and must have been depleted, but its drivers tried to get as far as possible. We have no record that it ever ventured beyond the eastern foot of Silver Island, but at least we know that it brought the water of which the Hall family was so greatly in need. It is quite justifiable that no water was available for beasts, although John Wood remarked that steers were dropping in all directions. When he was within ten miles of the spring, he had only two yoke left; but they sensed water ahead and commenced to hurry; soon they were on the trot and, at a distance of a mile, had to be restrained from running.

Madison Moorman crossed the desert during the last two days of July, 1850, and was sufficiently ahead of John Wood so that his company had recuperated at camp on Pilot Peak and had pulled out the day before Wood arrived. In addition to the other discomforts, Moorman complained of exhaustion caused by lack of sleep, from which, no doubt, all of the men suffered, as they had spent most of the night at Redlum Spring trying to collect water and grass and had traveled steadily throughout the next. Moorman's company used the final pint of their water at Silver Island, Madison giving his last few swallows to a favorite mule, with which the captain of his pack train, Dr. Thomas, remained while the rest went on. He wrote: "After travelling a short distance we met a wagon loaded with water which had been sent out by subscription to relieve the distressed. The teamster gave us as much as *we* could drink but would not let us have any for our mules. We told him of Dr. Thomas' situation and pushed on —seeing numbers of poor animals dead and dying."

The gap through Silver Island is low, so low in fact that from a distance it looks level. It was studded with the carcasses of beasts that had died and mummified hideously. As soon as the disheartened plodders had crossed over its shallow curve, the long expected Pilot Peak stood out ahead, bold and beautiful, a real mountain isolated against the sky. Between them and its beckoning comfort stretched twelve pallid miles of misery on which no human thing was allowed to die but only to struggle on, in dehydrated agony, past the stranded wagons, from which the animals had been unhitched and driven forward; past scattered carcasses that, fortunately, dried without rotting and were embalmed by the salt and the blazing sun, which melted the very suet under their stiffened hides.

Man by man, animal by animal, the long line moved uncertainly, a boa constrictor of wretched living things. So elemental and stripped of superficiality was every individual that one might have imagined the Judgment Day had arrived without the benefit of Gabriel's advance notice.

As they approached the salt-lapped mountain, a frenzy of anticipation possessed them. Unexpected funds of strength permitted them to stagger at a run across the last few rods of glaring white, the first few rods of green, and to fling themselves, harshly sobbing with fatigue and thirst, beside the sweet, trampled spring. In the great fount they drank and soaked, fell in, crawled out, and lay like parched and half-dead sponges, from a drained sea, which had miraculously again found water.

CHAPTER VI

Oases

FOR years it was our habit, when going east by automobile, to spend the first part of the night at Wells, Nevada, and to get up at two and boom across the great causeway over the salt during the dark hours. Not very many people who live out of the state are more familiar with the appearance of the Salt Desert during any given type of night: starlit, dusky black, moonlit and with shroudlike mists, or stabbed with lightnings and cannonaded with thunder from the Wasatch.

We always passed through Wendover, a small city on the Nevada-Utah line with its head in the Toano Mountains and its feet in the salt beds. And it was always night.

Through the years I had worked up an unreasonable dislike for the isolated town whose comfortable population slept so heartlessly in their beds while I rode past their locked doors, bolt upright, sleepy and uncertain as to whether my dinner had not been, perhaps, just the thing, or whether I merely wanted my breakfast.

"This will be once that we can really see the place at close range," I remarked as we slipped easily down the east slope of the Toano Range into the outskirts of the town. It was morning, but the desert spread below was already shimmering in the heat waves. "How are we going to get out to Pilot Springs? If there's a road, I suppose it will be terrible."

"I heard somewhere," my husband reassured me, "that the army built a good road to it for some of its customary obscure reasons. It may have been closed during the war, but it certainly will be open now. We'll go ask."

In pursuance of this idea, we inquired at service stations, cafés, bus stops, stores, hotels, and motor camps. (This doesn't sound like the truth, but it is.) An hour passed, and still we hadn't found a person in Wendover who ever had been out the twenty-odd miles to Pilot Springs. Seemingly, Wendover exists to speed the traveler on his way to some other destination, but the destination must be stereotyped. Pilot Springs is not an ordained spot. Cars zipped past on the perfect east and west highway so fast that crossing was a major hazard; down the hill, two little switch engines at the depot nuzzled each other and bounded back with a grand crashing of box-cars loaded with eastbound and westbound freight. Wendover had no particular advice for the eccentric who might want to go north.

Finally we found a man who had had dealings with the army, and he told us how to get there.

The road was good, a highway in fact, and led north along the eastern slope of Silver Island as it broke away from the Toano Range. Almost at once we came to a cluster of nearly deserted barracks nudged into a cove in the mountains. A sign said that this was the Wendover Aerial Gunnery School, and it struck me at once that the eighty miles of salt lying to our immediate right was exactly my choice as a target for the first few shots of a novice. Our road headed for a break in the Silver Island Range at a point higher and several miles south of the place where the desert-weary emigrants crossed it. When we were opposite the gap, we turned to the northwest and drove through.

We found ourselves well up in the rough little peaks of Silver Island. It is a midget among mountains, having all the contours of the Tetons but forever doomed to be small, unbeautiful, and weird, with its rocky sculpturing barely covered with gingery earth. Mr. Bromley remarked that it looked like the landscaping on the moon.

Once free of the pass, we had a choice of roads. The one to the right led northwest across the twelve-mile stretch of salt flat directly to Pilot Peak, while the left-hand road stayed along the higher ground just above the circumference of the salt valley, and was used in wet weather. It had rained the night before, and the white salt was pud-dled with gray here and there; so we took the left-hand choice and headed circuitously for the line of attractive-looking meadows that border the west side of the desert. As far as the melting snow water of Pilot Peak can flow in the shape of rivulets and springs, it pro-duces verdure and nourishing pasturage. The long shoulder of the peak slopes gradually down to the south. Beyond it we could see a natural opening in the Toano Range and knew it to be Silver Zone

Pass, through which both the highway and the Overland Trail proceed west.

Our objective was the first cold and gushing spring reached by the emigrants. It is at the north end of the chain of springs, and we drove in that direction as quickly as possible, ignoring the important trail landmarks on all sides and trying to reserve judgment or, if possible, not even to see them until the return trip. This is not simply a notion but has a good solid reason founded in efficiency. When we are reading trail data from daily journals, we naturally make a mental impression of descriptions which the diarist has written while he faced west. If we try to make use of these mental pictures while we are facing in the opposite direction, everything is wrong: what he described as "uphill" is downhill to us; when he writes "to the right," we must translate "to the left"; what was misery to him, with the late afternoon glare in his eyes, is pleasant to us, with our backs to it; and so on. On the rare occasions where it has not been possible for us to do our field work moving in the same direction as the prairie schooners I have taken dozens of pictures, all facing west; I have carefully checked mileage about every two miles and made meticulous field notes of the country as it appears while traveling east. Once at home again, I sit down and, beginning at the end of the field notes, work backward to the beginning, reversing every direction; writing "uphill" instead of "downhill," "to the right" instead of "to the left"; trying to remember that the oxen would be tired in the places where we were rested, and so on. After these are double checked, I throw away the actual field notes and attempt to forget the trip.

In this case we were to retrace our path almost at once; therefore, without taking a picture or a note, we drove on, hoping to find someone of whom we could inquire.

Ahead of us, and on another road that ran lower and nearer the edge of the salt, a small truck bobbed along erratically. We veered to intercept it, but the driver knew the country and evaded us without half trying. We were disappointed, and the usual mild recriminations went on for a minute or so while we drove through a gate and into a sort of outer corral. A sign said that this was the Charles McKeller Ranch, and we knew that we were still south of the springs where the trail came off the salt.

Between us and the clear-cut jagged silhouette of Silver Island were pole corrals and some low sheds built sketchily of the same peeled slender logs and roofed with sod on which grew weeds, grass, and even a lone wild rose. Beyond them toward the flat stretched the hayfields. Gnarled and knotty willows shaded a small house made of railroad ties mortared together with clay and with small square windows. Around this were scattered the appliances that an old bachelor keeps where they will be handiest: a coffee mill, a grindstone, a meat safe on a tree. Winding between the house and the trees was a rivulet fed by a spring, clean, imperceptibly moving, and with beautiful lacy reflections of the twigs entwined above it. In the water sat a jar of butter with a clean white cloth tied over it.

We called and a meadow lark answered from the pasture fence. A pure white cat, still warm from sleep but hospitable, emerged by some private exit and rubbed against our shoes, considerably damaging her immaculateness in the process. No one else was about. From the hayfield came the warm scent of grass in the sun, and from the corrals, the sharp, ammoniac, not unpleasant smell of horses. It was the magical morning hour that causes one unconsciously to walk upon the grass so that the crunching of the gravel paths may not disturb the silence. Again came the meadow lark's sweet shrilling, and a horse threw up its head and nickered.

I started for the curling edge of the salt to get a comprehensive view of the ranch with the sun behind me. "Look out for snakes!" My husband's invariable and peace-shattering admonition annoyed me. I shrugged off the warning and also my camera, which had been slung over one shoulder, retrieving the latter with some loss of dignity, and reached the edge of the hayfield that lay between the corrals and the desert. Here I "who-whooed" again.

"He ought to be here soon," a voice said behind me; "he may have gone up to the other ranch to feed the horses."

I turned and faced a man, a good-looking man in a freshly laundered khaki shirt and trousers. I don't claim to be a detective, but it was evident that he had not walked to this isolated spot: he hadn't walked at all. It was even more evident that never since they had been ironed had he sat down in those pants.

"Mr. Watt lives here," he explained in a friendly way. "He'll be back. I'm trapping and usually stay all night with him when I pass this way."

I regarded him with genuine appreciation. How came he to be so clean? I only need an hour in the sagebrush to look like a dusty Skye terrier in buttons. "Wait a minute," I suggested, "and I'll get the picture I'm after and walk with you to meet the rest of the family."

I got it, aided by many friendly suggestions, and in not more than three times the interval promised, we were walking back. An ecclesiastical-appearing horse with a long solemn face came and hung it over the fence. My companion, patting it absently as he passed by, turned to me: "I have my outfit with me." He pointed. "There it is, back of the corrals."

A small, rather oddly equipped truck was unobtrusively parked beyond the fences. As I looked, all the mysteries unraveled, for this was the truck we had tried to intercept. He had simply driven into what was to be his camp, dressed hastily, and prepared for visitors.

Visitors, it seemed, were scarce.

What were we doing and why were we concerned with this place? Why did anyone except himself prefer to leave the highway? His interest was keen.

Dr. Neff, Mr. Bromley, and my husband, being introduced, tried to do a much more complete job than the routine explanation which we grind out ten times a day in answer to inquiries and told him quite thoroughly what were our plans and purposes. Then, with the general finesse of a bulldozer removing a stump, my husband went after facts and figures of the desert. Fortunately for us, we had struck a one-man bureau of information. For thirty years Mr. Hale had spent his vacations trapping coyotes and knew the country in all its aspects. He displayed an irritating economy of words, but now and then I got a succulent bit as I hovered on the outskirts of the group. This fertile strip between the salt and the mountain sage slopes, he said, used to be strewn with the debris of the camps, and the twelve-mile salt flat which lay spread before us in such plain view was dotted with abandoned wagons and the bones of cattle; but most of it had disappeared before his recollection, and it was practically all gone now. Wagon iron had been at a premium in early Nevada, and ranchers had carried it quite a long distance. Then, no doubt, the Indians had wandered the whole scene of the holocaust in the winter, when travel was possible. Anything appealing to their acquisitiveness had promptly vanished.

"But how about the muddy spots?" I climbed into the conversation with a question. "If they were dangerous for the emigrants, wouldn't they be bad for the farmers too?"

"Well, I don't think many people went as far out as the mud beyond Silver Island, but there's no need to get stuck. I manage all right. I simply carry four strong boards the length of the wheel base of the truck and, by picking two up and putting them in front of the other two, make a portable road."

"Why in the world couldn't the emigrants do that with the floorboards of their wagons?" I exclaimed disgustedly, "especially when it meant life or death to them."

"It was the matter of water for the animals," he explained. "They were so hard up for water by that time that they couldn't fool around. A truck may need a certain amount of filling for the radiator, but it doesn't get on your nerves by suffering for it and it doesn't feel the heat. Then, too, I pick my days—wouldn't think of prowling around out there during a hot spell. The fellows going out to mine gold in California had to cross when they got here; if it was good and hot, the animals lay down and gave up instead of pulling out of mudholes."

Dr. Neff sat silently, as was his custom, in the open door of the car. About him the conversation had swung this way and that. Now and then he unwound his legs and tried a new pattern, but he said nothing.

He now contributed a sentence: "Here he comes."

We looked up and saw Mr. Harold Watt striding through the gate. The bachelor had returned. And what a bachelor! Without an ounce of fat on him, his displacement would be only slightly less than a deep-sea tugboat. Mr. Bromley, who is an inch or two over six feet, looked up at him in amazement. My proffered hand disappeared completely in his, and, as he stood relaxed against one of the willows, the cat sat comfortably on the toe of one boot to keep her white fur from the ground.

He took charge of the expedition at once. People had been here several times to see the trail, and he knew the routine. His conversation, comfortably larded with original expletives, was concise and to the point. He didn't omit anything or add anything. If it hadn't been for the expletives, which I was fortunately able to leave out without losing the thread of the story, I should never have been able to keep up with my notes. The men afterward expressed regret that I couldn't take shorthand, as some of the more unfamiliar terms, they felt, would have borne reconsideration.

"We'll have to go farther north," he said. "This is the Charley

McKeller Ranch; it used to be the Munsey place—the first homestead; but the two main springs are on two ranches above: first, the Pete McKeller place, and then the North Warburton Ranch. I have to go there anyway, sometime today," he continued, "to put down some hay for the horses in the corral. We can drive up now."

And we did drive up, getting a running commentary on the flora of the district that I hope I shall never forget: the sweet sage, of which I had never heard, like alfalfa, but only six inches high—all killed off by sheep, of which Mr. Watt did not approve; white sage, windblown and supple; curly sage, tougher and pungent; apple brush, with its little green apples that surprisingly burst into balls of white cotton; horse brush, very yellow-green with yellower flowers; rabbit brush, the sheepherders' wood pile that burns like kerosene; shad scale, a tiny scabby growth; all of these giving way, as we approached the famous springs, to rye grass (or wheat grass if you prefer to call it so) five feet in height and with full heads six inches long.

The spring on the North Warburton Ranch was the one first reached by the Donners. We stood beside it and looked east over the salt.

The full length of Silver Island, divided by two flattish gaps, spread in front of us. From the north gap came the trail. As it quivered into sight among the heat waves, it was possible to see the wheel marks with the naked eye. Several miles out into the salt the trail forked; one arm came straight toward us; the other branched southwest toward the Pete McKeller Ranch, where the true Pilot Spring is. It isn't often possible to detect the marks, Mr. Watt told us; the salt must be just the right degree of dryness to permit it.

Still farther to the north across the flat ran an old mining road where silver ore from Silver Island used to be freighted to Tecoma, then an important supply town.

We prowled around the spring awhile, keeping a respectful lookout for rattlers, which our host called "whistle tails," and then took a reasonably successful picture of the forks of the trail through one glass of Dr. Neff's binoculars, as I had failed to bring a telescopic lens.

The peaks of Silver Island were a hot-looking, brownish vermilion, like molten iron cooling. There was water there, said Mr. Watt, if the emigrants had only known—not enough for the animals, but a little. One spring in a cave yields perhaps ten quarts in twenty-four hours: in other words, it just drips. There had been a large herd of wild horses there too, not long ago, but they habitually crossed the flat to water somewhere on the railroad to the north, or else came on the all-day trip across the salt to Pilot Springs. They had deteriorated to the point where the government thought it best, and most humane, to get rid of them. Mr. Watt had helped to do this. They were just mustangs and diseased with a sort of brain fever.

We walked back past the Warburton cabin, made of logs brought clear from Idaho, and drove south again to the Pete McKeller place and to Pilot Spring, which succored most of the gold seekers. There are no traces left of the wreckage which once littered the ranch, the flat, and the whole chain of springs. It is enough to know that this fertile block, watered by the snows from Pilot Peak, is the keystone of the whole structure of Hastings' Cutoff. Without it the route never could have been conceived.

I wonder of which it did most, good or ill.

We came back and had our late lunch at Mr. Watt's house, he furnishing the fresh bread and coffee and we the filling for the sandwiches, which I made.

Dr. Neff brought in tuna and veal loaf, while Mr. Bromley added a can of cranberry sauce, cold from the icebox, and some cream for the coffee.

Mr. Watt, disdaining patent openers, cut open the cans with his pocket knife. Nothing could have been more smooth and flowing than the motion; he might have been separating a round from molded jelly.

"Do you see my hands?" he asked me, laying those newly washed articles over most of the exposed surface of the little kitchen table.

No answer being necessary, he went on: "What's funny about them?"

"You have three fingers the same length!" I exclaimed, suddenly noticing the fact.

"Yes, and some particular-adjectived petty officer in the U.S. Navy tried to turn me down once because of it. Said it might interfere with my adjectived efficiency. I figured I'd have to clean up on him to get in."

"Did you finally make the grade?" I asked, laying our repast out on paper napkins.

"Oh, yes," he replied indifferently, sticking another chunk of wood under the coffee. "I proved I was efficient."

An hour or so later we stood again under the heavy willows discussing the erratic wanderings of the trail leading west from Mr. Watt's house to Silver Zone Pass, which it shares with the highway and the railroad.

"From here," said Mr. Watt, "the old road follows the line of springs that you saw as you drove in. Your common sense would tell you that the wagons stayed on the sage slope just above the wet strip."

"Yes, this is one place where a person can know in advance just where to find the trail," my husband said thoughtfully. "The emigrants certainly weren't going to climb the peak, so they had to go south until they could travel over the slope. Besides, the water in the line of springs was too good to leave until they had to."

"Moorman climbed the peak," I interrupted. I have a talent for relevant details that weaken my husband's arguments without proving anything else.

"Well, for heaven's sake, he didn't get anywhere by doing it, did he?"

"No, the company was staying here four days to recruit the animals, and a few of the young fellows went up the mountain to see what they could see. I guess they were more tired than they thought or else the peak is bigger than it looks, for only one of them got to the top. Moorman wrote that the green spots they had taken for grass proved to be trees. They weren't used to high mountains back East of course, but you would think that the Wasatch Range might have prepared them for almost anything."

My husband got to his feet and took a long look up the peak, which, with the shadows deepening upon it, began to appear somewhat eerie. "I can't imagine men, already exhausted from the desert, wearing themselves out on a trip like that."

"I don't think they meant to climb it, actually; they were out hunting and just kept on going. They got a couple of rabbits and cooked themselves a stew, but they said they were three times as large as the 'common hares' they were used to, and much wilder. I'm afraid that what they ate were jack rabbits."

"Well, they were just as happy. Did you know that at first the Easterners called them jackass rabbits on account of their ears?"

I admitted the unladylike knowledge and commenced tentatively to roll up stray maps which had been allowed to wander.

The sun sank lower, the shadows changed, and Silver Island commenced to set out new arrangements of crag and canyon. Then, having stretched the elastic shadows to their limit, the afternoon let go and evening came. The little rolling slopes against Pilot Peak snuggled down and pulled the sage blanket over their heads. Time, the implacable, was leaving us behind again. Reluctantly, we repacked our boxes. We had had a splendid day and hated to see it end, but got under way at last. I, at least, had a project, a goal to be attained. This very night I intended to be one of the elect, sleeping behind the locked doors of Wendover.

*　　*　　*

The best way to see the route taken by the pioneers after they regretfully said good-by to the springs at the peak is to leave the highway and take the Montello Road, which turns north between Wendover and Silver Zone Pass and squarely intersects the old trail within a short distance. The wagons had followed the line of springs for about eight miles, probably, and had then come over the south shoulder of the peak, heading straight for Silver Zone Pass. The evidences remaining are easy to find but are what we call an "evolved" trace, having been in occasional use throughout the years. This dip between the ranges might be fourteen miles from the top of the shoulder to the top of Silver Zone. It is dry, dead looking, and hobnailed with dust-colored bushes about a foot high. Moreover, on a hot day it is breezeless and suffocating; but my character has been molded by strong men, and I plodded here and there, exuding Christian fortitude and perspiration and taking uninteresting pictures of the type which my best friends will not look at but which totally unknown persons call up on long-distance and ask to see as a favor. Certainly there is little to be said in their behalf except that they are possibly historic.

Bryant and his party, traveling through the dip between Pilot Peak and the Toano Range, found—of all unexpected things—wheel marks. They were the first emigrants to use the cutoff. Even *they* had no wheeled vehicles. At first the circumstance appeared inexplicable; but Bryant was a well informed gentleman and seldom at a loss. He remembered what he had heard of the Bidwell-Bartleson Party of 1841, who traveled north of the Salt Lake but slanted southwest to cross the mountains at about at this point, and he was able to explain the phenomenon correctly to his group of men. The pack train remained with the wheel marks for several miles, feeling a sense of companionship in this desolate place; but when the ruts went on into what is now Silver Zone Pass, the riders turned to the left and journeyed along the east side of the Toano Range for a few miles toward the south before crossing.

Four years before Frémont explored this way, Bartleson and his company had made a good choice in the unknown terrain that lay ahead of them. Silver Zone was destined to become the pass used by the cutoff. It was unlike Bryant to choose deliberately a route that had no advantages as against one that had many. Why did he go south instead of following Bidwell? And, what interested us far more, which way had Frémont's sixty mountain men gone the year before?

The next page or two are good ones to skip unless you are interested in the minutiae of trail history. In them I will attempt to explain why we think that Frémont used the pass and why the ordinarily cautious Bryant, with the next westbound pack train, did not.

In the first place Silver Zone Pass is a most inviting gap when approached from the east, and the contour of the shoulder of Pilot Peak sheds the travelers practically in front of it. In order *not* to use the gap, one must deliberately go past it and cross the Toanos in an obviously more difficult place. A party would need a convincing reason to do anything so contrary to the dictates of common sense. But Frémont's party was the first to use Hastings' Cutoff. He had no reason not to pick the easiest route, especially as there is water in the pass and none in evidence to the south. We can be sure also that Frémont's mountain men didn't miss the wheel marks left by the Bidwell-Bartleson Party. These and other arguments, to be told in their proper place, convince us that Frémont arrived in time at the summit of Silver Zone. Any westbound group would normally do the same.

But for a party proceeding east before the route became well marked by tracks, the story was different. Eastbound travelers made their entrance into Goshute Valley (sometimes called Steptoe Valley and lying west of the Toano Range) eighteen miles south of Silver Zone at Flower Springs. From there the pass was seen at an angle and was far less attractive.

Clyman, Hudspeth, Hastings, and old Greenwood, with their party, were the first to travel this route going eastward. They were trying to follow the dim tracks left by Joseph Walker's section of Frémont's company which had split at the first water hole west of Silver Zone. Heavy grass had grown in Goshute Valley and they were not able to locate the trace. For lack of anything to guide them, they proceeded straight east and camped in the Toano Range. The next day riders circled the country lying to the east of the mountains, and Clyman connected with the marks of Frémont's horses as they disappeared westward into Silver Zone Pass. The party then collected and trailed back along the tracks to Pilot Peak.

Interpreting, we find that the Hudspeth-Hastings Party crossed the Toanos east of Flower Springs and made a fresh trail north, leading past the eastern portal of the pass, to Pilot Peak. No wonder that Bryant coming west along these fresh tracks followed them. He had traveled with, and been advised by, Hudspeth. Even though the pass looked tempting, no doubt he remained on Hudspeth's line of march and crossed the Toanos where the Hudspeth-Hastings Party had negotiated them going east.

As the entrance of Silver Zone was reached by the Harlan-Young wagon caravans following Bryant and conducted by Hastings and Hudspeth, the two guides saw the advantages of the pass and used it. The white-topped prairie schooners coagulated into a line, for, although the pass is wide farther along, the eastern portal is narrow. The route of the cutoff was established.

The new highway has wiped out all trace of the normal entrance to the gap; but, as the modern grade persists and the old and war-worn automobiles get hot, many of us are glad to see a neat sign, "Water," and an arrow that points to the bottom of a small, steep ravine, straight down from the south edge of the road. This was the first place that the emigrants could get a drink after leaving the desertward verge of Pilot Peak, and it was known as "the springs in the ravine," or some similar designation. It never acquired a proper title. The trail was down by the spring. Henry Bloom wrote that the first fresh water found on this stretch was in a deep gully through which he traveled several miles.

Robert Chalmers added the information that there was no grass at all and that the spring was so very small with so many people crowding to it that, for a long time, he couldn't even catch a glimpse of it. He was patient, though, and his turn came. By dipping up water with his cup and pouring it into his tin plate, he was able to water his horse. Moorman and Wood speak of the water supply as a well dug in a ravine, and it is evident that, by 1850, when they saw the place, the output had been amplified. The water was muddy, of course, from constant usage; but it was cool and its users were grateful.

We left our automobile parked just off the highway and climbed down. The ravine is deep and the spring invisible from the road unless one gets out of the car and walks to the edge. About every three minutes a westbound car would stop for water, and the driver carrying some odd receptacle would dodge across the highway and slide down the path which fell steeply from the edge of the cement.

"This has been an important place in its day," I said as I tried without much success to get a good angle for the camera, "but it isn't very photogenic."

"It's important now, if your car happens to get hot," Dr. Neff answered me quietly.

A scrambling noise announced the more or less involuntary descent of another prospective water carrier and a booming voice agreed, "I'll say it is."

He was a stocky, red-faced man, jerky in gesture and speech, as if continually under a full head of steam. His gold-spangled dentistry gleamed and his wiry gray hair sprang out from his bald spot in Christmas-wreath fashion. As he bent to dip water, he presented an amazingly extensive surface of gabardine. His utensil was a dog's small drinking pan.

"Times haven't really changed so much, have they," I observed to Dr. Neff, "since Chalmers watered his animal here with a tin plate?"

Perceiving the newcomer's expression of annoyed noncomprehension, my husband decided that footnotes would be necessary and supplied them.

"Well, what do you know! So this was the trail! And a water hole, too; well, it's still doing business by the side of the road." He looked down the rocky little ravine along which several generations of roads have left slight evidence and then turned and looked up. "This place must have been a lulu before they got a road through. Where did the wagons go from here?"

"Up the mountain to the summit, west to Ruby Range, around it to the south, down the Humboldt River to the Sierra Nevada Mountains, and over them to California."

The fat man gave a low whistle. "All that for a wagon!" He scratched his head and in the process spilled most of his panful of water. "Sounds kinda interesting," he said thoughtfully and scooped up another supply. "Well, I may as well start climbing. Wouldn't dare take a drink. I'm so hot I'd short-circuit myself."

He scrambled up again and dodged across the highway with due care for the precious cupful he had managed to retain in the pan. "How many trips do you think it will take?" I asked.

"As far as I can see, he'll never get through," my husband opined as he hoisted himself to the highway and pulled me after him. "A good hot engine could boil that much out while he's going back for more."

Dr. Neff untied the canvas water bag from the bumper of our car and silently substituted its gurgling flood for the last few drops that were being shaken out of the tin dish.

Once the constricted eastern entrance to the pass had been negotiated, the mountaintop stretched wide and uninteresting, a simple stretch of upland junipers. Only a little way above us, clouds moved majestically. Below, tenuous Goshute Valley wandered purposelessly away into the south; on its far side, nestling against the unresponsive shoulder of the Pequops, was the bright green that indicated the spring at the Johnson Ranch; the mountains themselves formed a fair specimen of the rugged, decisive short ranges of Nevada that (quoting Dr. Neff) "jump up and down in one place but don't go anywhere." Our rearward observation noted the last evidences of the great desert which we were now leaving behind for good and all, and the forward look comprehended a scarcely less frightening prospect of tumultuous, pushing mountains.

I left the others and sat down beneath a juniper to write the things that must be recorded on the spot to be of any value.

Dr. Neff and Mr. Bromley were happily performing an appendectomy on the gas line of the car, with nothing visible outside the hood but their rear exposures. My husband stood with his hands in his pockets and advised. Strangely enough, his advice is often ingenious and workable but is never taken, being usually unorthodox.

I wrote steadily, glancing now and then at a map and oftener at the outline of Goshute Valley, trailing its interminable length north and south. I was doing an unprecedented job of successfully correlating the pink and green spots on the map with their improperly colored counterparts in the valley below me. The little town of Shafter was the only settlement in sight, and not even I could get confused.

I wrote steadily, pulling the familiar data easily out of the top drawer of my brain while my subconscious rummaged for something that didn't fit—something in our conclusions to date that refused to dovetail smoothly into its allotted space. I had to find it, because all the geographical information I was recording so busily was bulging and slopping over into places where it didn't belong. I put down my notebook and called for help.

"Say," I demanded when the cohorts had moved up, "what's wrong here? Frémont called the next watering place after crossing this range Whitten Spring, didn't he?"

Unqualified assent from all three.

"And the name is always applied to Flower Springs, isn't it?"

"Yes, it is," my husband agreed; "but I know what you're thinking about. Nobody would wander eighteen or twenty miles southwest to a totally unknown set of springs completely invisible in the sagebrush when he could *see* the spring at the Johnson Ranch, with acres of green grass right in front of him across the valley."

"And there had been no grass since they left Pilot Peak," said Mr. Bromley. "The horses were in no shape to pass up good pasturage."

"And, besides, if you remember," my husband added, "Preuss's map of Frémont's 1845 expedition shows that they went straight west from Silver Zone Pass. Preuss wasn't along, but Frémont gave him the data after he returned east."

It is unfortunate that the log which Frémont must have kept of his explorations that year has never become available to the public. When, many years later, he wrote his memoirs, I'm sure that it was not available to *him*. Something had happened to it.

One of the party, Edward M. Kern, wrote a few paragraphs of description. While camped at Whitton Spring, Frémont split his party and placed Kern in charge of the larger portion to find their way down the Humboldt River under the guidance of Joseph Walker. Frémont, with a small party which included Kit Carson, moved to the southward, or down Goshute Valley. Kern, with his group, crossed the mountains to the west of camp.

Personally, I believe that the spring at the Johnson Ranch is the famous Whitton Spring, although Moorman, in 1850, is the only emigrant diarist who (to my knowledge) ever called it by that name. Bloom and Reed, however, describe its location, stating that they traveled west from Silver Zone Pass and camped at a fine spring before starting south to camp the next night at a place answering the description of Flower Springs.

The map made by T. H. Jefferson while traveling with the Harlan-Young Party shows the trail going straight west from Silver Zone to what he called "Relief Springs" at the Johnson Ranch, another of his appropriate names. He also marked the spring with the caption "Chiles Cache." Evidently this oasis was the scene of another historic incident whose locale has been somewhat indefinite. It suggests that the wagons of the Bidwell-Bartleson company, of which Joseph B. Chiles was a member, were left here. They would leave no more tracks to encourage future travelers.

Bidwell tells of the camp at which they prepared their pack saddles and abandoned their wagons: "W. [Sept.] 15th. Started very early, day was exceedingly warm, passed through a gap in a ridge of mountains [Silver Zone Pass], came into a high dry plain, traveled some distance into it, saw the form of a high mountain through the smoky atmosphere—reached it, having come about 15 miles—found plenty of water [on the Johnson Ranch]—our animals were nearly given out. We were obliged to go so much further, in order to get along with the wagons: We concluded to leave them, and pack as many things as we could.

"T. 16th. All hands were busy making Pack saddles and getting ready to pack. While thus engaged, an Indian, well advanced in years, came down out of the Mountains to our camp. He told us by signs, that the Great Spirit had spoken to him, to go down upon the plains in the morning and on the E side of the mts. he would find some strange people, who would give him a great many things. accordingly he had come. We gave him all such things as we had intended to throw away; whenever he received any thing which he thought useful to him, he paused and looking steadfastly at the sun, addressed him in a loud voice, marking out his course in the sky, as he advanced in his invocation, which took him about 2 minutes to perform—as he received quite a number of articles, it took him a considerable part of the day to repeat his blessings. No Persian, in appearance, could be more sincere."

The water of the Johnson Ranch spring supplies the town of Wendover. It is pumped to the summit of the pass and runs the rest of the way by gravity. It must have been a mighty stream, pouring its waters inexhaustibly into the meadow, before being harnessed to serve the needs of a city. No wonder that Frémont remembered it years later when writing his memoirs.

Our next step was to corroborate the emigrants' descriptions of Flower Springs and to ask about the original water supply of the valley.

"Let's go over and eat our lunch in Shafter," I suggested. "Somebody there will know all the answers."

We always carry a lunch with us and have a certain amount of canned goods floating around under the load which we never intend to open and which in almost every instance has come home with us after our trip. Sometimes even the sandwiches come back to camp at night, as we invariably buy our lunch, if possible, for the sake of the additional chance to gossip about the lie of the land. It would probably be so today.

Shafter is a railroad town, pure and simple, or perhaps not so pure and, on second thought, probably not simple either. Its *raison d'être* is the intersection of the Western Pacific, whose weighty tracks trend southwest to disappear into Jasper Pass, and the Nevada Northern whose roadbed trails north and south on the floor of Goshute Valley. The town is built of whatever circumstances afforded in the way of material. Red boxcars offer a not too bad solution of the housing shortage, and tie houses indicate that this is Nevada, where tie houses have proved their worth. A few white frame cottages with red trim cling to the edge of the settlement.

We bumped into town, negotiated the tracks, which were high, and brought up at the depot. It was exactly noon, and not one square inch of shade could we find, so we left the car out to fry and reconnoitered for something to eat.

After a short hot walk we were rewarded by good coffee and sandwiches at a small establishment entitled succinctly "Beer." Here we perched on a row on stools and were presently joined, at our request, by an Indian of indeterminate age, with most of his front teeth missing. He stayed for a while but soon took his refreshments with him and went to sit on the floor with his back against the wall.

From him and from W. J. Thomas, owner of the store, we obtained enough information to make a good start.

First and most important, the Flower Springs *are* about eighteen miles from the Johnson Ranch, in a southern direction straight down the edge of the Pequops. So far, fine, I thought. "Were there any other springs near the Johnson Ranch?" my husband asked when he got a chance. Only the ones right there, he was told. There was no natural water that was fit to drink in the eighteen-mile trip. Once in a great while water used to stand at Little Lake, but it was alkaline. "Are any of the Flower Springs warm?" he inquired.

There are, it seemed after some argument, different kinds of water in the Flower Springs, some sulphur and some sweet and good, while the south springs are fairly warm.

How about the passes? I wanted to know. There were three important ones, they told us, close by. Jasper Pass, that used to be called Flower Pass before the railroad came, leads west from Flower Springs, over the Pequops, to Mound Springs. The Western Pacific has tunneled through it and goes that way. It is the easiest of the passes. Rocky Canyon Pass leads west from the Johnson Ranch, over the Pequops, to Warm Springs, a group similar to Flower and Mound Springs. It is the highest and hardest. Little Lake Pass splits the difference in everything. It is midway between. The stage line to Tobar went that way, but, although there is water now at Little Lake, it is not natural; the wells were dug. Even Shafter, in the middle of the valley, has no natural water of its own. I think it is likely that Bidwell took Little Lake Pass.

We went out satisfied. Evidently there were no other oases to confuse the issue. The migration went first west, then south. From Silver Zone to Johnson to Flower. In later years a road went across the hypotenuse of the triangle, straight from Silver Zone to Flower, but it was not so in 1846.

Shafter was steaming into action as we left the café. Several men were at the depot. A slim, vivid girl with red hair came running out of a yellow cottage and let the door slam after her. She had a letter in her hand and we decided that a train was due. In fact we could hear it. We crossed the tracks hastily and moved southwest through masses of yellow flower spikes, the size and color of lupine.

*   *   *

The eighteen miles of trail from the Johnson Ranch to Flower Springs were tedious, neither enjoyable nor particularly bad.

The longer trail from Silver Zone Pass, slanting southwest to Flower Springs, was even more tiresome.

It has occurred to us that the slanting trail, the hypotenuse of the triangle which had the Johnson Ranch for its apex, was at first only used when traveling east. The eastbound traveler came from a land of lush abundance, with springs and grass in profusion. His horses were in no straits. There was no need to take the shortest route to grass and water, which would have been north from Flower Springs to the Johnson Ranch; he could slant over to the pass at Silver Zone and be done with it. His horse could go on short rations for one night, and a day's journey would be saved.

We found Flower Springs, sometimes called Flower Lake, to be a grassy, almost imperceptible depression set into the sage. By measurement, this green spot is three-tenths of a mile across and is filled with a coarse broad-bladed grass. It remains quite hidden until one is almost upon it. The term "lake" is justified, because water stands, to the depth of an inch or two, among the grass roots, in cattle tracks, and upon the white ground. It looks milky where the earth is visible through it, but it seems clear enough when viewed among the green growth. From the more or less flat surface of the lake rise four or five main mounds, with more tucked in between. They are bouncy, and are filled with various amounts of water of decidedly different kinds. We noticed a prevailing smell of tules in the gusty little breeze, which promised rain before the day was over. At the point of the lake nearest the road, a tie house with a shed constituted, probably, a line cabin for some ranch. Two horses whinnied eagerly in the sunlit silence. No one was at home, and we entered the corral through a fence made of poles of various lengths set on end and wired together. Dr. Neff carried a bucket, for we never miss a chance to see that the radiator is kept full, and the horses followed him closely, lonesome for human companionship and eager to drink out of the bucket, though water and grass in abundance made it a sort of horse paradise. Around the house and fences great clumps of rye grass shot up, shoulder high, in vigorous growth. I looked at it curiously, because usually, when I have a chance to examine it in the late summer, the heads of grain have been stripped from it by the Indians, who, I understand, boil and eat them. Ahead of us, and beyond the water, rabbit brush exploded into yellow bloom. Nowhere did we see the dainty blue flower which is abundant in spring and has given the place its modern name.

Bryant, after camping on the east slope of the Toanos and descending the next morning to Goshute Valley through an extremely rocky narrow gorge with perpendicular walls, came finally to Flower Springs, having made that day eighteen miles. It was, he wrote, "an oasis of about fifty acres of green grass, reeds and other herbage, surrounding a number of springs, some of cool fresh water, others of warm sulphur water. These waters rise here, and immediately sink in the sands. Our information at Fort Bridger led us to expect a spring and grass at this point, and in order to make sure of it, we extended the flanks of our small party some three or four miles from the right to the left."

The spring of which the informant had told Bryant may well have been the one at the Johnson Ranch. Somehow the expanse of oozing wells, which is often called Flower Lake instead of Flower Springs, doesn't seem to fit the words "led us to expect a spring and grass." In that case it was probably Joseph Walker who supplied the information, as we know that Bryant met him at the fort on July 17th and discussed the Hastings route, which Walker did not like nor recommend.

There must have been something irritating about the atmosphere of Flower Springs, for Bryant had to rush between two of his eight men to prevent them from shooting each other; and Reed wrote, after leaving the place, "left the Basin Camp or Mad Woman Camp as all the women in camp were mad with anger   and made this day to the two mound springs   14."

It looked very much like rain, and, although we fully intended to see the pass through which the trail negotiated the Pequops, we were afraid to take the car any farther. The men began to walk casually along the old trail from the spring toward the mountains, and I, as a matter of precaution, hastily gathered a camera, extra film, and notebook and started, ding-dong, after them. The afternoon was hot and muggy. Crickets whirred exasperatingly. I never can tell whether there are two or a thousand. Then we struck the edge of a burned-over area and found no more signs of life, not even the fat little horned toads which had been scooting across in front of us. Squat sage bushes, bereft of their dull green, raised blackened arms that could no longer hide the trail but only pointed the way to where the old roadbed headed for the dry and treeless gap. The building of the Jasper tunnel has obliterated much of the evidence.

Of course Dr. Neff and Mr. Bromley vanished at once; construction of any kind has more allure than a century-old trail.

My husband prowled into the general hodgepodge and commenced to poke around.

"Look out for snakes," I called, imitating him irritatingly. Nevada was having a "snaky" summer, and it was impossible to forget them. We seldom heard them buzz but frequently saw them slithering out of our way into squirrel holes, with battered rattles disappearing last, much the worse for wear, like the ears of a disreputable tomcat. I have a working agreement with my family: if the rattler stays above ground and shows fight, they can take time out to kill it, and, beyond a few ineffectual shrieks, I say nothing; but I draw the line at digging a rattler out of a hole with a pocket knife, a corkscrew, or any of the paraphernalia we are apt to have on our persons. Under such circumstances I'm a noncombatant. Let a polite rattlesnake alone, is one of my maxims.

For once I drew no fire from my husband. "I *am* looking out," he answered absently. "I wonder why they made bricks here."

He held up a hand-troweled specimen of yellowish clay, made sure that it had no interest for him, and threw it away. In following its trajectory, his glance lighted on what to me looked like a most uninteresting piece of junk. "My gosh!" he said reverently.

"Now what?"

"Just look at this," he breathed. "It's a linchpin."

"Is that good?"

"Good! What's the matter with you? It's a real find."

I turned and faced the situation without undue rapture. "Looks like a simple piece of ironmongery to me. What's it supposed to do?"

"Linchpins haven't done anything for about fifty years," he educated me. "They used to run through a hole in the hub and pin the wheel to the axle; now they use plain nuts."

I refrained from an undignified retort which instantly occurred to me and went over to look. It was a tapered iron pin about ten inches long, with a shaped head. At its thickest part it was over an inch through, and it sloped down to half an inch where it had snapped off in an irregular break.

My husband regarded it with affection. He was elated, I thought, out of all proportion to the importance of his find. "I'll bet they used them on the dump carts when the tunnel was built," I objected crossly and went back to my camera. My ill humor, being principally based on the temperature of my epidermis, didn't faze him in the least. He dropped the large end of the pin in the side pocket of his jeans and went whistling up the road first carved by tall, narrow-tired wheels and cut by heavy hoofs.

I tagged along slowly. Because air is scarce on the mountains, it seems that I always have to do a lot of extra breathing.

There wasn't really much use in climbing, I thought. You get to the top of one mountain and Nevada can trot out another—juniper covered ridges one through fifty. We had surmounted the Pequops and ahead of us, beyond the next valley, lay the long north slope of Spruce Mountain.

I climbed a little higher and got my second wind. Maybe the mountains were worth while, after all, for a change. I wondered if the emigrants felt that way about them. The sage flats mean well, but they do get monotonous. Moorman, I remembered, enjoyed this summit. It was "very fine," he said, until they struck the sand and sage at the bottom again.

We were enjoying ourselves, too, in our own incredible way, cutting cross sections here and there through the century and holding them up to each other's appreciative view.

In order to hold up the choice bits I had just remembered, I had to whistle at my husband's unresponsive back for a long time. He stopped finally, being tired, and I caught up.

A soft wet wind was wandering through the Pequops. Soon it would rain and thoroughly soak mountains and deserts alike—and us too, probably, if we didn't hurry.

But we didn't, and it did.

CHAPTER VII

In the Shadow of Ruby Range

WEST of the Pequops the route followed by our grandfathers in their covered wagons was seemingly as forgotten as the chart of Noah's cruise in the Ark.

Three large valleys separated by two ranges of mountains intervened between the last recognized ruts of the wagons (those at Flower or Jasper Pass) and the spot where Hastings' Cutoff is known to converge into the California Trail just west of Elko. In all our years of searching out lost sections of historic trails, we had never come up against such a proposition. Here was a chunk of virile landscape the size of a New England state in which we were at liberty to stall our motor, break our springs, puncture our tires, run out of water, gas, food, do anything at all, and probably nobody would be the wiser, unless, when all was finished, we were.

It seemed best to handle this section separately and differently from the remainder of the cutoff, which was moderately well placed by those who were in a position to know.

With this in mind we planned to establish a permanent camp somewhere on the west side of Ruby Range and to devote as much time as was necessary to the business of locating the elusive fragment of trail which we knew struck the range amidships on the east side, turned and went south along its line of snow-fed springs, crossed low Overland Pass toward the far end, and turned north again to find the Humboldt River.

We had to have advice. A stranger doesn't just wander out and put up a tent in the sage country of Nevada—not to stay a month anyway. So we went for help to Elko, where we have two friends, Dr. Secor, a physician, and Dr. Gallagher, dentist and well known sportsman. There we settled down for the week end in a cottage court and telephoned to find which way to turn next.

Dr. Secor is much interested in the geography of the Overland

Trail, and some years earlier he had taken time from his busy day to show us a difficult section of the Humboldt River route. He certainly proves our contention that no one knows the more obscure roads better than the physician of the community. Dr. Gallagher is a surpassingly successful fisherman and hunter; roads to him are means by which he arrives at trout stream or deer-haunted mountain. This section of the state is sportsmen's paradise, and in his quest for mule-tail deer, grouse, sage hens, ducks, geese, bass, and trout, he has covered most of the rough country in the two counties, Elko and White Pine, which contained our disputed territory.

On Sunday, said Dr. Gallagher, we would start out in his car and find a camp site west of the Rubies, meeting the ranchers of Huntington Valley. Then he would pilot us through Harrison Pass of Ruby Range and introduce us to the ranchers of Ruby Valley on the eastward slope. We would then return by Secret Pass, the most northerly of the three passes which break through the stupendous peaks of this short, high chain of mountains.

When this was happily settled over the telephone, the men went out to get the car greased—only two men, this time, as Mr. Bromley was not with us. As soon as they disappeared, I unpacked and hung in the bathroom such dresses as I expected to need. Then I turned on the hot water in the tub and simply left them hanging. I never press a dress while traveling; any wrinkles steam out easily, and the rayon jerseys do not need even this simple treatment. I selected a gray-blue with white dots, put some Mexican silver combs in front of my braids, added matching earrings, and felt dressed up. We would have dinner and see the town; but first and most important, we would have dinner.

In its way, Elko is a gay place, bearing the same relation to the eastern section of Nevada that Reno and Las Vegas bear to the west. It remains smaller than Reno, probably because Utah and Idaho are less heavily populated than California. However, such persons from adjoining states as care to make a drive of 150 miles can find a snappy evening's entertainment in Elko. The town is bisected by the railroad tracks, but there is a hotel on either side.

The short walk required to get to the hotel of our choice was interesting. Like most Nevada towns, Elko has its full quota of Indians; in fact there is a small rancheria on the northeastern edge of town, and its less industrious inhabitants may be found on the streets at all hours. They are usually tired. When an Indian gets tired, he props his feet and leans against a wall; when an Indian woman gets tired, she sits flat on her spanker anywhere she happens to be, with as complete detachment as if she were on a remote side hill, and falls into astral contemplation. There was one sitting against the front of the hotel, near the door, with her feet straight out in front of her; unheeded, we circled the terminal moraine of her skirts.

Near her a sickle-faced Mexican lounged against a lightpost singing, and two weary and dusty riders entered the lobby ahead of us, clumping on their slant-heeled boots.

The dining room was full and we had to wait, but after a while we got a table and had our dinner. Through an arch I could watch the slot machines, some new, some old. In Nevada they just wear out in service, seemingly never being disturbed for any other reason. With fascinated attention I watched a man put a pocketful of nickels into the cast-iron stomach of the one nearest. By "pocketful" I mean all that a man's pocket will hold; he had several dollars in nickels. He shed them one at a time and went off into the bar. I still watched, hoping that two modest tourist ladies, who giggled a little and tried it next, might collect on his investment, but their coins produced no regurgitation.

Then a major commotion in the back of the dining room denoted the departure of a family, travelers undoubtedly, going back to the auto-court cabin to put the children to bed. The father paid his bill absent-mindedly and ushered two older girls out between the tables. The mother plucked her fat baby from the highchair and took a five-year-old by the hand. As they passed the slot machine, he broke away. "I want some gum, Mommie," he told her urgently. "Mommie, let me get some gum."

Energetically he tried to climb up to the slot, using one hand while the other gripped a coin.

"That isn't a gum machine, Bobbie," she admonished him wearily. She looked tired enough to drop, and the baby was heavy. "Come with Mommie."

"I wanna put my nickel in."

"I tell you this isn't that kind of machine. If you put your nickel in, it's gone. You don't get any gum. You don't get anything."

"I wanna anyway, Mommie. Lift me."

The mother looked around, met my sympathetic eye, and shrugged.

"It's his money," she told me and slid her free hand around under his upheld arms, pulling him up on her hip high enough to reach the slot. "All right. Now put it in and pull the handle. It makes a nice noise."

It made a lovely noise. Five cent pieces commenced to roll out. The cup ran over and still they came. Bobbie hung limp on his mother's hip and watched them without surprise. After all, had he not put in a nickel?

I have never seen anything short of an earthquake bring such immediate action. The occupants of three tables crawled around on the floor. Bobbie had no hat, so we filled his little pants pockets. They left the dining room just as the father came back to see what was keeping them.

"See, Daddy," said Bobbie contentedly displaying his wealth. "I put my nickel in the hole. Mommie said I wouldn't get anything, but I did."

There must be a moral to that somewhere, but I don't feel up to it.

Outside, the Indian woman had vanished with the sun. The Mexican had sluiced his vocal chords with more drinks and was floundering in a morass of geographical indecision, making a splendid start toward one bar only to retreat despondently to his lamppost and get oriented for a tentative start toward another.

Even so, I love Nevada in the evening. A faint pink stained the flat tilted planes of the Rubies with their trailing blurs of snow. Some of the Elkoites sincerely believe that the sunset glow jeweling the peaks is responsible for the name Ruby. We watched it fade into gray, while a pair of doves sitting on a wire crowded closer together and moaned, two mourners at the funeral of the day. By the time we reached our cottage, it had grown dark.

Dr. Secor was sitting outside in his car enjoying what was probably his first quiet moment of the day. "Here I am," he greeted us cheerfully, "and looking forward to seeing the maps of Hastings' Cutoff, and the diaries too. You brought them, didn't you?" he added anxiously.

"Surest thing you know," said my husband.

"We wouldn't get very far without them," added Dr. Neff.

We all went inside and spread them out. I had given a good deal of thought to his visit and had things ready. With quick concentration he was soon immersed in the marked passages. Presently he looked up. "A good many years ago," he said, "another man and I rode horseback along what we took for the Donner Trail from Flower Lake west. I have thought since then that I am probably the only man in this section who has traveled it, but I'm beginning to have my doubts."

Silence descended again, and presently Dr. Neff handed him Beckwith's railroad-survey map made in 1853. One glance was enough. "Damnation!" he burst out. "I'll bet I'm the only man who *hasn't* been over it. The trail went right through the gap where the Jasper tunnel was built, and I have never had time to travel by train."

And then began what I considered to be the crux of our scheme for relocating camp sites and trails—the correlation of our research in libraries and at home with the geographical knowledge of some picked local person. And the proper person often takes a lot of picking, for he can either save us days and weeks of time, or, by misinterpreting what he reads, he can cause us to waste so many of our vacation days that the whole project must wait another year. After an evening with our data, Dr. Secor took an ordinary county map and marked the likely route on it. He made marginal notes of the ranchers we would meet in the different sections, and at dubious points he gave advice and suggested where to go and whom to ask for more information. He told us where and when we would have to leave the car and walk. Armed with this marked map, we could fare forth and go to various mountain passes and springs with a certain knowledge of finding them.

After he had finished, it was hard to see how the project could possibly fail.

*   *   *

"I hope you'll be comfortable in your camp," said Mrs. Gallagher, who entertains with an absolute minimum of effort and was enjoying herself. "South Fork is a good trout stream; you'll be just off the reservation; and the store at Lee is the only place to buy anything that you'll find for miles."

"It was the best place I could think of," agreed Dr. Gallagher, surveying the ruined remains of his fried chicken and evidently deciding regretfully that nothing more could be done with it. "You really should have two cars, though. Some of the country you're planning to go over isn't traveled at all. If you got stuck, you could just sit."

"We're going to have a second car. I've agreed to rather an odd proposition," I admitted. "I guess I'd better tell you about it."

"We have all agreed to it," my husband supported me with unusual promptness, "and *I'll* tell about it. About a month ago, the history-minded folks of San Francisco celebrated the city's birthday with a lunch at the Presidio, and I happened to be the speaker. We were given some invitations to send out allowing the invitee to pay for his own meal, and Mrs. Paden conscientiously mailed them to a list of people who were known to be interested in the history of the West. Some of them she knew and some she didn't. The next day one of them, who happened to own an autographed copy of her first book, recognized her writing and called up to thank her. Wasn't that the way it started?" he interpolated, looking at me.

"That was it, and I liked his manner over the phone. He sounded nice."

"He's regular, or I miss my guess. Anyway, he asked her what we were doing of interest this summer and found that his vacation coincided with ours in time and approximate place. So he asked if he and his wife might drop in at camp—if they could find it—just to see how we were making out with our project."

"And I," I took up the story, "was nervous because we didn't have a second car for the work over the mountains, and suggested that they stay a few days if they liked, and take an excursion or two."

"Um-m-m-m," said Dr. Gallagher.

"Oh, I know I was taking a chance," I apologized, "but he sounded as if he would take things as they came; and afterward I talked to his wife and liked her, too, and we really were in a jam."

"Do you think they'll come?" Mrs. Gallagher wanted to know. "And what's the name?"

"I hope so. He said Yes right away, but we had to do some stiff persuading with his wife. She had more reason to wonder what she was being let in for than we did. The name is Mewhirter; not one you hear every day."

"He's a solid citizen of San Francisco and the Peninsula," my husband reassured her raised eyebrows. "The only trouble may be that they won't realize the kind of country they have to take their car over."

"Yes, they do," I put in. "They read in *The Wake of the Prairie Schooner* about how we crossed the Humboldt Sink, and decided it might be interesting. Well, they got *too* interested and got stuck in the alkali slickings; they had to wait until night and walk out to Parran, and they just got there in time for breakfast. If they are still interested in emigrant trails after that, they can take anything and be good sports. Their car is the same make as ours, with interchangeable tires, and, if their son comes, there will be a Ford coupé too. It ought to be a perfect setup."

*   *   *

And so the first of the week found us established in a more or less permanent camp near the small store at Lee, thirty miles from Elko, awaiting the arrival of the Mewhirters. We were in a grove of old cottonwoods through which ran a narrow ditchlike offshoot of the South Fork of Humboldt River. We had two tents to sleep in, but the rest of the housekeeping had to be done outdoors. If it rained, well, it just rained.

A canvas spread in the shadiest spot held some cushions and our box of maps and notes taken from journals, from the study of which addenda under soporific conditions we arrive sometimes at the oddest conclusions. A three-burner gasoline stove occupied one end of a long board table nailed to a couple of trees, but I also had an old-fashioned little wood fire at the edge of the ditch where I was sim-mering a stew.

While not exactly our own vine and fig tree, it was at least our own gasoline stove and fly spray, and I was satisfied with it.

"Where in the world did you get this meat, and what do they call it?" I asked my husband, who had some hours ago returned to camp with that portion of the groceries he had been able to remember. "I've been cooking it most of the morning and it's exactly like hunks off the spare tire."

He paid no attention, being quite absorbed in making a choice between two dozen or so lurid pocket-size mystery books which our friends had collected for our mental relaxation during vacation.

"Well, I didn't expect we could eat it for lunch, but we'll be lucky if we can get a knife through it by night. I'll toast some cheese sand-wiches; the coals are about right."

I buttered bread, sliced cheese, and made some huge square sandwiches. Dr. Neff silently handed me the right number of clean whittled sticks, and I propped the sandwiches upright on a piece of tin beside the fire. As they got hot, the cheese melted, ran down onto the hot metal, and smelled wonderful. The coffee bubbled itself into the proper state. Dr. Neff took the cream out of the icebox, closed the box lid and sat on it while we entered into one of our interminable discussions (in which I discuss and he says Yes and No firmly) about which smells the best, coffee and bacon or fried potatoes and onion. I had just reversed a sandwich, burned myself on hot cheese, sucked it off, and was getting a basin of water from the ditch when we heard two cars coming down the hill from the store at Lee.

The noise extracted my husband from the depths of heartless murder, and we all trotted over the uneven ground to guide the Mewhirters to the camp site we had picked out for them. There were two cars. "Thank goodness they all came," I gasped as we hurried.

Mr. Mewhirter got out and came around the car with the most flattering expression of well-being, just the way my husband inspects a likely riffle before casting. He had reached the place he wanted to be. "This is my son, Trove," he introduced easily, and I turned to take the hand of a tall, self-possessed young man whose expression behind dark glasses I could not read, but whom I liked at sight.

Mrs. Mewhirter just sat in the car and I went over to her. "I'm not going to get out until I find out whether or not you want so many," she declared firmly. "Nothing went the way we expected; we had to shut up the house and all come—even the dog. This is Sharon," she said, indicating a pretty sixteen-year-old daughter who was just a little put out at being forced into a strange, and probably uncomfortable, environment but appeared willing to make the best of it. "And that is Muffet." Muffet, a large yellow dog, ruffled as a marigold, hung her tongue out and panted pleasantly. "She's fluffy-minded but she means well."

"You don't know how glad we are to see you—all of you," I told her fervently. "Just get right out of this hot car and, when you have cooled off, come over to our camp. I'm going to run back and rescue the toasted cheese sandwiches and make some more for you." The dying down of the coals had conveniently produced a perfect product, mellow inside and crisp outside and just smoky enough to be good. Dr. Neff built up the fire while I constructed some more sandwiches for a second round and cut cantaloupe. I covered the golden halves with oiled paper from force of habit, but our camp at Lee had fewer unoccupied insects with leisure to become interested in our food supply than any place I have ever stayed.

Presently the contingent from the other camp appeared, each carrying a chair and beating down a grassy path that was to become pretty well worn during the next week. Coming last and herding her family with an air of pleased proprietorship was Muffet. Her ears were cocked, her tongue hung out, and her tawny hair was tufted in all directions like a burst firecracker. She barged around for a few moments, looking for interesting ankles, and vanished.

Alice Mewhirter set two quarts of ice-cold milk on the table, produced a cake, and commenced, capably, to pour coffee for those who wished it. With a sigh of gratitude I recognized the fact that from now on I was sharing camp duties with an expert, took a big round bite out of my first sandwich, and leaned back gingerly in my chair, where the heavy shadow of the big cottonwoods lay thickest.

The breeze was cool. It always was. I suppose the nearness of the great snow-topped peaks tempered our days. There was nothing particularly beautiful about the location, lying, as it did, away from the river between fenced meadows; and it was necessary to walk uphill some three or four hundred yards to the store for drinking water, passing on the way all the outbuildings and a large chicken yard. But it was comfortable, if not spectacular, and we were very grateful for a cool camp.

When everything but the last cup of coffee was gone, we got down to serious planning. Our first project was to locate the second "mound spring" of the diaries, which Dr. Secor had told us was probably the location still called Mound Springs that lies between the Pequops and the next elevation west, Spruce Mountain. Mr. and Mrs. Mewhirter were to go along in their car. It was not likely to be a difficult section, and we left the question of whether or not Trove and Sharon should come to be decided later. Trove had brought a rod, and the South Fork is a good stream. It doesn't often outrage the ordinary intelligence by producing nine-pound trout, as do the springs of Ruby Valley, but it does very well by the expert fisherman. In the course of the afternoon he slung his creel over one shoulder and went off, and from then on he kept the camps festooned in fish.

Sharon contentedly poked through our paper-covered library. Presently she selected a garish specimen displaying a skeleton hand grasping a pair of bloody scissors and, settling down under her mother's slightly disapproving eye, began at the last page and backed into it.

It was a lovely settled day. We didn't go anywhere. I washed all the clothes not absolutely attached to anyone's person, swept the tents, raked the camp and cooked and cooked. It takes a day like that about once in two weeks to keep a camp going. We were all working in silence—that is, most of us; the silence of my husband was probably occasioned by the fact that he was undoubtedly asleep—when a small but noisy riot started in the chicken yard. I ran out into the open and saw a barrage of feathers and flapping, squawking chickens whooshing over the fence. From their midst emerged Muffet, trotting calmly and heavily, with a big chicken in her mouth. The noise evaporated like spilled ether.

We converged on her in horror. This was the most convenient spot in the county, and we had every intention of being model campers and retaining our privileges. Someone pried her unresisting jaws off the feathery body. It was already cold and stiff and lay on the ground, with pallid eyelids closed, in all the supreme unattractiveness of a defunct fowl. It had been dead a long time. Muffet's misdemeanor evidently had been merely trespass, and she stood guard over her find with a pride that attested her sterling worth.

"She didn't kill it, that's certain," Lyle Mewhirter said equitably. "Maybe she thought she was retrieving something." He picked up the chicken by the end of its wing feathers and, annexing our garbage can as he went by it, took the whole thing downriver to bury. Muffet, with a disarming air of solid citizenship, went along to see the job finished

The camp, being thoroughly stirred up, went about its late afternoon duties. I started setting the table for dinner. The exploratory fork still bounced off the stew. "I should have brought the pressure cooker for this altitude," I confessed, "but really I didn't dream that it was so high. What is it here, six thousand?"

"Just about, I guess." This from Doc, who was concocting a hybrid mixture of pancake batter and corn which he contended would be easier to chew.

My husband had dipped a basin of clear running water from the ditch. He now inserted his head and came up snorting. For some reason that is entirely beyond me, most men do this, much to their apparent invigoration. He stopped in mid-snort. "Why didn't he bury it?" he asked of unresponsive nature; "that's what he started out to do."

He stood up and dripped coolly on to his shirt while staring down the river path. Mr. Mewhirter was returning, striding along through the cottonwoods and swinging the empty pail. Behind him, obediently at heel, trotted Muffet with a big feathered body in her mouth.

"Golly!" gasped Sharon, "that isn't the same chicken."

Once more we converged. Our whole idea was to get this one out of sight. Pay for it, yes, but later and under less embarrassing circumstances.

Seeing that the common focus of our eyes was three feet behind him, Mr. Mewhirter turned. "What in the name of common sense—Muffet!" he thundered, "where did you get that dead hawk?"

Muffet laid it down gently and looked hurt. Alice Mewhirter took her over to the tent and tied her up. "I'm sorry," I heard her say, "but if you must express yourself in barnyard fowl and such, you'll have to stay put. It's too nerve racking."

We went quietly back to dinner, ate the beef, and resigned ourselves to indigestion.

CHAPTER VIII

Grass Country

IN the middle of a July morning three cars, carrying seven people, pulled up next to the fence enclosing the Mound Springs. It wasn't a difficult fence, being built simply to keep wandering cattle from drowning themselves headfirst in the peculiar water holes. The rest of the people went over or through in a conventional manner. I went under. What will happen to me on top of a fence is always uncertain, but if I can lie down on the nice dependable ground, give one half-turn and come up on the other side, it makes little trouble for anyone.

The first party to cross the Pequops into this valley was the Bidwell-Bartleson company, and they didn't find water. Of course they might have missed Mound Springs in the dark, but it rather sounds as if they had come by way of Little Lake Pass.

The distance from Flower Springs over the Pequops to Mound Springs was variously stated as eighteen miles by John Wood, sixteen by Moorman, fifteen by Chalmers, and fourteen by James Reed, who often underestimated. Travelers on the cutoff didn't have the advantage of the fur trappers' wisdom to tell them how far they had gone, as did the emigrants on the regular Overland Road; but, by 1850, the Mormons were selling little guidebooks, imperfect but helpful, and Moorman procured one from the men at the adobe hut in Tooele Valley. The Mormons on their way to found Salt Lake City had designed and installed a workable roadmeter which made Clayton's guidebook of the Mormon Trail north of the Platte the most dependable of any in circulation among the Forty-niners. It is likely that subsequently they used the roadmeter in calculating any important distance and that the guidebook sold to Moorman gave him fairly true mileage.

Moorman wrote: "A travel of sixteen miles brought us to grass and water in a place that resembled very nearly the one last named [Flower Springs], with this difference, that the spring issued from the top of a considerable mound that would shake to its center from the steps of one man, yet scores were up on it at once. A man let his mule come upon it to drink from the little branch that ran off from the spring, into which the animal stepped and almost as quick as thought was as far down as the pack would let him go. It took pretty hard pulling to get poor *mula* out, which occurrence made others around more cautious. There can not be too much caution observed at these places, for there is great danger of animals being seriously injured if not entirely lost."

Trove and I started up the slope of the mound together. He jumped on it to watch it shake, but I let well enough alone. At the first ill advised hop one leg disappeared to the knee in a queer substance that looked like weed-grown ashes. After that I trod lightly. At the top we looked across the still surface of some dark and opaque water. I hesitated uneasily and wondered if the lip where we stood extended over it for any perceptible distance. Involuntarily I took a few steps backward and stood poised ready to make the descent in ten leaps if my feet started to sink again. We were discussing the probably depth of the spring when Muffet passed us, walked into the water in a highly suicidal manner and, when about ten feet out from the edge, began slowly to sink. Inch by inch she went down, until only her fluffy forehead was out of the water and her long ears floated.

Trove whistled and she rolled her eyes at him and remained still.

"You don't think she's being sucked down into the thing, do you?" I was worried.

"No, I don't. I think she doesn't want to come; but I'll admit she looks stuck."

He whistled again and I called, "Come on, Muffet," persuasively. "Good puppy."

But that excellent dog remained submerged and even went down an inch. Trove started to pull off his jacket but paused with one shoulder out. Mound Spring was not an alluring place to jump into casually. "Let's try leaving her," he suggested and hurled a large clod ahead of us down the slope. I trotted obediently after it and he came along behind.

Muffet flashed past, snowering both of us from her flailing tail, and had taken a large bite out of the clod before we arrived.

"How did she manage to get out?" I asked breathlessly. Keeping my footing had prevented me from watching.

"Just stood up and walked out," he said, with some appreciation of the humor of it. "She was lying down."

The obstacle to be surmounted between here and the next valley was the north slope of Spruce Mountain. We went over it on the course of the trail, with no difficulty worthy of the name, had our lunch on top among the piñons and junipers, and came down the west descent to a wide flat valley, where we made good progress.

The trouble with jaunting along on unworked lengths of the emigrant trail is that you may at any moment have to give up and go back. As we went in a procession of three cars, mile after mile, this possibility weighed heavily. A field trip which progresses successfully until the last hour can be most unsuccessful from a standpoint of comfort if (as has happened more than once) we have to retrace our way back in order to get out of a dead end. The farther you have gone, the worse it is. In this instance nothing of the sort happened. In fact very little of any sort happened. Once, our car, in the lead, frightened a coyote so that he forgot his ordinary caution and was caught in a trap. Trove, bringing up the rear in the Ford, had to get out and shoot it to end its suffering. Now and then we met the huge, tolerant Hereford bulls that wander at will through the rabbit brush with one or two favorites from their harems. When riding, I can see their virtues. It's when I'm afoot that they render me positively cataleptic.

Moorman wrote that his party, several times in this afternoon's trip of about twenty miles, mistook mirages for lakes of water. We could not help thinking that the "mirage" seen by Moorman's company was actually Snow Water Lake, (a flat, pale piece of water which is in plain sight from the slope of Spruce Mountain) If so, they had certainly reversed the usual procedure and had mistaken the real for the unreal.

Toward late afternoon we arrived at the Warm Creek Ranch. The camp site in this vicinity is not so well defined as any of the others encountered after leaving the Jordan River. The wagons had come to a country with plenty of room, plenty of grass, plenty of water. The only lack was in finding sage enough to burn, so that the tendency was to scatter camps. Then, too, the trains often arrived here after dark, having made an exceptionally long trip from Flower Springs. A doctor rode into this camp, almost dead with fatigue after thirty-six miles in the saddle, and found an anxious old Dutchman with a little boy who came out into the trail asking for medical help. Screams of pain came from out the dark where a man lay with crushed ribs caused by a fall from his horse. The doctor went into action and the man was made comfortable. It was just an ordinary trailside occurrence. Even the good old Samaritan who had interrupted his precarious journey to remain a day most uncomfortably with the sufferer until a doctor should happen by was one of the ordinary personnel of the Overland Trail to California. One diarist told wonderingly that a man who had delayed several days to nurse a helpless invalid back to health was the only man of his group to get his wagon through to California intact; so it is possible that good was repaid with good then as now.

A low gap, long to travel but almost flat, led through a branch spur of Ruby Range, or Humboldt Mountains, as Frémont called them. At the end of the gap the emigrants found themselves in Ruby Valley, one of the fair places of the earth.

The jagged crown of the Rubies holds its snow long after it has gone from all but the highest peaks of the Sierra Nevada—snow in white woolly caps from which ravelings break loose and appear as frothing creeks hanging whitely down the mountain. Like the snows of Pilot Peak, they feed a multiplicity of well-like springs; but, unlike the lonely peak, the water here is so abundant that it soaks through the adjacent valley, forming two main lakes—Ruby Lake to the south and Franklin to the north. In a wet season they are worthy of their title, but ordinarily in summer they are glorified marshes tinseled with small shiny ponds and confettied with red and white cattle.

From Franklin Lake a small sluggish river runs north. It was named Franklin River by Beckwith during his railroad survey in 1853-1854, and Moorman characterized it quite well as a "small muddy creek of indifferent water."

Most trains nooned at Franklin River and reached the foot of Ruby Range toward night. Travel was so easy, the animals so refreshed, and the men so eager to make up for previous delays that they made notable journeys each day. Topography had a great deal to do with it also, of course. They had been stopping at water and grass where (and if) it could be found. Now it was everywhere. They could go on to the limit of their endurance.

Seven miles beyond the "muddy creek," and making twenty-two from the vicinity of Warm Creek Ranch, Moorman "encamped for the night at the base of the main ridge of Humboldt Mountain on the brink of a clear, rippling little stream flowing from the fields of eternal snow. The pasturage was of the best—blue grass, timothy, wheat, clover and many other grasses clothed the fertile soil in a garb of waving verdure. Several of the men started up the mountain in search of the black-tail deer, which abound through this region, while another started to the lower grounds after sandhill cranes, which kept up a deafening song. The huntsmen returned at dusk without success, and after supper an hour was whiled away by jest and laugh and merry song."

At this point we lose the benefit of the data from Bryant's meticulous journal. He did not turn south along the course of what was to be the cutoff but, coached by Hudspeth before they parted company, turned off toward the Secret Pass along the course of Joe Walker's section of the Frémont Party which Hastings and Hudspeth himself had traveled going east. The pass is a "dilly," sagy and rather wide at the start but narrowing into a grim and rugged slash which the horsemen avoided, going over the tops of the rolling mountains instead.

The Harlan-Young Party, led by Hastings, were the first to face the necessity of getting wagons to the west side of the Rubies. In their judgment it was best to go around the short mountain chain rather than over. It was probably the best choice, although the mountains, which chance to be low near Secret Pass, do not look formidable. But the elevation, even on the flat, is about six thousand feet. It might have been too much for the tired animals. There was a chance here to gain the four or five days that meant safety for the Donner Party later, but the wise ones of the migration decided against it. The wagons started south.

The modern road keeps much the same course as did the cutoff; it turns south and stays between the mountains and the lakes. It is a little higher up on the sagy slopes above the marshland than was the trail, for a road must be dry enough for all-year-round travel, while the emigrants only used the cutoff in midsummer. From a vantage point where we drove over the instep of a foothill, we stopped to take stock of the situation. The valley lay below us robed in such green as we had not seen for weeks. Crude blue gems shone on her bosom. Not all our reading had prepared us for such luxuriance.

We drove on from one to another of the galaxy of springs that edge the marsh. Beyond them the grass-matted flat was netted by a reticulation of rivulets stemming from the springs that merged gradually into the two shallow lakes.

Columns of white steam rose ahead from the boiling springs on the Smith Ranch. If our old friend Bryant had gone this way, we would no doubt be informed as to the temperature of the water and the circumference of each spring; but we didn't measure them. We were too busy piloting Muffet between the hot pools on an improvised leash of twine which only her innate good nature prevented her from snapping at any given moment. We had watered her at the car until that spongelike animal was completely foundered; and it worked very well, for she showed no interest in the deceptively hot ponds of all sizes.

John Wood mentioned them without elaboration. He was too full of enthusiasm for the beautiful cold springs which could be used to quench thirst. Moorman gave more detail. "I did not count them," he said, "but there cannot be less than twenty, nearly all varying more or less in temperature. One of the springs I supposed to be twenty feet in diameter, of unfathomable depth and boiling like a pot. From the appearance of the ground around, which is perfectly bare of vegetation, they sometimes overflow. They attract the attention of every passer-by, and this strange phenomenon of nature is only beheld with wonder and surprise."

Bidwell wrote on September 21st: "We came to some hot Springs, which were to me a great curiosity. Within the circumference of a mile there were perhaps 20 Springs: the most of which were extremely beautiful, the water being so transparent, we could see the smallest thing 20 to 30 feet deep. The rocks which walled the Springs, and the beautifully white sediment lodged among them, reflected the sun's rays in such a manner, as to exhibit the most splendid combination of colors, blue, green, red &c., I ever witnessed. The water in most of them was boiling hot. There was one, however, more beautiful than the rest: it really appeared more like the work of art than of nature. It was about 4 feet in diameter, round as a circle, and deeper than we could see—the cavity looked like a well cut in a solid rock, its walls being smooth and perpendicular. Just as I was viewing this curiosity, some hunters came up with some meat, we all partook, putting it into the spring, where it cooked perfectly done in 10 minutes—this is no fish story!

"The earth around the Springs was white with a substance which tasted strongly of Potash, and the water in the springs was of this quality."

It was, I am sure, the advent of the peculiar hot wells upon the horizon of the Donner Party that led Reed to designate the whole flat as Mineral Valley. There would be no other obvious reason, but, then, James Reed was an individualist and did not always react as other people did. He was of the majority in one respect, however. They all gave the valley a name. It was too singular and too lovely to be left out of the conversation. A name was essential. Had a guidebook entitling it been available, it would have come down to posterity under whatever name was used, such is the power of the printed word, which speaks to everyone. As it was, each man coined his own. John Wood called it Fountain Valley. "From the innumerable springs here to be seen," wrote Moorman, "I designate it Spring Valley, as I am ignorant of its real name, if it has any." Blackburn called it Thousand Spring Valley, and Jefferson listed it on his map as Valley of Fountains.

I think it is probable that John Wood was carrying the Jefferson map, because of this and other similarities in titles, but it had a small circulation and was little known.

Naturally, there were Indians in the mountains. And they gave trouble. Reed tells that George Donner lost "little gray & his cream col. mare Margrat." The red men were of the Shoshone persuasion, "sulky, thievish and blood-thirsty," said John Wood. They had plenty of everything—nut-bearing piñons, fish, fowl, and game—so that their friction with the emigrants took a different form from that of the half-starved Diggers of the lower Humboldt River, who regarded the columns of animals as a fruitful source of much-needed meat. The Indians of the Rubies wanted only to be let alone. Their sorties were in the nature of halfhearted battles, gestures to frighten the white man from their paradise. And if they spied a few wanderers and could shoot them safely, they were shot and left lying. The Indians of the lower Humboldt killed the animals so that they must be left behind. The Indians of the Rubies vindictively shot the riders. Of course a good horse was always acceptable, and George Donner's cream-colored mare undoubtedly bore a Shoshone brave for the rest of her days.

John Wood had heard that there was a packers' trail only fifteen miles long over the center of the range, eliminating the long trek around it to the south and saving several days' journey; but his company was poorly armed and they were afraid to leave the main trail. This was one time, we should be happy to know, that John chose the easier course; for five men who adventurously took the short cut were killed that day.

It seems evident that the short cut went by way of modern Harrison Pass.

* * *

We broke our continuous trek along the trail to return to our headquarters by way of Harrison Pass and see the country traversed by the packers' short cut. We were in something of the same fix as the emigrants, who seemed to work harder on Sunday than on any other day, except that they worked in camp while the animals rested and we worked out on the road. In our case it was the opportunity to find the ranch owners in the house instead of out in the field that kept us on the alert.

It was dark when we reached camp, and we were tired but nevertheless had to plan for an early start tomorrow. So, when both camps were illuminated by fires and lanterns and the pots of ham hocks and beans were heating, Sharon and I walked up the shadowy road to the store to get fresh bread for the sandwiches.

We were among the horses before we realized it.

Some indistinct figures were still dismounting and some were unsteadily heading for the entrance to the little grocery—Indians from the reservation demonstrating their impregnable right to a Sunday-night spree. They weren't any more dangerous than certain types of their white brothers under similar circumstances, but I don't care much about either at close quarters. Sharon and I ducked inside; it seemed advisable at the time; but there, slightly better illuminated, was a row of similar heavy-set figures squatting against the wall opposite the counter. They had no English for conversational purposes and didn't make a sound.

I threw a quarter on the counter and said "Bread," which I got. Neither myself nor the young fellow back of the counter thought of the change. He was a Mormon lad, with all of their ingrained distaste for excess of any kind. I didn't envy him his evening, as we hurried outside again.

We reached camp far faster than any of the staggering figures could have followed, unless they rode; made up the sandwiches and, as the crowd on the hill became noisier, decided to put out all the lights and go to bed. There were five tents and seven people in camp. We didn't expect (nor have) any hurtful experience, but thought we wouldn't be at hand to invite a late call.

I took a mystery with me and read for a while with a flashlight inside my bed roll. I felt quite serene again. After all, nothing untoward could happen to a person who was warm in bed reading comfortably about murder. Suddenly we heard galloping horses— just like the Westerns, I told my husband. "Too darn much like the Westerns," I heard him say as he pulled on his shoes in the dark. The whole bunch rode whooping into our little grove and, either for fun or accidentally, crashed their ponies through a fence. They powwowed about it for a while and then tore at full gallop up the hill again.

By this time the men were out and I had laid aside my synthetic paper-covered excitement and, with my eye to the screened window in the back of the tent, was having some of my own. My stomach felt as if I had eaten a nervous lobster. There was nothing to do that seemed both right and effective. But my husband (whose ideas have a habit of working) insisted on going halfway up to the store and, with Mr. Mewhirter's help, closed a heavy gate that, to judge by the depth it was imbedded in the ground, hadn't been swung on its hinges for years. Then they stepped back into the willows and waited.

In five minutes the teetering cavalcade was back, pounding madly along on the ponies, and brought up slam against the gate.

I couldn't see in that direction from my window, so I stepped outside in the shadow and knelt down at the door of the tent to peer under the pendent branches of the cottonwoods. A little fuzzy kitten materialized out of somewhere and climbed my knee to purr like a refrigerator in action. I was frantic to hear what was going on and bounced her off into the grass. Snatches of a voice engaged in oratory reached me and I drew a full breath again. If they had stopped to argue, they couldn't get up impetus to come so fast. It was a dozen or so ponies tripping over tent ropes and flinging inert braves here and there among the bed rolls that I really dreaded.

There was nothing at all to stop them; but the psychology of the closed gate had worked. They rode slowly up the hill again and, this time, kept going.

We went to bed again; but the kitten wanted to come in. She *really* wanted to, and she was a persistent animal. She sat beside the head of my cot just outside the tent for most of the night and mewed. Occasionally, because she was really quite comfortable in the folds of a tarpaulin, she purred. Once in a while, as I grew immune to those noises, she rose on her hind legs and sharpened her needlelike front claws on the canvas next to my ear. So, after all, it was a half-pint kitten, and not the Indians, who kept the night uneasy.

*   *   *

We took up our trail tracing at the boiling springs and drove south. The day was a glass bowl sloshing full of sunlight, and it smelled deliciously of white clover. Starting from the space between Franklin Lake and its southern neighbor Ruby Lake, the old packers' trail climbed over Harrison Pass. The jagged peaks fell off into dark canyons, and at the mouth of one of these an ancient relic of the Shoshone tribe, known as Old Barley Sacks, lived for years in a hut adorned with saddles, bridles, and various trappings from Fort Ruby.

There were springs everywhere and, opposite us to the east, Ruby Lake shone tin-bright. Under the most spectacular of the peaks, Cave Creek, almost too cold to drink, flows from a cave into which one may row a boat, and covers itself from the sudden light with massed elderberry bushes. The Game Refuge Headquarters are on the creek, and here, according to Reed's journal, the Donner Party camped.

From the next hill we could see Overland Pass and the Toganini Ranch, where is found the last of the enormous springs and the site of old Fort Ruby. The name has stuck, but the fort has evolved into a ranch. As we approached, we noticed that the buildings were the combination of log and sod that seems to fit so well into the scheme of Ruby Valley. In the yard stood a huge freight wagon, falling into disrepair.

The ranch is owned by Mr. Harris; but Mr. and Mrs. Carl Maves were leasing that year, and we told them our desire to cross the last and most southerly pass of the Rubies, sometimes called Overland and sometimes Hastings' Pass. The range was dwindling fast. The pass is low and short and it looked feasible. We didn't need much in the way of a road, we told them, just enough space between trees and a reasonably low center.

But they couldn't even assure us of that, said Mr. Maves. No one had been over it for a long time. He couldn't remember if an ordinary car had ever made the trip.

That was true, Mrs. Maves said, and added that a cloudburst had ripped out a portion of the old road bodily on the western side of the pass, if what she had heard was to be believed.

If we couldn't go clear across, we asked resignedly, could we go to the top?

Yes, they thought so. Mr. Maves had been there not too long ago and knew that it was passable for a truck.

Back through Harrison Pass we went and circled to the west end of Hastings' Pass, where the cattle of the Sadler Ranch range. At the ranch house we presented ourselves and asked three young-looking booted riders about the possibility of crossing.

They regarded us with the kindly pity of those who ride horses for those who do not, dismounted, and walked up a knoll with us. From its top they pointed out the route we must take.

Overland Pass was visible from the hilltop. It was rather low and looked anything but formidable, much lower than Harrison Pass, which soared over the range at a pretty stiff elevation; and much less labyrinthine than Secret Pass, which had disappeared at low level into the maw of the mountain in a disturbingly final manner.

No, they didn't think it possible to get over, but we were welcome to go up and have a look. It was passable as far as the top, although a recent cloudburst had done a lot of damage. Someone from the Juaristi Ranch had been there rounding up cattle.

When we reached the car, introductions proved that our informants were Nora Shangle, one of the top exhibition riders of the state, and her son and daughter. I reversed all my ideas of riding as an avocation. It must be a most relaxing sport, for, in their similar broad hats and jeans, they looked more or less the same age.

The next day we again crossed the range, went to Fort Ruby Ranch, and prepared to negotiate Hastings' Pass.

"But first," said Mrs. Maves, "you really ought to go out to old Ruby Valley stage station—that is, if you can make it. It's only a mile or two straight out into the flat; but you practically have to break trail through the tall grass, and the high center on the old stage road is bad."

"I didn't realize that we were near the stage route," I told her.

"Yes. The stage came straight west from Ruby Valley Station to the pass. The cutoff angles into the pass from the north. Through the pass is the only place where the later travelers on the stagecoaches traveled the cutoff—and they probably didn't know it," she added.

We succeeded in reaching the little station. It is intact and as picturesque as anything to be found in the way of a stagecoaching

relic. The pygmy building stands eight feet high at the eaves, eleven at the peak, and has two rooms twelve feet square. The logs of which it is built are bleached to a cream color, and the rocks of the chimney are variously colored against the solid yellow of the flowering rabbit brush. It makes an attractive picture and one not easily duplicated. Until a couple of years ago one of the two rooms had stacks of papers and magazines from decades back. Mrs. Maves had told us with concern that they had recently vanished. I stood and looked at the fireplace, envisioning the station keeper and the stock hand reading away the winter days, and hoped that whoever had salvaged their library had placed it where it would do some good to students of that far-gone era. I felt a flash of real pride in the stalwart little building which seemed to brace itself and dare the encroaching rabbit weed that so far had rather astonishingly refrained from over-running it. It was so lonely and so tiny that it looked pathetic, like a toy forgotten, as we left it and moved along the stage road toward the mountains.

I thought again of little Ada Millington trundling along in her father's old prairie schooner while the fastest and most spectacular stages the world ever produced whirled past them. Her baby brother was ailing and was not destined to recover. In a day or so he died. If only, the mother thought, she could get his little body to Carson City, where they intended to live! Her heart contracted in horror at the thought of leaving him out in the wilds where they would never come again. Somehow she persuaded a softhearted driver to take him on the stage. The hired man went along to take charge of the necessary arrangements at the end of the journey. From then on Ada watched for the stage stations, because, nailed to the nearest telegraph pole (then brand new) she always found a note telling of their progress.

Telegraph poles! That reminded Mr. Mewhirter of something. He was a Pacific Telephone & Telegraph Company executive, and was interested in everything that had to do with communication—and he is capable of most intense interest. He remembered that, of course, the old line went up through the pass with the stage road. He would walk, said he, and proceeded to do so. It was no hindrance, because he could make better time on foot than we could with the cars. At the end of the morning he got back behind the wheel triumphantly with an ancient wooden insulator which is now in the museum of the company.

Overland Pass is 6,789 feet in elevation, almost 1,100 feet lower than Harrison Pass. We nooned at the spring close to the summit and south of the trail. The emigrants used it for the same purpose. Muffet, emerging from the car, promptly cooled herself in the overflow from the spring. It was boxed or she would have sat in that. We didn't care. We had a thermal jug and were independent of the source that had supplied hundreds of travelers.

The old trail was deep and kept crossing and recrossing our road. The sage was as high as the car. Just west of the summit and north of the road was a very old cabin.

The cloud had burst on the western descent, wiping out a hundred yards or so of thoroughfare, but it didn't matter to us. The detour we were forced to make around the washed-out section was scarcely more rough than the regular trail.

On the west slope Moorman found a brush hedge, made of up-rooted sage. It extended a long distance, and he rightly supposed it to be constructed by the Indians for assistance in their rabbit drives. Blackburn saw it too. "their was a high fence," he wrote, "made of brush and small pines well this bothered us again. who made the fence. it looked like it was made for deer and we let it go at that. the company that came through here [emigration of 1846] could not have made it for the fence ran clear over the mountain."

I had spoken to Mrs. Maves about these windrows of pulled-up sage, and she said that there had been similar hedges on Ruby Range within the memory of present inhabitants.

"Near the brush fence three deer jumt up," Blackburn continued in his inimitable casual style, "and crost the road ahead of the horses and our best hunter grabbed his gun and sayes les have some venesen for supper and started arround a hill to get a shot and we lost sight of him. went on a little distance and waited. an hour or more. and he did not return two of our men went to look for him. they hunted all over but could not find him. went on to the first good camp an stopt. sent two men to look. they scoured the country good but without success. we weare in a fix and so was he. Brown says the indians have taken him and that is the last. we all thought the same for their was plenty around here we sat arround the camp fire wondering what to doe look at that fire on top of that hill sayes one ile bet thats him. les goe to it sayes another. and off two started to the fire and took an hour to reach the place. they approached causily for fear of a trap. and found him roasting venesen he said he was going to live while did live and he built the fire so we could see it for he was lost and could not find the road. well," concluded Blackburn philo-sophically, "we come out of that lucky."

Overland Pass proved to be wide and shallow. We saw blue timber grouse and sage chickens; an embattled snowshoe rabbit stamped her front feet like a scared but stubborn sheep; a long skinny mink streaked across the road in front of the car. And now, as we ap-proached civilization with its fences, a large mule-tail buck, with great antlers in the velvet, stood beside the road and stared at us in a magisterial manner. Then, rising in the air with the effortlessness of a dirigible, he folded his legs under him and sailed over a gate.

At the foot of the gap the stage of the sixties had held due west across Huntington Valley to the Diamond Range.

The Sadler Ranch, on Mitchell Creek, lay below us. We went down toward it into a rolling flat. Small shoulders run down from the Ruby Mountains and separate the meadows where the ranch houses are built. The valley of Huntington Creek is long but narrow, and full of fine range land. Jefferson and John Wood called it Glover Creek. About fifteen miles from its beginning in Headwater Springs, the trail strikes it near the Sadler Ranch and immediately crosses, roughly paralleling it for possibly twice as far on the west side. The Valley is an attractive rural picture. Heaped and trailing hay wagons take their uncombed shock heads from field to stack; white-faced cattle lie in the road; sway-backed work horses of heraldic outline rest Roman noses on one another's rumps and switch one another's flies in perfect harmony.

The phone line through this section is a marvel of patient ingenuity. In order to raise the one wire high enough to keep cattle from sampling it, crooked poles have been secured to the tops of the fence posts and the wire strung along their tips. These poles are quite evidently branches from the small trees growing above us along the mountainside. Anyone who realizes the labor necessary to acquire telephone communication on the more remote ranches will never again regard it as a commonplace convenience.

Eight or ten miles below the Sadler Ranch, Huntington Creek disappears for a short distance, so that Reed was impelled to call the place Sinking Creek Valley. The place swarmed with Indians. When it seemed advisable, they loved their white brothers; when it seemed safe, they did not. The account of Lienhard is the only one that gives much about the Huntington Valley Indian situation in 1846. His company met an Indian from this tribe who was digging up edible roots. He was amiably inclined and demonstrated how to do it. Finding this well received, he caught a live grasshopper and showed them how to increase the calory content by imprisoning it in a sandwich between two roots. The next day he came back and offered some for sale; but one of the party who had partaken of roots, sans grasshopper, had been painfully sick in consequence. Lienhard, in refusing to buy, showed the Indian by "gyrations of his body" how much pain the man had suffered. Everybody had a good laugh except the main character in the drama, and the roots went back to the Indian village, where they were more appreciated. Farther down the Humboldt there was a pitched battle, but nothing is said of trouble here.

Chalmers, in 1849, knew that the Indians were stealing mules, but he evinced no nervousness at passing their village thirty-odd miles down the valley of Huntington Creek. His party met the squaws first, out gathering the heads from the wild rye grass. There were about fifty teepees in the village. Most of the inhabitants wore clothes of one kind or another picked up on the trail, just a bit of this and that worn for ornament only. So-called "decency" affected them not a bit, and the need for warmth was too far in the future for them to heed. They came out en masse to beg, and they would trade anything they had for a knife or a gun. Almost invariably they were armed with bows and arrows.

By 1850 the war was on. Moorman's camp in Huntington Valley was attacked at midnight of August 11th, a sort of mock war intended to frighten the guards and stampede the stock. Balls whizzed over the heads of the men watching the mules and aroused the whole camp. The campfire fizzled out pungently under a bucketful of water, and the men leaped to their guns. The Indians were invisible in the dark and the emigrants did not fire a shot, holding their blast until it could be effective. The red men collected among the shadows and yelled hideously by turn for most of the night. Toward morning, after a lull, a horrible whooping began, only to be answered from several directions. The white men thought uneasily that reinforcements had arrived, and possibly they had; but the Indians did not feel strong enough to engage in actual battle and retreated over the hills. Contrary to most beliefs, Indians did not as a rule attack in the dark. Dawn was the favorite time, and then only if they were in overwhelming numbers. There could be no doubt of the courage of many individual braves, but mountain men said disdainfully that the wounds suffered by Indians were usually in the back.

Morale and moral fiber were beginning to wear thin in the emigrants' camps as well. Sheer weariness gnawed at their self-command. Two men "had a chunk of a fight. one got his arm broken & the other his ear nearly bit off & otherwise bruised. the weapons used were double-barrel shotgun clubs teeth & after the fight," wrote the Forty-niner who told of it, "we hitched up and traveled."

Just like that—hitched up and traveled with no more ado. The fight may even have cleared the air a bit. The pressure of absolute necessities was becoming too irksome for those not constituted to bear up under it: the need for fresh animals as the old stand-bys gave up or were stolen day by day; the need for better food as the three "B's," bacon, beans, and biscuit, began to cause dietary diseases; the need for unobtainable medical care. All these combined with accidental mishaps to wear down the strongest nerves.

Some twenty-five miles down Huntington Creek, on the Cord Ranch about five miles from the small settlement called Jiggs, Smith Fork runs down from the Rubies and the creek loses its identity as they merge. Smith Fork runs a shorter distance, twelve or fifteen miles, before merging with the South Fork of Humboldt River, which also comes from the towering fastnesses of Ruby Range.

Smith Fork is flat and treeless, with cut banks widely spread from the stream bed to carry the winter floods. While still flowing through an open canyon, a mile or two before reaching the South Fork near Twin Bridges, it passes what was, and still is, called the Soap Mine. Moorman enjoyed Smith Fork. "We nooned," he wrote, "upon a beautiful little creek full of spotted trout, of which we caught a fine fry which made us a good supper. Our course for twelve or fourteen miles was North, then, with the little stream down which we were travelling, we turned to the West, passing through a Kanyon.—In the bank of the creek where it angled to the West we discovered a soap mine—there seemed to be any quantity of this substance, as good soap as ever was made; the existence of it can only be accounted for by some chemical action, an oil and an alkali having united."

In order to investigate the "soap," my husband, Mr. Mewhirter, and I walked across a hot field full of sage and stickers, waded Smith Fork, and walked a quarter of a mile more in the **V**, between Smith Fork and South Fork, which is on the Ben Guerena Ranch. The "mines" are holes dug horizontally in the low bluffs that edge the east side of the bottoms and are full of unpleasant slimy stuff that didn't suggest any cleansing agent that I had ever seen, and is used by the local ranchers to cure saddle galls on horses. It acts like antiphlogistine. The mine doors were timbered and a tiny car ran on rails into the hole. It was intensely interesting to us to note how little the country had changed in a century.

And here news began to percolate through the 1849 camps that Hastings' Cutoff was about to deposit them in the Humboldt Road—not near the Sink, as they had expected, but about 215 miles upstream from it. Chalmers, arriving rather early in the season, heard the disagreeable news ten or fifteen miles up the South Fork. It seems almost as if they had shouted the word from one wagon to another. It spelled something very like disaster to the listeners. There were one hundred people in his group, he said, that had only food enough for two or three days. They had started from Salt Lake City with food for twenty days and expected to be in California in fifteen.

Bloom, in 1850, wrote that his provisions which had been expected to last until arrival at Sacramento were nearly gone. He then had about 430 miles to go, over two hundred of which were along the meager Humboldt Valley, which was without food for man or grass for animals in amounts that would take care of the gold-rush migration.

Most of the hardy souls of the migration heard the news with a few moments of depression, perhaps, or of anger, then shrugged it off and went fishing.

They had come thus far. They could go on to the end.

CHAPTER IX

The South Fork of the Humboldt

THE canyon of the South Fork is some six miles long. We walked. A jeep would have taken us through all right, I think, although some of the sage was monstrous, with trunks six inches through, and the cattle paths were labyrinths. A horse would have been the answer to prayer. However, we had neither horse nor jeep, and felt that we could walk the distance, and be done with it, while we were negotiating for transportation.

We entered the canyon at the south end. The breeze was brightly nonchalant, but something about it spelled rain before night. The first objects of interest were jagged pinnacles high on the right bank. Mr. Mewhirter found an ox shoe below them. He has the sharpest eyes for interesting relics of anyone with whom we ever have hiked over the trail.

I never see anything of the sort, being too busy watching for bulls. There are no places of security along the trail. It seems to stay as far as possible from trees. Even a ten-foot sage bush boasting a six-inch trunk is not much of a refuge, and I live in misery in places such as this canyon, which was studded with cattle.

We discovered, during our sojourn in Elko, that the old-time residents of the Humboldt Valley do not credit the story of the emigrant wagons passing through the canyon of the South Fork. It sounds improbable when one knows the terrain as well as they do and has never read the journals that record the passing; but it is a fact.

All journals mention it, but Moorman tells it briefly: "we entered a very rugged Kanyon of six or seven miles' continuance. We crossed four or five times the very rapid and deep little river, and sometimes, to avoid a crossing, we would leave the wagon track and risk a hazardous bridle way on the steep and rugged mountain side, from which an awkward step of our surefooted mules would have hurled us a hundred feet into the river foaming in the depths below. Several of our animals stuck fast in the miry banks and to extricate one of them hard pulling at ropes and deep wading into mud and water was necessary."

The wagon track mentioned by Moorman is still in evidence. Many winter storms have gradually encroached upon its width until, in several places, only one wheel track is left. The wagons, needing more clearance, always crossed more times than was necessary for the less unwieldy pack trains.

Lienhard wrote that the Harlan company wagons made six crossings; but John Wood, of course, couldn't seem to manage with so few, and forded twelve times. He said it was incredibly bad, and no doubt it was. Some of the fords can be seen plainly, the ruts running into the river and resuming on the far side. Sometimes the wagons took to the bed of the stream for a surprising distance. Once, while the men were exploring one of the crossings, I looked over a hundred feet or so of sage tops and encountered the white-lashed eyes of a Hereford bull. He regarded me curiously and went on chewing. I blenched. I had never done it before, but I did a good job. Fright pinched up goose pimples on my legs and crawled through the roots of my hair. There was no safe place to go, so I executed a small but brisk stampede into a thicker mesh of sage roots, faded into them, and prayed that my husband hadn't forgotten his inestimably precious better half. Having long ago taken the initial precaution of holding my breath, there was nothing to do but let it out again; and I crouched, a perfect example of a human vacuum, both lungs and brain, on extremely maculate ground where, for generations and generations of white-faced Herefords, cattle had bedded.

My husband passed by. It is even possible that he hurried. I heard the whiz of a rock casually thrown and a thud as it hit about a ton of prime beef on the hoof. The beef heaved itself sideways to bring one eye to bear in my husband's direction and, after finishing the particular piece of bunch grass it was consuming, moved off with all the dignity of an ocean-going steamship.

It was a long time before I could work up any interest in things historical again.

It rained about noon. Thunder crashed with Wagnerian intensity, and we ate lunch to its orchestration, with moisture running off the eaves of our headgear. My husband s hatbrim was wide and turned up all the way around. Every so often it would fill with water, give way in the back, and spill the contents down his neck. That and an unalterable interest in food helped me to regain my poise.

Landmarks are scarce in the canyon. We greeted Ten Mile Creek, where it runs in from the right bank, with acclaim. The trail happened to be on that side at the time, and the wagons forded it easily. The growth of sage is stupendous, but it can be attributed to the fact that modern cattle have their bedding ground there. Tiny lavender daisies, big dusty-yellow daisies, red Pentstemons, and royal purple thistles add bits of color; killdeer scud along the river's edge and witty-legged quail run for a distance and take, whirring, to the air.

The trail sometimes left the river, but I, after meeting the bull, never did. I just stayed with what protection the abrupt banks could afford and waited for the trail to return. Where the canyon narrowed, we found a good many rocks scoured by wagon tires. Soon it squeezed into a gorge with high cliffs. This must have been where Moorman's company took their mules along the top of the bluff.

Lienhard gives the only word picture of the Harlan Party in transit. "We had next to travel," he wrote, "for about 6 miles through a narrow canyon, and were compelled to ford the stream six times. Here one of our oxen played havoc by laying down in the cool water on account of which the wagon toppled over, wheels up, which dumped the entire baggage into the stream." It sounds rather amusing put that way, but presumably it was not one of their better afternoons.

After a while Bullion Creek entered from the left. While the men were wading around, examining the take-offs for the fords and a mound on the left bank that really resembles a grave, Mr. Mewhirter stepped on something sharp, reached a long arm under the swift current to investigate, and got his fingers under a wagon tire imbedded in the gravel and silt. It took some patient prying to get it out, but when extricated it proved to be almost five feet in diameter.

The canyon is an untraveled place since its five busy years a century ago—or, I should say, is untraveled by the public. There is plenty of sound and motion.

Besides the dozens of cattle, coyotes slink swiftly along the deep-set paths between the heavy sage. Rattlers poise like belligerent corkscrews. Swallows nest in cliffs whose height is doubled by the glassy water and wheel and dip in swooping arcs. Ducks splash noisily as they take off from water to air. Magpies make their rendezvous in

the willows. Beautiful white cranes stand motionless on one leg to watch for unwary fish. No doubt occasional fishermen whip its riffles, but we saw no one on the two occasions when we apologetically invaded its privacy.

Moorman completed the trek through the gorge and arrived at the junction of the cutoff with the old Humboldt Road on August 14, 1850. There were pack trains at least ten days ahead of him. Information concerning the cutoff is so hard to find that it seems good to include a paragraph from the journal of Silas Newcomb, who took the regular Overland route from Salt Lake City to California. He wrote on August 3rd, 1850: ". . . nooned on the river bank a few miles below where a South branch of very considerable size puts in. A larger opening in the mountains denotes the spot. At this point Hastings Cut off from Salt Lake ends. . . . have said that this route was impracticable but we find that a company of packers among them Messers Allyn Vedder and Marsh who arrived at the river today and are said to be the first [party] behind [us] have come through starting only three days after we left the city."

This proves the possibility of a pack train on Hastings' Cutoff, with inordinate good luck, gaining three days over a company traveling by the regular Humboldt Road. Most packers did not make such good time. Wagon trains never did.

Unfortunately, the companies of 1846 did not have such good fortune. When they reached the Humboldt Trail, they found a communication whose date informed them that the Boggs Party, which had chosen the regular route at Fort Bridger, had passed three weeks before. Its members were planning to make their way to Oregon by the newly explored Applegate Road. Ex-Governor Boggs was a prudent man. He wanted no part of the struggle then reaching its climax on the coast.

California was not yet a state; it was a predicament.

But the gallant companies with Hastings kept their faces set firmly toward their destination. Reaching the end of the South Fork canyon, they turned their wagon wheels into the ruts of the Overland Trail and followed the course of that insignificant river, the Humboldt, that played such a large part in shaping the destiny of the West.

IT was about 160 miles from the end of Hastings' Cutoff to the place where Lassen's Cutoff started into the unknown. Meager and grassless miles they were, but blessed in the minds of the emigrants with the security of many traveling wagon trains and the knowledge that there was no better alternative they might have taken.

The Humboldt Valley route was a known quantity. Joseph Walker explored its course from end to end in 1833 long before either cutoff came into being and more than ten years before a way was found to take wagons across the barrier of the Sierra Nevada. The chastened travelers of Hastings' Road rejoined their more conservative comrades moving down the valley and drew a long breath of relief.

No person who had diverged onto Hastings' Cutoff (as far as our knowledge extends) ever committed the imprudence of leaving the main trail again. It was those who had stayed with the circuitous course of the regular route who became impatient and, when the Humboldt River made its great swing to the south, started west on Lassen's Cutoff, derisively known later as the Greenhorn or Cape Horn route.

CHAPTER X

By Way of the Rabbit Hole

LASSEN'S so-called "cutoff" into the Sacramento Valley of California appropriated as its easterly approach to the Sierra Nevada Mountains, and through them as far as Goose Lake, the Applegate Road to Oregon. At Goose Lake the older road took itself into the north. From there the resourceful Peter Lassen evolved a route which followed Pit River for many miles, went through the valley which is now artificial Lake Almanor, balanced down a ridge along the course of Deer Creek, and relinquished responsibility for its exhausted travelers north of what is now Chico. Where Deer Creek strikes the Sacramento Valley, Lassen lived, from the year 1844, in a little mud house and was lord of a large domain.

Both Lassen and the Applegate Brothers were reviled by the Forty-niners who traveled the course, receiving whatever vituperation was left after damning its grassless, waterless deserts and cursing the spiteful Indians who haunted its canyons and mountains. Nothing was too bad to call the authors of this route which, next to Hastings' Cutoff was the worst stretch of road on the Overland emigrant trails. But as a matter of fact, the Applegates, in seeking out and establishing the new road in 1846, were activated by altruistic motives; while Peter Lassen's reasons were merely simple and personal. He wanted a more direct road from the emigrant trail along the Humboldt to his ranch at the junction of Deer Creek with the Sacramento River. In 1847 he went back to Missouri. With him (so prove Read and Gaines in their critical notes on Bruff's journal) traveled John J. Myers who claimed to have gone to California in 1843 and to be able to guide any party from the Humboldt trail, by the southern Oregon route (Applegate Trail) to the "head of the Sacramento." Bruff believed that it was Myers' knowledge that made it possible for Peter Lassen to set out with a company of twelve wagons and to guide them over what, to him, was unknown country. I will go one step farther and say that it seems indisputable that John J. Myers was the John Myers listed among the thirteen men of the Chiles-Reading Party who came south from Oregon by way of Pit River in 1843, which would have given him the necessary geographical knowledge.

This sidelight may explain the sang-froid with which Lassen piloted the first wagons into the mountainous Pit River country. Any previous route had to be greatly modified, however, to accommodate the wheeled vehicles. He had a great deal of difficulty and rumor has it that he mistook Mount Shasta for the mountain that afterward bore his name and, one hazy day, led the angry emigrants far out of their course; but eventually he arrived with them at their destination.

He had succeeded. He became excessively fond of the road. It was his. He hoped to found a settlement on his ranch that would be a trading center for the northern part of Sacramento Valley.

The exploring and opening of the Applegate Road to Oregon had two basic reasons. The first was personal: Jesse and Lindsay Applegate, on their journey into Oregon in 1843, had each lost a son, drowned in the Dalles of the Columbia as they rafted their wagons down the great river. They sought a route with fewer natural hazards for Oregon colonists. The second was patriotic: In 1827 a treaty had been signed by England and the United States agreeing on temporary joint occupancy of the Oregon Country and specifying that a year's notice should be given before it could be terminated by either nation. The situation was unsatisfactory and both countries wanted the affair settled, the United States asking for a northern boundary of 54 degrees and 40 minutes north latitude. President Polk was elected with a popular slogan of "Fifty-four Forty or Fight" and asked Congress for authority to give the notice. In the spring of 1846 the residents of Oregon felt uneasily that they might be in a very hot spot indeed before the year was over. More than ever it was imperative to attract a large American migration and, still more important (so thought the public-spirited Applegates), to insure their safe arrival.

The emigrant route passed three British "forts" or trading posts, Fort Hall, Fort Boise, and Fort Walla Walla. True, up to this moment the English had been kind—even generous—but trouble was in the air. The slowness with which news traveled made everyone wary. It was thought safer to bring the migration of 1846 to Oregon by a new route.

Money was publicly subscribed and a small exploring expedition set out. It broke up because of internal disagreements and reorganized with Jesse Applegate as captain, the first captain, Levi Scott, going along to do his share. Besides the brothers, Jesse and Lindsay, there were thirteen men who traveled south from Oregon in the last week of June. They planned to intercept the thoroughfare to California opened to wagons in 1844 by the octogenarian Caleb Greenwood, which followed Joseph Walker's route down the Humboldt River (from where it rises near what is now Wells, Nevada, to where it sinks in the desert some twenty miles west of Lovelock), and then was continued by Greenwood on a new route by way of Truckee River. The Applegate Party were hazy as to just where they would connect with this Humboldt Trail, but would be guided by the location of the hoped-for water holes in the desert region they must traverse before reaching the Humboldt Valley. One limited water supply they found very simply by following converging rabbit tracks, and it has borne the name Rabbit Hole Springs from that day. Other water was located—sufficient, they thought, to supply the yearly migration to the Willamette Valley—and they struck the Humboldt River still hopeful for the success of the new route. Near the junction of the main Humboldt River with Lamoille Creek, they were sighted by Edwin Bryant and his party, who were just completing their venture on the almost equally new Hastings' Cutoff.

The two parties of horsemen were thrilled to the core by the unexpected meeting. They might easily have missed one another; had Bryant's pack train been ten minutes later, the Oregonians would have passed from sight.

It was evident that the 1846 migration was well on its way to the West Coast. If the Oregon-bound wagons passed Fort Hall and the turnoff to the Humboldt River before the Applegate Party arrived, it would be too late to reroute them; the effort expended in exploring the new road would have come to nothing, at least for that season.

Jesse Applegate solved the problem by a forced ride to intercept the wagon column, persuading a few to return with him and use his supposedly safer route. The Boggs Party responded, and J. Quinn Thorton, who had chosen the northern route and safety when the Donner Party turned south to dare the new and hazardous Hastings' Cutoff only to rue it bitterly later. Now a similar choice was put to him, and he chose a new and dangerous route in his turn. The comparison held, and he later rued it bitterly and vocally. The Applegate Party as a whole believed that the new road would save the Oregon travelers three hundred miles; Jesse more conservatively, estimated a saving of two hundred. Also, it was said to be supplied with all the necessities of travel except for a dry drive of thirty miles. Such was the hope of all concerned (probably including the Applegate Party itself) as they left the valley of the Humboldt and went west into the Antelope Hills.

*   *   *

It was in September that my husband and I turned from the splendid Nevada highway No. 40 just west of Imlay and crossed the Humboldt River on a little wooden bridge. Dr. Neff was vacationing on the Klamath River, and we had not been able to reach him. In fact his one dutiful postcard had omitted any mention of an address.

The unanticipated lull at my husband's office had come during his absence, so we asked Alex C. McMillan to go along for the ride or whatever the week-end trip might happen to offer. We always invite hesitantly, for trips with the Padens seem usually to provide more excitement than comfort; but the choice was excellent from our point of view: Mr. McMillan asked for no comfort whatsoever if the ride in question took him through mining country and, in addition to being a handy man with any excavation implement needed, from a shovel to a ditch digger, would, if occasion demanded, go bear hunting with a Flit gun. Part of the country we hoped to see, notably that around Rabbit Hole Springs, he had visited before; but the first hundred miles would be new to my husband and to me.

The two men rode in front. I occupied the left quarter of the rear seat, continually pushed at by the stack of impedimenta necessary if (as seemed likely) we had to stay all night somewhere in the desert. Every time I leaned over for a camera something moved in under me and I had either to fish it out or sit on it. I soon found that it was easier to sit on it, if it hadn't too sharp corners, as something else always slid in during the process of removal. On top of this stack of boxes and bed rolls, dignified on his own pillow, sat our old fox terrier, Pepper. Pepper loves to ride and is an excellent and experienced traveler; he hadn't a doubt but that it would be a lovely trip.

Beyond the little wooden bridge over the Humboldt, we stopped for shade under the only trees big enough for that purpose that we would see all day. They are ancient cottonwoods, gnarled and leafy, but they are not yet old enough to have been on the scene when the Applegates went up and Bryant traveled down the valley one hundred years ago. There were no trees along the river then. Down the winding current a mile or so, seen below the steep-cut white clay banks, are the shining waters of the Rye Patch Dam. Most, if not all, of what was called Lassen's Meadows, and which provided grass for the desert crossing to the west, is covered by these waters. Here, in trail days, was a busy place for those who chose this moment of their journey to demonstrate (disastrously) their initiative.

The camps of those about to deviate from the usual trail stretched in all directions. Cattle grazed luxuriously, we are glad to know, making up for the lean days just past and gathering strength for what was to come. Men cut grass and cured it somewhat in the hot sun. Some swam the river, narrow but surprisingly deep, pushing wagon beds while others pulled with ropes; for, strangely enough, the grass on the other side was always more desirable. Here the travelers of 1846 through 1848 and the unbelievable migration of 1849 were as comfortable as they ever seemed destined to be.

The Lassen Trail broke away from the regular Overland Trail at a point somewhere under the waters of Rye Patch Dam where the river used to make a short bend to the south. Here was a fine new barrel painted red, said the Forty-niners, and in it, hit or miss, was a miscellaneous hodge-podge of messages left for those who followed. The collection was dumped, pawed over, and replaced by someone from practically every company that passed. A good many writers of daily journals mention receiving letters in this self-help post office. Sometimes the message said that the writer was taking the much discussed cutoff and advised the newcomer to do likewise. Sometimes the writer of the missive had been warned against the cutoff and passed the warning along. Possibly there was no place where opinion was so honestly divided as here. The Donner tragedy doubtless was in a great measure responsible for sending hordes of people over this new route whose one doubtful advantage was the low crossing of the Sierra Nevada Mountains.

A geographical accident also played its part in persuading undecided emigrants in favor of the cutoff. The Humboldt had just made its great curve and was flowing southward accompanied by the regular trail. The Lassen Road took off to the west. It seemed to go in the right direction.

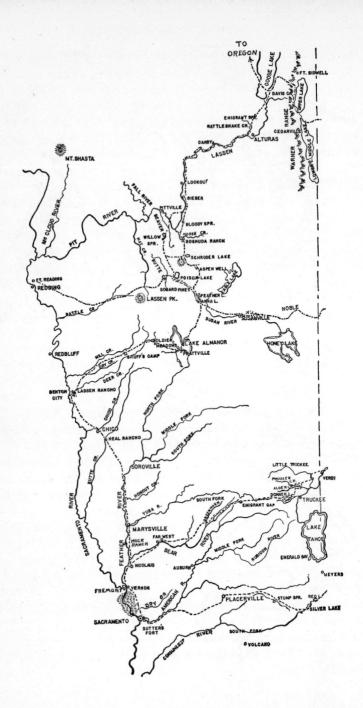

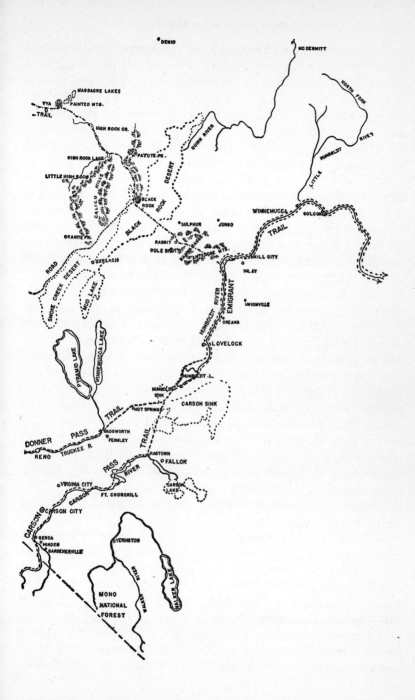

The elevation of the Humboldt River is not inconsiderable—about 3,900 feet—but we soon started up toward Antelope Range. After our month in the Rubies, we were surprised to find the Antelopes shrunken—faded too, as if they had been left too long on the line; but they were in front of us and, attractive or not, had to be negotiated. To our right was rather a good gap, flat and easy; but we never seem to want easy gaps; apparently a gap never goes anywhere. We always have to charge up the nearest mountain.

When about thirteen miles from the bridge by road and perhaps eight or nine by trail from where the old barrel stood at the junction in Lassen Meadows, the cutoff angled in to join the road. Together they entered a curving wash in the sloping hillside. Dry rattling rabbit brush and brown bushes, small and dead looking, prevailed. Now and then we would encounter a group of large shrubs covered with luxuriant and brilliant gold blossoms. We did so now where the road came curvingly to a spring some twelve miles from the meadow. Bruff, who gives by far the best description of this portion of the cutoff, says that there were three springs here, all of them, as I understand it, on camp roads and separate from the trail proper. As no one would pass without going to one of these watering spots, it was a case of tossup. This was an excellent place for persons who might have lagged behind their train, or gone on ahead, to become separated from their companions. Whichever water hole the individual chose was apt to be spoken of by him as Antelope Spring, and I doubt whether many persons knew which, if any, was exclusively entitled to the name. All of the springs, so called, before reaching the Black Rock Desert are merely damp spots, with possibly a trickle of overflow. By carefully excavating these, the emigrants made basins that held several gallons; but the first company to arrive took all that had collected, and the rest had to wait for the trickle.

J. Quinn Thornton could get only a half-pint apiece for his thirsty cattle and sat up until two o'clock in the morning to fill one keg for the following day's march. By this time the Applegate Party proper had forged on ahead to improve the road for the emigrants whom they had persuaded to follow them, and there was no one to whom Mr. Thornton could complain, so he took refuge in his diary, giving as his considered opinion that it was a repulsive country. As they emerged from the hills into the desert, he improved with practice and informed posterity that "it seemed to be the River of Death dried up, and having the muddy bottom jetted into cones by the force of the fires of perdition."

There is no doubt that the suffering, death, and destruction inseparable from the story of the Applegate Road came as a surprise to the Applegate brothers themselves. They had had some rough going on their way to Oregon with the Cow Column in 1843 and had come through successfully. They had had some waterless stretches, so called, the longest being a sandy trek of less than thirty miles between the watershed of the Kansas River and that of the Platte, which they made in the rainy season, while their cattle were still strong and well fed. Then, toward the end of their overland journey, their animals endured thirst for many days because the only available water lay at the bottom of the Snake River gorge, to which, after being unyoked, they were driven down at night. There had been discomfort in a high degree, even suffering no doubt, but the stock was able to keep going. They had never had experience with cattle in a desert like Black Rock. Then, too, they could not have foreseen the tremendous numbers of the gold rush, swept on inevitably by the pressure of those behind, turning blindly up this experimental road in their fumbling search for a way around the dreaded deserts ahead. Some say that one third of the overland migration of 1849 turned off on the Applegate Road, or, as they called it, Lassen's Cutoff. They were enormously too many for the grass and water supply of the first sixty miles—a supply that had not even sufficed for the few wagons of 1846. But the Forty-niners were travel and trouble hardened by the time they reached the long nerve-racking valley of the Humboldt, and daily staked everything they held dear on the happenstance of what might be around the next bend. They embarked, without encouragement of any kind, upon this road which broke away toward (rumor had it) a low spot in the Sierra Nevada range. A casual entry in the journal of Amos P. Josselyn, written as he was about to leave the river, emphasizes how ignorantly hundreds turned from the beaten track. "We understand," he wrote, "that three years ago there had some 3 or 4 wagons started through here but could not learn anything about the road. There was 8 wagons started in yesterday led by Magee."

This may have been Milton McGee of the Chiles-Reading Party which came south from Oregon along Pit River in 1843. The supposition would explain his willingness to lead the second party attempting to take wagons along the road opened by Lassen in '48. In that case one might have expected him to be in the company guided by Myers and our old friend Hudspeth who, we know from other journalists, were on the Lassen Trail early in the season of '49; Myers having been a comrade of McGee on the 1843 expedition. Myers and Hudspeth evidently had started out to pioneer a short route to the gold mines and actually had succeeded in opening the new cutoff from Soda Springs to Raft River called indiscriminately by either of their names. But existing evidence seems to show that Magee was ahead of them in taking the turnoff into the Lassen Trail in '49, as either Myers or Hudspeth was too well known for his presence in the lead party to go entirely unremarked. As a lesser indication: when the party led by the latter men was noted by journalists farther along on the trail, none, to my knowledge, mentioned Magee.

Once over the Antelope Range, we bowled through a high valley covered evenly with sorry brown shrubs in a tufted candlewick effect. It was occupied by a small mine headquarters of the more primitive type. An ore cart had wheels made of solid discs cut from logs; the wood pile was of brush pulled out by the roots and stacked ten feet high; there was a galvanized iron building, empty as a blown egg, and a broken windmill. It seemed deserted. At a crossroad we said eenie, meenie, minie, mo and went to the right, fortunately, as it happened, for the trail turned up soon after and went with us into a canyon we had seen from the summit.

This rugged and sage-grown gash through the Kamma Range is known poetically as Rosebud Canyon. Delano called it a "defile" and Bruff described it as a pass with definite indications of gold. Within a mile or two we began to see vindications of his opinion in miners' tiny cabins up gullies to the right and left. Spills of small iron-stained rocks ran down the mountain on the one hand while, on the other, rounded excrescences of dull gray boulders clustered on the canyon side like abandoned wads of chewing gum. Presently, about thirty miles from Imlay bridge, we saw our first signs of life: a mine and buildings, four very small trees, and a tank that looked wet. They were on the right side of the canyon proper.

"It's not in operation now," Mr. McMillan corrected my guess, "but it was not too long ago. I think there's somebody here."

As we drove between the buildings, all the somebodies promptly arrived. A Mr. Smith who said he had been the "dragline man" was in charge since the closing down three weeks before. With him was a pretty little wife with five good-looking and well mannered children. "Why, wherever do you go to school?" I asked the oldest who was all of thirteen and a Boy Scout.

"Dad takes us over the hill to Sulphur. That's on the Western Pacific Railroad and there's a school there. He comes and gets us at night."

"How many of you go?"

"Four of us—all but the baby."

A casual wave of his hand gave me the impression that a town might be just the other side of the hill. I could see that my husband was getting directions to our next objective, Rabbit Hole Springs, from Mrs. Smith and that the other two men were discussing the mine; so, as the boy seemed exceptionally keen and was quite willing to talk, I went on asking questions. "There are some buildings painted green up a side canyon to the right; they're back just a mile or so, and I think there is a well there. Do you know what they are?"

"Oh, yes, that's Rosebud. And up the side canyon several miles more is Rosebud Mine."

"Thanks, that settles that." And I made a note of it. "Before we came to Rosebud, we passed a cabin up a branch canyon to the left. I think there was water there too."

"Yes, I know that place. It's Rosebud Spring."

"And this main canyon is Rosebud Canyon?"

"Yes, ma'am."

"For mercy sakes, why?" I asked Mrs. Smith, who looked up just then.

"I think somebody had a sense of humor," she contributed.

We found on inquiry that it would be necessary to come back after seeing Rabbit Hole Springs and take the road to Sulphur which left the Smith domicile and went directly over the hills. So we left with promises to see them again before the day was over and started on the five-mile drive to Rabbit Hole.

It was here that we passed on our left hand the colored hills that called forth admiration from the emigrants even in their distress. They appear to be clay, and the shades are as prettily blended as if white paint had been added to each: a rich yellowish cream color was next to a pale turquoise, and a faint salmon-shaded hill lay next to one of oyster white which, in turn, blended into burnt sienna and saffron. There was not a spear of green growth in sight.

Bruff wrote: "Road N.W. through several hundred yards of high clay bluffs and hills, of the most delicate and beautiful warm tints, in horizontal strata." Then he added, with less enthusiasm, "Road-powder blinding & chocking one."

Delano wrote also of the tinted hills and, while he is telling us about them, he may as well take us on to Rabbit Hole Springs which lay just beyond and around a dog's-leg turn in the canyon. ". . . we pushed forward," he wrote on August 16, 1849, "anxious to reach the promised spring, for our cattle as well as ourselves stood greatly in need of water. The day was excessively warm, yet we hurried on, and descending a couple of hills through a defile, we passed the most beautiful hills of colored earth I ever saw, with the shades of pink, white, yellow and green brightly blended. Volcanic mountains were around us, and under ordinary circumstances we could have enjoyed the strange and peculiar scenery. Turning westerly, we pressed on through a small basin beyond the defile, when, after ascending a little elevation, the glad shout was raised, 'I see where the spring is!' Several wagons had stopped in the road, and a knot of men were gathered around a particular spot, which marked the place of the glorious element, and with parched tongues we went up. Judge of our disappointment, when we found the promised springs to be only three or four wells sunk in the ground, into which the water percolated in a volume about the size of a straw, and each hole occupied by a man dipping it up with a pint cup, as it slowly filled a little cavity in the ground. Each man was taking his turn to drink, and we had ample time to get cool before our turn came to taste the muddy water; and as to getting a supply for our cattle, it was out of the question. Beyond us, as far as we could see, was a barren waste, without a blade of grass or a drop of water for thirty miles at least. Instead of avoiding the desert, instead of the promised water, grass, and a better road, we were in fact upon a more dreary and wider waste, without either grass or water, and with a harder road before us. We had been inveigled there by false reports and misrepresentation, without preparing for such a contingency, as we might have done, in some measure, by cutting grass on the river. Our train came up, followed by others. What was to be done? It was thirty-five miles to the river and about the same distance to the spring ahead. Should we go back? Our cattle had already gone without food or water nearly thirty hours. Could they stand it to go back? Could they possibly go forward?"

A month later, and at the same time of the year at which we, ourselves, were traveling, Bruff arrived at Rabbit Hole in slightly better case. He had found, and cut, grass for three days' forage for his animals. They were dreadfully thirsty but not starving as were the cattle of less provident captains. Quite possibly it was not so hot as when Delano put such unanswerable questions to unheeding Fate, and during the month wells had been dug. Bruff wrote: "Afternoon the road branched around a low bluff to the right; where, in 200 yds, I found, near an orange colored clay spur, a well, or tank, of water, and a crowd of thirsty men and animals surrounding it.—A few yards to left of this another—similar hole, filled up with a dead ox, his hindquarters & legs only sticking out,—above ground. Dead oxen thick about here, and stench suffocating."

I have not stressed the fact that in trail days a frightening assortment of dead stock punctuated the miles all the way from the river and were becoming more numerous through this last stretch of the canyon. Bruff, who was nothing if not a detailist—bless his heart for it—saw fourteen dead and one dying in the morning and thirty in the afternoon which brought him to Rabbit Hole. It was actually twenty miles from here to the next water, that at the Black Rock across one arm of the desert ahead of them; but, although the Rock was in plain view, distances were so deceitful that people became confused and returned to the tantalizing promise of water held out at Rabbit Hole when they might better have gone ahead. Delano told of a "poor fellow from Illinois, named Gard," who came back, "after having gone onto the desert about six miles. His cattle were exhausted, and it was impossible in their present condition to go either forward or backward, and it appeared to us all that his case was sad indeed, with a family of small children. If his cattle had given out entirely," continued Delano, "the emigrants would have done all they could; yet, in a burning house each one is apt to think more of his own safety than of his neighbor's."

We, in our turn, a century later, found where the road branched around the low bluff to the right. The trail was so rough and sidling that we decided not to drive any farther. We would have to turn back here, and we rightly decided that this was Rabbit Hole and that the springs were somewhere in the offing. They certainly were not in sight; so the men started off in opposite directions, calling to me to stay with the car. For a while I could hear the rattle of their progress through the brush and then nothing at all. It was noon, and the day encompassed perfect silence as a cup holds liquid. It was almost a relief when a swarm of deer flies joined the party. The car became too confining under the circumstances and Pepper and I got out. What they live on when I am not present has always puzzled me.

A low tableland was at my right. It ended in an abrupt drop gashed with ravines and gullies and seemed to be of a white-clay composition. The men now came running down the bank; both had found water in different places but alike in that they were on the very lip of the plateau.

"This is Rabbit Hole Springs all right," said my husband happily, "and there's one right up there. There's a little mine beside it and they have enlarged the basin until it's quite a pool. I'm going to circle around and drive up on the plateau." Then, hopefully: "Will you wait and see what's up there or do you have to see this one?"

"I have to see this one," I announced and got out. What my husband has found and mentally catalogued he loses any desire to see again. There might not be any springs up on top and I would just be out of luck. A spring in the hand is worth two in the sagebrush, I figured, and commenced climbing while they turned the car around.

I crossed over a shaft and a pile of tailings in a ravine, going up until I found, tucked away under the great bunches of rye grass, a little pool of water. Above it was an ugly galvanized iron tank. Desert men say that rye grass is a sure sign of human habitation at some time or another, but the tank was even surer. Rabbit Hole had become civilized. However, we saw no one here; nor had we seen anyone but the Smiths all day.

When we swung up on the plateau and stopped the car close to its precipitate edge, we found ourselves at the top of another ravine. It was swathed in the same desert vegetation as the rest of the hills, but vested with some life and moisture. Its bushes didn't rattle as we pushed our way through, but bent and bowed amiably. Here the rabbit tracks had converged on a little trickle of water which filtered from a source hardly more than damp. Here successive wagon companies had dug wells and more wells, some of them life giving, some corked with the rear construction of oxen who had plunged in to die soggily and render the water useless. Toward the bottom of the ravine a stone house shelters modern Rabbit Hole Springs, for, in such a dry country, all drinking water is of value.

Back on the plateau two little board shacks have been built. Nailed to one was a notice, written both in English and in Spanish, that, commencing on some long-gone date, this portion of Humboldt County was to be used for bombing practice. It must have annoyed the lizards. I couldn't see that anyone else would ever find it out, at any rate not from this sign.

Near the head of the ravine is a mound that is evidently a grave, heaped in the middle and weighted with heavy rocks. It may be old, or it may not be; Bruff found a grave here. His description of the tableland where we now stood ran like this: "Along the edge of this Plateau are a number of springs as they are called, but are actually wells, dug from 3 to 6 feet deep, and from 4 to 5 feet diameter; containing cool, clear water but a little saline,—about half filling the wells. Two of these springs were about 4 feet apart; in one was a dead ox,—swelled up so as to fit the hole closely,—his hind-legs and tail only above ground. Not far from this was another spring similarly filled. There was scarcely space for the wagons to reach the holes, for the ox-carcasses. W. of the plateau springs, the road follow'd an indentation formed by winter floods, down into the plain; and close on the right of it was a deep rugged gulch, containing 2 spring-holes, choked up with oxen; while the ravine for 100 yds. was thickly strewn with their carcasses. Here, and around the other springs, I counted 82 dead oxen, 2 dead horses and 1 mule;—in an area of 1/10 of a mile. Of course the effluvia was anything but agreeable. On the spring bluff we halted for the night, watered, and served out grass to the mules. In the very heart of this Golgotha, was a fresh grave, on the head board of which, (piece of a broken wagon), was this inscription:

> " 'M. De Morst,
> of Col: Ohio
> died Sep. 16th. 1849,
> Aged 50 years,
> Of Camp Fever.' "

It is noticeable in many accounts that more oxen died than mules or horses, in the proportion of about forty to one. It may be that there were many more oxen on the desert—more alive as well as more dead. Or it may be that men took better care of their horses and mules, as being valuable and claiming more of their affection, so that, in the division of water, they got a greater share.

As to the man who died of "Camp Fever," who can wonder?

It was noon and quite pleasant with a faint breeze. One of the small buildings gave a patch of shade on a spot where it was possible to sit and we had our lunch—yes, "in the very heart of this Golgotha" we ate lettuce-and-mayonnaise sandwiches, made on the spot for freshness, and gave our terrier more water to drink than Thornton could get for his famishing oxen.

*   *   *

Back at the **Smiths'** we filled the radiator with water from their tank and took casual instructions as to how we were to circle to Sulphur, where the children went to school. There we would find a road across Black Rock Desert to Gerlach, something like forty miles southwest. I looked at our highway map. "When we get to Sulphur, our troubles will be over," I announced decisively. "See, the Gerlach road even has a number—It's forty-nine."

"Very appropriate," my husband nodded. "Probably *too* appropriate," he added grimly. "Where will we contact the trail? It went northwest from Rabbit Hole," he explained to Mrs. Smith; "but you were right, we couldn't follow it in this car. Maybe a jeep could get through."

"Yes, they dashed around in there with jeeps during the war," she agreed. "It was a bomber base, you know; but you just take this road up over the hill to Sulphur, and then the road to Gerlach, and I guess you can estimate where you cross the trail on its way from Rabbit Hole to Black Rock."

"And you can be sure of one thing," said Mr. Smith with emphasis. "You will get a good look at the Black Rock Desert."

We swung out of their yard and over the brow of the hill to the east. Almost immediately we saw an abandoned steam shovel in an open sandy gully below the road to the right. Closer inspection revealed hovels scattered as if a giant hod carrier had dropped a load of broken and dusty bricks. Stranger still were roofs here and there, dozens of them seemingly, without any houses under them.

"This must be the place Mrs. Smith told me about this morning," my husband remarked, stopping the car. "She said that some four hundred people lived in this draw, some in dugouts and some in simple holes in the ground, and panned out a dollar or so a day. That was in 1937, when we had more peace than prosperity. The children evidently explored the place after everyone had evacuated the gully, when the ban was placed on mining for gold during the war. They said the newspapers left lying around ranged in date from 1937 to 1941."

Never have I seen anything so desolate. There was not one vestige of shade. The low shelters were too squat to cast a shadow; there was not a tree in the miles of bulging yellow mountaintop visible from our vantage point and which seemed to have puffed up from some leaven within, like bread dough, still bearing the marks of the kneader's knuckles. I took a picture of the community. It contains, as it lies on the table in front of me, two abandoned steam shovels and five dwellings above ground. These architecturally prominent edifices have been constructed by piling railroad ties one on top of another. They are likewise distinguished by having outhouses after their own design, but smaller. Dotted around the gradually rolling slopes of this sage-covered sand hole, which covers a matter of acres, are the black spots indicating cave entrances—not dugouts, caves. I may not be exact in my definition of what constitutes a dugout, but personally I have always held out for a front elevation, something in which to hang a door. The dugouts here were of two types: one started out as a tie house in front and wound up as an excavation into the hillside; the other was merely a peaked roof set on level ground and heaped over with dirt until there was nothing to prevent little Johnnie from rolling his hoop over the ridgepole except the absence of a hoop. There was no sound on the mountain but the muted pulsing of some insect, like the very heartbeat of silence.

At first I was upset by the notion of civilized people living under such conditions. It seemed beneath our lowest standards. And then I remembered three days we spent in Boston during the heat wave of 1936, when the brick slums baked and invalids hung out of windows or died in their sweat-sodden beds. I surmised that this place had fewer germs.

Just then words came from my astounded partner. "To think," he exclaimed, "of Americans living like gophers in holes!"

"Furl your flags," I advised; "it's only one more proof of our adaptiveness. If I had to live in this dusty hot gully I can't think of a better place than a cave."

On the top of the mountain we met a jeep, the first car of any description we had seen on the road since leaving the river. The man in it yelled cheerfully but had no hand to wave; and as he went past, hanging firmly to the wheel, I could see portions of the far landscape between him and the seat. I have no doubt that the picture thus framed between his ascending rear and the pitching jeep contained at least two deserted prospect holes, for this whole section of the Kamma Range is pitted and studded with holes and dumps, as if a herd of giant pigs had rooted it up and left it.

Presently, on the far brow of the mountain, we came to three forks in the road, a recurrent crisis usually productive of trouble. There were no signs, of course. Those who use these roads know where they are going without the formality of signs. We tried all of them and exhausted part of a valuable afternoon and our patience. It was three o'clock when we saw buildings ahead.

If there were a bump on the Black Rock Desert the size of an Indian mound, Sulphur could hide behind it; but there were no bumps near by. I shuddered Spencerianly as I jotted the mileage in my field note book. Sulphur was painfully visible.

The first thing we passed was a beanbag of a schoolhouse braced under the weight of its big flag. Between it and the railroad track are the dumps. Why Sulphur should have so much to discard and who discards it will always be an unsolved question; but there were the dumps, seemingly twice as much in acreage as the rest of the settlement, which, indeed, is only the customary railway buildings, a grocery, and a house or two. There were discarded cars, old iron, machinery, gigantic ten-foot wheels such as they use in lumber camps but which, as we hadn't seen a tree all day (except at the Smiths'), I figured must have some other purpose; rolls of chicken wire, old gunny sacks, anything and everything—all the better brands of junk—such lovely things to use should we get into deep sand. A wire fence hemmed them in, and we sat impotently and wishfully outside, like big-game hunters at a circus.

A nice-looking man appeared, blue-shirted and with heavy leather gloves to protect his hands. He was the only person we glimpsed while in town. My husband, always interested in things educational, said: "I see you have the school here for the district. How many children do you have enrolled?"

The man looked whimsically at the small patch on the seat of education whose flag, whipping bravely in the wind, seemed about to rip it out bodily. "Six," he replied briefly.

"Does that include the Smith children?"

"Yes, it does."

"Well, then, in a month you'll only have two, because they're going to leave."

"Yes, we know that. One of them is ready for high school; but somebody will show up with children. I don't think we'll have to close."

And probably it will work out. Some woman with three children and a teaching credential will arrive to lift the school at Sulphur out of the doldrums.

"Is that the road to Gerlach, running along the tracks?" I asked— "the one that is marked '49' on the map?"

"Yes, you can't help going to Gerlach if you take that road; but it's pretty bumpy if you stay by the tracks. There's a fork about seven miles from here, and you'd better take the right-hand turn. It goes out on the desert, where it's smoother."

"The desert is what we want to see, anyway, especially Black Rock," my husband told him, and went on to explain the purpose of our trip. The man's face lightened as his opinion of our normalcy rating went up, and he entered into the necessary figuring with a good will.

"You'll be going at right angles to the trail—just about." He narrowed his eyes and took a long look west to where the dark, excoriated Black Rock Range stretched its low forbidding length down from the northeast, ending in a decidedly repellent crag lower than the rest. "That's the Black Rock; and it's plenty big when you get up to it," he added with emphasis.

"Then we will cross the trail when we get opposite the Black Rock?" my husband asked.

"I suppose so. You'll be able to see the canyon across the desert to your left, where the wagons came out from Rabbit Hole Springs; they went right for the Black Rock because the first spring is there."

"Yes, it points at them just like a finger. Will we be able to see any signs of their passing?"

"I wouldn't think so—too much sand blowing around out there; and it's been almost a hundred years."

"All right, we'll look around, though, when we get out where they must have crossed."

That's what we thought!

I once more joined the debris in the back seat and we crossed the tracks, turned left along them, passed the depot and a house or two, and then my rearward vision regaled itself with more junk. But our interview with the man—a person of undoubted breeding and intelligence—had raised my opinion of the vicinity. It might even have a few points to recommend it, in sundry unthinkable ways.

"Ye gods!" This from Mr. McMillan, who was driving. "What a swell road for a helicopter!"

I rubbed the top of my head, got up off my knees, to which position I had fortunately returned, and decided to look ahead instead of out the back window. The road was rough—not a doubt of it—and apparently had suffered the effects of a cloudburst. Black Rock Desert wouldn't be much better on a rainy day than on a hot one, I thought; and a hot day on this sweltering flat would stew the very cartilage from one's bones. It was warm yesterday, so Mr. Smith had told us, and with a very stiff hot wind. Today, horribly weather conscious as we were, seemed perfect; we couldn't have asked for anything better.

I settled back to wait for the place where we would cross the trail. Excitement was probably over for the day. Trusting in the unquestionable rectitude of a printed map, I knew we were on a main road. Let it be rough; who cared? We were driving through a desert growth of large bushes. In Rosebud Canyon these same bushes had been gaudy with bright golden blossoms. Out here they were an unpleasant passion-fruit yellow and looked hot. They were getting farther and farther apart, too. Soon we would be out of them; we could see the last outposts ahead on the bare wind-riffled sand.

Seven miles from Sulphur we came to the forks and, relinquishing the twin apron strings of the railroad track, we turned to the right and went off on our own. The white earth was gently bumpy now, like boiling milk and the solitary greasewood bushes were larger, as they had collected great heaps of wind-driven sand and had continued to grow up and through the mounds. The wind had blown beautiful patterns and riffles there, and I got out to take a picture.

In fact I took one each way. The first one, looking south to the canyon of Rabbit Hole Springs, showed it to be much farther away than was Black Rock in the one I took facing north. I estimated that, having sneaked in from the side, we would soon cross the trail at about two-thirds of the distance into the desert that the emigrants had had to negotiate. And it was high time, too, as the shadows were growing long. The greasewood bushes threw beautiful lacy patterns on the white sand; and the wind riffles, which I noticed were increasing in size, had each its own. Our car, normally black, was flour-white and cast a long black shadow streamer to the east.

We started again and so did the wind. It swept the desert and shook the rugs. We traveled in a blinding cloud of what Bruff described as "road-powder." It seemed to be a combination of sand and an impalpable dust that coated my dark glasses at once. I wiped them; but it was a futile gesture and I simply discarded them. It was then that we discovered that the road was gone. The car slowed helplessly. We were on pure sand.

Mr. McMillan shoved his foot to the floorboard and yanked off his dark glasses; the powerful car moved slowly ahead. We didn't dare to stop. He didn't even dare to shift gears. We didn't dare to lose that road, and it wasn't straight. It hadn't been straight for a hundred yards at a time since we left the railroad, but wound around among the dunes. I hung out one window and my husband out the other while the driver glued his hands to the wheel, his foot to the floorboard, and his eyes to the faint shadow at the left side of the road that wasn't quite like the rest of the desert. "To the left! To the left!" we would yell in unison as the windshield grew thicker and thicker with dust. "More to the right. Now left again." We were making a laboring twenty miles an hour, which doesn't sound fast but is too fast to be feeling for a road you can't see. I had visions of how unpopular I would be flagging down the Western Pacific with a flashlight; even the inhospitable haven of its tracks and a possible section gang was a mighty long walk.

"If we leave this roadbed, it will be curtains," said Mr. McMillan, whose nervous system is, I am sure, encased in reinforced concrete and who seldom recognizes trouble even when it arrives. I, who see it at a great distance, go on dumbly to meet it, and usually find it to be a mirage, was more staggered by his simple statement than I cared to admit. "Yes, really embarrassing," my husband understated briefly.

We curveted along for about two miles. It was like going for a swim in thin library paste; but finally the piled sand seemed to be getting less.

Our driver released the breath he had been holding and said, "But we aren't going to." And neither one of us had to ask him what he meant.

Presently we came to where the road surface showed again, just little islands of it peeping through a choppy lake of sand. The first island surprised us and we overran it. On the second one we stopped and with one accord threw the doors open and sat in them with our feet in the road. Personally, I was as spineless as spaghetti.

"We can at least clean the windshield," said my husband finally as he tossed the stub of his cigarette on the sand and turned his back on it; no need here to guard against fire. He started the engine and pushed the gadget that throws water on the glass. The busy little wipers went to work.

"That's better," said Mr. McMillan gratefully and started again.

"Why didn't we think to turn it on when we were trying so hard to see?" I mourned, and my voice sounded weak.

"Even if we had thought of it, we couldn't have found the button to push," Mr. McMillan said reasonably. "Nobody had time to take his eyes off the road."

The hot wind of yesterday had been a real sandstorm out here. Every track older than our own was obliterated. Even though we were on a dead line between Rabbit Hole and the Rock and we knew that hundreds of wagons had passed this way, yes, and that dozens of the great schooners had been abandoned and lay within our vision, we also knew that every evidence had long since vanished in the action of the wind and the winter storms. We were close to the Rock; it appeared to be about two miles away, but was probably farther. Unless one has a known distance as a guide, it is impossible to estimate in the desert; but we knew it to be twenty miles from Rabbit Hole Springs to the hot spring at the Rock and so had some manner of yardstick.

"Well, this is it," I said. "This is where we wanted to be and now we're here—probably right on the trail, and what does it get us? We can't travel it and we can't see it."

"Oh, yes we can," my husband corrected me. "We can see about fifteen miles between here and Rabbit Hole. Of course there are a couple of miles in the canyon that we couldn't travel, but we saw them from the top of the hill. The rest of it is in plain sight. Here, take the field glasses."

I took them and he was right. There lay the terrible Black Rock Desert, the color of a dirty sheet. The emigrants dreaded (and rightly) to cross it. Eighty-two dead oxen raised a mighty "effluvium," said Bruff, at Rabbit Hole. What a stinking stretch had been these burning and malevolent miles of blighting sand! The struggling procession threw off dead cattle like chips from a lathe. Mirages of cool water and dark trees, such as I could see on all sides simply by removing the field glasses from my eyes, enticed many cattle from the path. They could not be held by the men, who were themselves exhausted by fatigue and heat, and so ran wildly into the dancing heat waves mercifully to drop and leave their hair-matted skeletons where they did not add to the stench along the road. Even so, the portion of the cutoff that lay across this heat-belching desert was putrid and re-pellent with carcasses sprawled grotesquely on all sides and even in the trail.

As a man's safety and that of his family was measured by the remaining strength of his animals, oxen were not left lightly to die. All animals were saved, if humanly possible, by water and grass carried out from the hot spring with its small patch of verdure at the Rock.

"Do you think we can ever get to Black Rock and see the spring?" I asked in a small voice, for I had hoped that the desert might be of the type of Humboldt Lake bed, twenty miles west of Lovelock, where a car might be driven at will.

"Not through this kind of sand," said my husband, dashing my hopes. "Maybe from some other direction in a jeep, or by bringing saddle horses in a trailer; but we won't manage it this year."

I knew better than to ask if we couldn't take time to walk. It really was not too hot; but the distance was indefinite and we were still sitting on an island of road without much confidence in what lay ahead. "All right, if we can't, we can't," I capitulated. This was not the first time I had had to postpone a greatly desired objective, and, so far, we had managed to see them all in the course of events. "We'll be back some day," I told the crouching black granite-boweled rock as we left it behind—"not that you care, of course, but it'll make me feel better." It is my one contribution to the cause of research (which now seemed to be getting a little blue around the edges) that I do manage to get into things: just give me time.

We had no more difficulty. The desert changed in character; the sand stretched flawless—hard and packed. Presently tracks of the omnipresent jeeps commenced to spider-web its paperlike surface. We left the point of Black Rock Range far behind and with the glasses had a sweeping view of the salt-lapped miles up its curving flank, where basins of boiling water gushed over, cooled, and watered acres of rank rough pasturage that put new life into the cattle of the migration. Beyond the range rose Payute Peak. To the west, with a narrow valley between them and the peak, ran the Calico Hills, long, low, and parti-colored. Behind them, but projecting farther to the southwest, ran the Granite Range. All these bounded a great desert which seemed, to our solitary selves, to be in one of its more deserted moments, while, swinging around, I could face, out of the opposite window of the car, the Selenite Range uplifted on the southern edge.

As the afternoon sun sank lower and the wind died, we were entertained by mirages and the odd effects produced by any trifle left on the sands. "There's a car ahead," exclaimed my husband; "first, except the jeep, all day."

"No, it's too big for a car; must be a truck," Mr. McMillan, who was still driving, gave as his opinion.

Two miles later we passed it—a tiny bush by the roadside which had caught and held a low mound of sand. It was eighteen inches high and about three feet through. Bottles gave exceptionally fine scenic effects, as, approaching Gerlach, we had ample opportunity to judge. That otherwise admirable town must live completely out of bottles.

It is a railroad division point. A local engine at the depot was snorting and backing through its collar to the accompaniment of clouds of steam. We drove up the main street, glad to see people and cars again. It was six o'clock and we were hungry. We had quite a choice: Johnny Capooch Shop, the Washoe Grocery, the Miners' Club, Blondy's, and one or two other sources of food and drink. We chose one where a conspicuous sign said that it could seat one thousand people but would like to take them twelve at a time. I peeked in the window and saw six and gave the high-sign that there was room and that it looked clean. A bony man in high-crotched overalls slipped refinedly out to blow his nose in the gutter and went back in again to fork some more potatoes into himself. We followed him, leaving Pepper in the car breathing defiance at a German shepherd through the window, while, on the sidewalk sat a placid white cat which they both would have liked to chase but didn't dare.

Our chicken-fried steaks were thin but so enormous that they hung in ruffles over the rims of our plates and the mashed potatoes and peas had to be stacked on top. Every bit of it could be cut with a dull spoon, but I just couldn't contain it all. Besides, the German shepherd had taken himself off and the cat was getting boring; something had to be done for Pepper. Social niceties didn't seem appropriate at the moment, so I began to cut up the extra meat and make a dish of two paper napkins. The other diners at the counter, seeing that I was about to feed my dog, garnered their scraps, and we scraped together a meal such as he had never seen before. I put it on the ground around the side of the building, where, much to his disgust, he was forced by sheer lack of will power to share it with the cat.

Our trailwork here was done. We were to drive after dark to the land of cabin camps and cement highways and make our next attempt to go to Black Rock after the winter was over. While the little hills were still blushing rosily at its approach, the night swooped down with a rush. A smooth but lonely road poured fluidly past our wheels; a swollen moon struggled up behind the Nightingale Mountains and rolled over the top, lighting the whole landscape. Greeting it, a coyote—virtuoso of the greasewood flats—started his yipping yodel.

It had been a good day, an easy day beyond our expectations, one of the days you are proud of when you view it in retrospect. I was glad it was over.

CHAPTER XI

Black Rock to High Rock

ELOW the Great Hot Spring at Black Rock, weary men bathed in the overflow. In its basin, almost three rods in diameter, the water was too hot to touch, but down below it was not as warm as their steaming bodies. While the blistering day went through all gradations toward a bitter cold desert night, this natural bath formed a touch of genuine luxury. There were some women in camp. Delano had found one alone a few miles out on the desert, weeping over her thirsty little son. He gave her what water he had, which in turn she thankfully gave to her baby. She had reached this haven by now. We know, too, that there were others. But in 1849 it was a man's world. The very small proportion of women whose husbands or fathers had brought them on the gold trail, although treated like queens when encountered, were not expected to be among those present. The difficulty of getting a bath was one of the molehills out of which the pioneer women had a perfect right to manufacture mountains. They perspired fervidly under the enveloping canvas of the wagon tops and nagged their husbands into bringing them enough hot water to wash the little girls.

Dr. Bradway wrote in his journal that the water contained lime, iron, and magnesia; was about 180°, and when cold tasted sweet and palatable. Modern ranchers simply state that the water contains fluorine and that if cattle drink it for more than a few months their teeth fall out. The draft animals soon ate the twenty acres of coarse grasses watered by the overflow, and latecomers were forced to drink and move on for pasturage. They were glad to go, for the ground sounded hollow when stepped upon and made the stock uneasy.

Black Rock itself was a forbidding pile that looked like cinders melted together, peppered around its base with fragments of lava. A closer view showed this 450-foot volcanic cliff to be various dark shades of brown and purple, and its top was filled with hundreds of crows. Doubtless the beneficent attendance of these scavengers was to be regarded in the nature of a lesser miracle; but their presence, noisily tearing at the clumped carcasses of those animals who had reached water too late, was not pleasant. Here, as heretofore, dead oxen predominated. Bruff counted in the latter part of today's journey 150 dead oxen, three dead horses, and five mules, fifty of which were in the immediate vicinity of the spring. The men could hardly wait to go on to the better pasturage which they could see ahead.

* * *

We went to Black Rock in August. It had become imperative to complete the two most inaccessible portions of the cutoff or give up the project. The fifty miles of trail lying north of the Rock was the first difficulty. The last fifty miles before reaching the Sacramento Valley was the second; but we would worry about that when we reached it.

No ordinary car could make the trek from Black Rock to High Rock Canyon—not even approximately. For years we had hesitated to take horses because of the hardship of the three-day trip. My husband decided that we would try to find a jeep in the vicinity. It was a splendid idea as far as it went, but handicapped by the factors that there are no telephones in a stretch of country a hundred miles across and that we didn't know anyone to whom we could write for information. When one thinks of the Black Rock Desert, however, one is apt to think of the Western Pacific, whose tracks skirt the southern edge. We put our problem to Homer Bryan, assistant general manager, and he competently arranged the details.

Early in a warm evening we arrived at Gerlach without much idea as to the nature of his plan. The nearest telephone was at Wadsworth, sixty miles away. We took up residence for the night in a little one-story building consisting of a long hall, from front door to back, with perhaps ten small cubicles on each side, for all the world like an egg box. The bath occupied one of these and was exactly the same size as the bedrooms. The hotel is probably for the convenience of the railroad men who break their run at this point, and it is clean and adequate.

In the morning we found that Anna Belle Albrecht, station agent, had arranged with Mr. Jackson, the rancher who chanced to live nearest Black Rock, to receive us and, at least, to consider giving us the use of his jeep. She also had persuaded Mr. Taylor to guide us to the ranch. We pooh-poohed the idea of a guide, although we were most appreciative of the courtesy that prompted it; but after following Mr. Taylor and his daughter, Gwen, for thirty miles of puzzling desert road along the foot of the Calico Hills, with a set of spidery wheel tracks disappearing into each canyon and out toward each spring-watered clump of willows, we grew more and more grateful to the hospitable people who were putting themselves out to save us possible trouble.

There are quite a few Jackson ranches, well stocked and busy, but it was our good fortune to find Mr. Jackson, Sr., at home and in a receptive mood. He hadn't been into High Rock Canyon for years. He would drive the jeep himself and have a change of pace for a day.

He had it all right. Whatever our day's jaunt may have lacked, it wasn't change.

With some misgivings and most of our equipment, we left Mr. Bromley and Dr. Neff to make camp when it should become cool enough. The spot they selected was a desert spring where Mr. Jackson raised vegetables. Willows cast a dense shadow. They had plenty to read. We found out later that they had the company of a six-toed cat who evidently kept them from becoming bored or, for that matter, even relaxed.

Mr. Jackson's jeep was a majestic, roofed affair, tall for its length, with doors that buttoned. I sat in front beside the driver. My husband was behind me, precariously perched on a rolled sleeping bag. We started straight for the center of the great cream-colored skating rink of a desert, then suddenly veered toward Black Rock. One set of wheel tracks cut the brittle crust ahead of us. It was nice to know that we had a predecessor.

In winter much of the wide-spread flat is snow covered or sometimes a shallow lake. It seemed strange to remember, on this warm desert day, that Frémont with his men, on their way south from Oregon, spent New Year's Day of 1844 plodding toward the Black Rock, where they could see a column of steam from the Great Hot Spring. They reached it at noon the next day and "passed the rocky cape, a jagged broken point, bare and torn." Four animals gave out during the day by reason of the heavy, muddy traveling and lack of proper forage. This is hazardous country at any season. The white sands, which are sodden in spring, become abstemious in June and grow steadily more glaring and arid all summer, harboring their keenest hostility until August, when, on a hot day, the things they can do to the ill equipped traveler are legion. We were glad to be accomplishing this particular piece of field work in August because in that uncertain month the trek of the Forty-niners was at its height; but we were even more glad that it was not a hot day.

The dry lake bed is edged with dropsical dunes tricked out in greasewood. We entered them about half a mile from the Rock, on its west side, and zigzagged between them toward the northeast until we met, and had to circle, the Great Hot Spring. It is an ordinary appearing body of water but, if lifesaving be deserving of medals, it should be polka-dotted with bronze.

This is the first of a chain of hot springs that stretches along the western foot of Black Rock Range and, during pioneer days, watered a strip irregularly about two miles wide. Ranchers have managed to increase the scope of irrigation in modern times until, in some places, the green extends almost to the Calico Hills. The narrow arm of desert that used to lie between the two ranges is disappearing.

As the companies moved on, we find fuller detail written in their journals; the feet were now more willing servants of the brain, leaving minds free to receive and to record impressions. A little rivulet of water, not hot enough to steam in the already superheated atmosphere, was yet alarming, so one journalist wrote, to the quirkish minds of mules; and a team of six surmounted the obstacle by leaping it, one or two at a time, jerking the top-heavy wagon after them. Some of the boiling springs themselves were only a few inches across and showed but little in the tall coarse grass; a misstep into the bubbling water served to lame the blunderer for days. In larger specimens of these cauldrons dead cattle were partially submerged, with the flesh boiled completely from their white tendons and bones.

The next water is three miles north, at the Casey Place. It has more pasturage, possibly five hundred acres, and was the Mecca of the famished animals. The springs, amounting to a dozen or so, are all hot. Mr. Jackson spun the jeep around them, ripping through the tall rye grass and sunflowers of the oasis. "This is a touchy sort of place," he observed calmly, for he is an imperturbable man, of even manners. "I lease it for grassland; and last year, when I was digging postholes to mend the fence around the water, my spade broke through the crust right into a boiling spring with pressure up. It spouted high enough to hit me in the face."

The springs on the Casey Place provided the locale for most of the characteristic thumbnail word sketches given in the journals of the emigrants: Here a man has coffee which he has vaingloriously brewed by setting the pot in the edge of a spring. Another is holding the end of a string to which is tethered a duck, picked and cleaned and boiling merrily. It won't be very tender before he gets tired of waiting and eats it with salt and frying-pan bread. Many have been without a hot meal for over fifty hours, and the smell of bacon permeates the air. In a convenient lukewarm runlet the women are washing, and some of the men too, wringing their clean-by-courtesy clothes and draping them over the bushes. From the main springs runs a stream of boiling water sufficient, possibly, to turn a mill, or so the men speculate as they watch its volume and speed. Forty rods below, a woman steps backward into its deceptively cool-looking current, and her thin high scream—a razor edge of sound—echoes back from the mountains to blend with the hoarse shout that answers. They strip her stocking from her foot and ankle and the skin comes too. She is lucky; had it been closer to the spring, the flesh would have cooked as well.

Somewhere near here, camped in the tall grass, fifty wagons with their weary quota of humanity—members of the first trains to turn on the cutoff in 1849—are waiting for Magee to come back, the same more or less legendary Magee who, with eight wagons in his own company, may be said to have started the influx of Forty-niners over this unpleasant cutoff. His cattle are recruiting while he reconnoiters, and, because his stock is still here, the crowd feels sure that he will return to guide them. Possibly Magee realizes that he himself has found more than he bargained for; possibly he even feels a sense of responsibility for the emigrants who have blindly followed and caught up with him and his teams as they recruit at the hot springs.

Two of his company, Milligan and Patterson, are out on the desert with water and grass, reviving and bringing in the cattle which have dropped by the way. They succeed very well, losing only one. Experienced and well equipped men seem able to negotiate the desert, even in hot weather, with only nominal losses. It is the ordinary man with a family, owning only one wagon and doing his own driving, who suffers most. At home he may have been a merchant or a minister. There is nothing in his experience to warn him that his extra stock may stampede suddenly toward a mirage and die in the attempt to find the evanescent paradise of trees and water. All sorts of preventable catastrophes happen to the man who can not foresee them. Magee's company work hard during his absence and get their stock in shape for further travel.

And Magee comes back. We know this, although no one puts it in so many words, because by evening the rest of the travelers "bait and catch up" and may be seen straggling out of camp, one at a time, onto a seven-mile stretch of deep sand. The consensus of opinion, loudly voiced, seems to be: "Drive ahead; if Magee can go it, we can."

And so the first large detachment of Forty-niners leaves the hot springs, and, as they pull out, word comes by the grapevine through the wagons that Mr. Gard and family, whom they left stranded at Rabbit Hole, have made it through to Black Rock Spring, with all his cattle on one wagon and everything else left behind. That particular worry, tinged with a certain suggestion of bad conscience, is wiped out, leaving them in better fettle for the night's journey.

*   *   *

I was relieved, and I think my husband was also, to leave this "touchy" spot of geyserlike boiling water and to trundle the willing little jeep along the northwestward-bending arc of the Black Rock Range. Because all water was found at the foot of the curving mountains, the wagons were forced to pursue a longer journey than the direct line would have been.

To give us a breeze and also to facilitate photography, Mr. Jackson swung the windshield up until it occupied a horizontal position at the top of its framework. Every time we stormed a patch of rye grass we harvested the crop into my lap with this knifelike arrangement. It made a vicious ripping noise and was quite an amusing experience.

Now and then a deep gully crossed our trail where flash storm waters had rooted their way down from the mountains. Some of these were big enough to swallow the jeep bodily. They were easier to negotiate, however, than the narrower ones, which the determined little car dove into, climbed up, bridged for an alarming second, dropped into again with the rear end, and then finally swarmed out of in compound low.

We had to go a quarter of a mile out of our way to see the oddest of the springs. They are set side by side like hard, round, wicked eyes, with a narrow raised bridge of earth between them. Some peculiar property makes them hotter than boiling, or so the local ranchers insist. Mine is not to make reply, reason why, or any other rhyming rigmarole. If they say the water is hotter than boiling, it's all right with me. Perhaps it holds some foreign substance in suspension; perhaps there is pressure maintained in some obscure fashion. The twin springs are called Double Hot; and don't dip your finger in either of them out of curiosity, or it will emerge with the top layer of flesh well cooked.

All this time we had seen tire tracks here and there along the way. Probably a small truck, we thought. It had detoured for unknown distances around the storm gullies but had always come back to our course along the trail.

At this juncture we struck the deep sand. It was probably the "seven miles of sand" traveled by Magee at the head of the Forty-niners. The truck struck it too. In fact it had almost imbedded itself in a big soft dune. From the evidence, its occupant had camped right there and spent a good long time shoveling it out by hand. I cast a ghoulish look around for skeletons; but the camp was deserted, and the truck had evidently gone back under its own power.

"Somebody was going out to Harding City," said Mr. Jackson. "That's the lost silver mine, you know. He hated to turn back, I'll bet."

Sometime in 1849 an emigrant named Harding (or Hardin) picked up a lump of metal which he thought was lead. He threw it in the wagon and, as he needed bullets, melted off one end and happily went hunting. It's the same old story; every mining country has a similar tradition. Years later someone persuaded him to have the remainder of the lump assayed, and he found it to be silver. Harding hunted the rest of his life for the place where he had picked it up, and so did his acquaintances. Many others have made the trip through the years, and prospectors still come, hoping through a miracle to make the strike. Quite a community sprang up in 1866, at the peak of the excitement, but gradually faded until it became a depopulated ghost town.

"We won't get completely away from evidences of tires," Mr. Jackson said in conclusion, "until we get beyond Harding City, for I was

out there myself, in the jeep, this spring. Most of us around here
think that the trail was straightened out between 1849 and Harding's
second trip so that it described a more shallow arc and struck the
mountains at a different place. That's why he couldn't recognize
anything."

As we swung on toward the "city," we hit another wash and
bridged it, getting our front wheels across and tying up on a sage
bush so that we could go no further. We had committed the unpar-
donable sin in handling jeeps: alternate wheels were off the ground.
No amount of coaxing works in a case like that. The men patiently
set about building up a rock ramp under a rear wheel while I stayed
in the car and served as "candlestick," swinging the balance of weight
from one wheel to the other as requested.

When traction was established, we backed away and then made a
run at the gully, crossed it successfully, and climbed to a sort of
sandy ledge.

"This is Harding City," said Mr. Jackson waving at two ruined
rock walls. "We'll eat lunch here."

The ruins were of white sandstone blocks and rose on the edge
of the ledge. With the imposing bulk of Payute Peak as a background,
they made a striking picture. Two pits walled with red stone showed
where the stamp mill used to stand. A large iron flywheel lay flat
among the scrubby growth. Somebody had believed in the presence
of the nonexistent silver sufficiently to bring in machinery. There
were no house foundations—there was nothing else at all.

While the men were discussing the eccentricities of the flywheel, I leaned over the broken coping and peered into one of the pits. It had long been a minor ambition with me, if circumstances were right, to make the welkin ring and become more conversant with just where that melodious item may be found; but I am a silent person under stress and I suppose that two or three really top-notch screams have been my lifetime quota. Right now, with my hand an inch from a rattlesnake's scarred tail, I rang the old welkin until it practically shivered to pieces—and landed four feet straight back in the brush.

As soon as I got my balance, I ran around to the other side of the pit to get a view from a safer spot. Of course both men had arrived by this time, and we saw that tragedy had struck a few hours before. In slithering through an opening between the rocks, the rough edges of the rattles had caught and held. The snake was hanging limply against the hot rock wall. Beating sunshine will kill a rattler very shortly if he cannot find shade, and hanging head down hadn't helped.

My enthusiasm for exploration was temporarily dimmed, so we went back to the car and had lunch—non-salty sandwiches and a choice of grapefruit or tomato juice, canned of course. It is a good selection for a dry, hot trip and seems to be what most people want when it comes time to eat, even if the lunch provides other things.

Then we simply stayed in the shade of the jeep for a while, in the middle of the deserted settlement. We were lucky, and a cool breeze swept over the raised ledge where the mill had stood, inhabited now by the deceased rattlesnake's family (invisible, thank goodness!) and miscellaneous lizards scuttling around through the shad scale. At first glance there would seem to be nothing to commend it to the senses. Nevada's historic spots often do not measure up very well by standards that we are accustomed to use—comfort, obvious beauty, safety, or what not; but there is certainly space unlimited, blue sky, gray-green mountains, and the indescribable smell of breeze over sage. Under their spell it is possible to catch something from each hour to enrich the years ahead.

A small meadow watered by springs lay to the left beyond Harding City. It is called Little Double Hot, but it has not the intense heat of its larger namesake. No doubt it had its full complement of camps during the migration. Stones, dull black and rusty-red, lay all around. They also had been hot at some distant period.

The Indians of the lower Humboldt apparently had not begrudged the caravans the privilege of starving their cattle across the desert, but the particularly pedicular tribe which they now encountered was not so unconcerned. Beginning north of the hot springs, the stock was in constant danger from sporadic arrows. Sometimes the little brown men managed to kill a stray, immediately take such meat as they could lop off, and run away into the mountains. Efforts to catch and punish them resulted in nothing but humiliating failure.

We had no road but the trail itself. The previous winter had been hard on it, washing out six or eight gullies to a state impassable to anything on wheels but jeeps. So far they all had been raw and new looking. At the bottom of the last and largest Mr. Jackson stopped and, for the first time, suggested that we get out while he drove up and over the edge. "I've got forty dollars' worth of iron weighting down the front," he said, "but you never know; it might go over backward." We now came to old evidences of former cloudbursts, where the washes were grassgrown and full of sage and were, in consequence, even harder to cross. A big-trunked sage bush forms a thoroughly effective obstruction, and we found ourselves on top of several, in the course of the day, that I thought for a while could hold us aloft indefinitely.

When opposite the western face of Payute Peak, Mr. Jackson pointed to a clump of trees in a small meadow part way up the mountain and told us the story of the death of Peter Lassen and his comrade, Clapper, who were killed at that spot while hunting for the Harding silver. A third man, Lemericus Wyatt, was with them. He was sixty years of age and weighed two hundred pounds. An arrow went through his clothes as he ran heavily toward shelter. The horses had stampeded down the mountain and he had no hope at all for his life. Miraculously, as he staggered on, he observed his own horse emerge from the dust cloud and come back. It had, he said, always been hard to catch; but now it stood while he mounted bareback, and then rode madly away with nothing but a picket rope to guide the faithful animal. The improbability of this circumstance and the known fact that Peter Lassen was always friendly with the Pah-Utes caused some to think that Wyatt might have killed his two partners himself. But Fairfield, in his splendid history of Lassen County, brands this as false. Lassen had made enemies among certain other tribes. The killing could, in all probability, be laid at their door.

Wyatt arrived at Susanville, after a terrible ride of 140 miles, and told the news. A party went out and buried the two men where they fell.

Many years later the brethren of the Masonic fraternity wished to reinter Lassen's body in an accessible spot where they might do him honor as the man who brought the first Masonic charter to California. It was done; and not one, but two large monuments in his memory stand under a mammoth yellow pine near Susanville, on the site where he first made camp when coming into the county that later bore his name.

"We call the creek that runs through the meadow up there, Clapper Creek," said Mr. Jackson pointing up the rugged slope of Payute Peak; "and we all hope it's Clapper that's still buried beside it; but, after the Indians and the elements got in their work, it's probably a tossup which body they took away."

Since lunch we had seen no evidence of travel but so many storm washes that Mr. Jackson was moved to say that the old trail would soon, at that rate, be impassable for anything on wheels.

Split Canyon is a rocky section of mountainside cleft to form a canyon, and makes a landmark visible for a long distance. When nearly opposite it, we came to sand grass, about a foot high and with a feathery top. In winter, when there is plenty of water, it makes good pasturage; and the government has put in a drift fence to prevent the stock from ranging on it during the summer. Beyond the fence we came at once to the cattle, whitefaces, who graze at will until the annual roundup. Mr. Jackson began to look around with proprietary interest for his own brand. A matronly cow stood by the road marked on the hip with a J slash J. Her sucking calf was branded differently. From my book knowledge of cattle etiquette, I expected a stiff reaction; but we didn't get it. "Those things happen," said Mr. Jackson tolerantly. "We lose twenty or thirty a year in one way and another. Guess they got separated for a while."

After passing Payute Peak, the Black Rock Range is known by another name; and we turned away from it toward Mud Meadows, the modern equivalent for Mud Lake Valley, or Salt Valley of emigrant days. The buildings of Soldier Meadows Ranch, shaded by a row of tall trees, were at some distance to the right. Israel Hale found a train of United States troops camped there in 1849. They were from Oregon and were to meet and assist some troops on their way from the States to California. Probably the name originated in this incident.

They were harvesting in Mud Meadows, and we drove between cultivated fields without stopping. We would have fair roads for a way, until we passed through the area of ranches and came to the entrance of High Rock Canyon.

The emigrants hailed Mud Lake Valley's fine grass and abundant water. The cattle strayed into it happily but not too securely, for the Indians, accumulating rancor and bravado, made nightly forays, killed a few, and drove others off into the mountains, which were here cut by crooked canyons. Some of the results of their labors were in plain sight near the trail and forestalled any enjoyment which the sight of enough grass might have engendered in the travelers. Delano ran upon a freshly killed carcass. "The horse lay near the road," he wrote, "and the gentlemen Digger epicures had cut off his head, and taken a large steak from a hind quarter—generously leaving the remainder of the poor, raw-boned carcass for the maws of the white devils, who had brought it so far to grace an Indian Board."

On the night after he wrote this, several more animals were shot— shot with such amazing force and accuracy that, in one case, a stone-pointed arrow went through the backbone and protruded six inches on the other side; and more cattle were rounded up and raced into the hills.

It was the usual policy in such cases to gather a volunteer force and, pursuing the retreating Diggers, force them to abandon their ill gotten supplies in the interest of speed; sometimes even exchanging gunshots for arrows. Delano's comrades did so in this case; but nothing came of it except the privilege of seeing their fugitives high above them on a cliff making gestures of derision, in which art the Indian of the times was both imaginative and indecent.

The volunteer party returned, having lost face with the Indians, and a sort of resolution was made and kept, for a while at least, that the wagon trains should travel always within supporting distance of one another.

In Mud Meadows the wagons turned west toward another range of mountains, apparently without a name. Beyond the first rampart of these low hills, High Rock Canyon provides an easy passage; but it does not extend far enough to the east to connect with Mud Meadows. Fly Canyon comes through, but it is so choked and impassable at the eastern entrance that the wagons were forced to climb up the smooth hillside and had to be lowered with ropes midway of its length.

On our way toward the hill where the wagons climbed, we drove into two large hot springs, one after the other; and I was really nervous both times, for they looked exactly like the deep well type. I couldn't help being intensely relieved when we rolled through in a regulation manner instead of plopping to the bottom.

My husband, in his enthusiastic attempt to see just how the wagons went down into Fly Canyon, stepped on an insecure slab of rock and found out; unfortunately, however, he was not equipped with the stabilizing ropes. It happened that no one saw him give his convincing imitation of a prairie schooner going downhill on the loose, and he didn't tell anyone for two days.

Years ago Miller and Luxe, the western cattle kings, owned land in the vicinity, and they built a road to do away with the rope descent. It is a precarious hillside shelf road and badly washed at that, but amply wide for a jeep. I got in and submitted to having the doors buttoned; presently we arrived safely at the bottom.

After a very short distance in Fly Canyon, we climbed to a flat open space, High Rock Lake Ranch. The lake justifies its name by filling with water once in ten or twelve years, but ordinarily it raises crops like any ranch. We drove through the north end and turned into the portal of High Rock Canyon. Little High Rock Canyon lay beyond the ranch, its entrance being south of our route. It looked higher and more rugged than the larger one we were about to explore.

I was prepared to be disappointed in High Rock and consequently was pleased out of all proportion when it proved to be an inspiring sight and a real curiosity. The walls are almost perpendicular and several hundred feet high, crowned with rimrock. The canyon floor is reasonably flat, dotted with springs and limned in greenery following tiny rivulets. Delano wrote: "It was a canon, or narrow, rocky pass through the mountains, just wide enough for a smooth, level road, with intervals of space occasionally, to afford grass and water. On each side were walls of perpendicular rock, four or five hundred feet high, or mountains so steep that the ascent was either impossible, or extremely difficult, ——and it seemed as if Providence, foreseeing the wants of his creatures, had in mercy opened this strange path, by which they could extricate themselves from destruction and death."

Farther and farther we drove into the canyon, between beautiful fluted cliffs. Rye grass grew so high and thick across the trail that pecks of it must have showered over my knees and feet during the time we were there. A cave marred the cliffs to our right. We went in, but it was blackened with soot and we could see nothing of interest.

Delano described a cave. "It was twenty-five feet long," he said, "by ten or twelve wide, with an arching roof fifteen feet high, and the remains of fires, grassbeds, and burnt bones. . . ." Yes, this must be the same Indian cave; and there were others close by. Camping, as Delano's company did, in the middle of their primitive village was just another infringement on the rights of the resentful Indians whose homes were in the caves.

Of course if these indigenous Nevadans, like the Shoshone tribes of Bear River, had chosen to stay right where they were beside the trail and exploit the emigrants, they could have done so with profit, and no harm would have come to them. But they were timid, unintelligent, hungry, and dangerous and would have no dealings with the white men. The line of moving emigrants, like a Juggernaut (a cliché which I cannot be restrained from using in connection with the westward migration), went right over everything—including cooking fires and grass beds. While camped in the very midst of so many denlike dwellings in the rocks that they dubbed it Digger Town, Delano's company were quite astonished at being attacked by Indians, and drove them off, wounding several, after which they posted a strong guard and went to sleep, apparently without pausing to think that they were between the villagers and their abject shelters.

"Beyond the canon," said Delano, "we came to an opening of forty or fifty acres, covered with clover and wild oats taller than my head, where, with most of the other teams, we laid up for the day." He meant only that the first section of High Rock Canyon had come to an end, widening into what is now the Powers Ranch, and rolling into little hills. The trail goes somewhat to the right and then drops down again into the second section of the canyon, which reappears in the same form but with lower cliffs. We took Mr. Jackson's description of the way in which the trail regained the canyon, for we have never seen it. Our field work in the west end of the canyon had been done some years before, and a short middle section was omitted.

We didn't see it now for a very good reason. The trail, which so far had not found any way to stop the jeep, became ingenious and buried it. The old runway grew deeper and deeper and more and more gutted by rains, until the top of the jeep was on a level with the ground. Then the gouged-out trail commenced to narrow until it was too pinched and constricted for passageway. We had to back a couple of hundred feet to get out, after which we decided to return to camp before darkness caught us in the canyon.

Traveling eastward, we were reminded that Frémont's men had plodded in that direction, hunting for "Mary's Lake" (near the Sink of the Humboldt), and camped there, on the night of December 30, 1843, in high spirits because there was abundant grass. "It was," wrote Frémont, "a singular place to travel through—shut up in the earth, a sort of chasm, the little strip of grass under our feet, the rough walls of bare rock on either hand, and the narrow strip of sky above."

As we returned into the valley of High Rock Lake Ranch, Mr. Jackson suggested that we go to the ranch house to fill the radiator. It was easy to suggest but proved hard to do. Here was a large sage-filled valley with a ranch in the middle. Somewhere a road ran from the edge toward that middle, but just where defeated us. It was impossible to see any passageway through the sage. We had to circle the valley until we found the entrance.

As we neared the house, it was evident that the men were haying and had worked late. It smelled like supper. We had pulled up at a decent distance from the door when a large man stepped out and boomed, "Get out and come in the house," after which he went back.

Mr. Jackson piled out of the left-hand door and I out of the right; my husband rolled over the tailboard and we all obeyed orders. Something about that smell just gathered us in. It was the Swingal Ranch and our host was Ogle Swingal himself. We were expected to have supper; there was no possible doubt about that, and we made no fuss. The group of six or seven had just finished and we took their places, gratefully eating what happened to be left. We consumed clam chowder and biscuit, potato salad and cake and canned prunes with coffee, while Mr. Jackson and Mr. Swingal compared notes for the season. I gathered that they didn't meet very often.

Half an hour later, when we had left the house and had succeeded in getting out of the Swingal mystic maze by circling a couple of

haystacks, Mr. Jackson told me a few anecdotes about that colorful character.

He is, it seems, the strongest man that ever came into this part of the country—a bachelor living alone with his hay hands, refusing to drink or smoke, and usually moving circumspectly for fear of hurting someone. Mr. Jackson once saw him lift a full metal tank holding fifty-five gallons of gasoline. He balanced it a moment on the tensed muscles of his stomach, then gave it a heave and landed it in the bed of a truck where three men had been endeavoring to put it for so long that he grew nervous waiting for them. "I must be failing," Mr. Jackson quoted him. "That strained me some."

After we had driven safely back through the two hot springs and made an undamaged return to welcome solidity, I was ready to enjoy the trip home. It would be shorter than the curve along which we had come—only thirty miles compared to fifty—on ranch roads in a state of reasonable repair. And the desert night would be cool but perfect from the present star-specked twilight until dawn, should our journey take so long.

At eleven o'clock, after just twelve hours of riding, we came within sight of lanterns at camp and broke an otherwise perfect record by passing the first car we had seen all day. Dr. Neff and Mr. Bromley heard us and turned on all the car lights for our guidance; but, even so, it took us fifteen minutes and a mile or so of traveling—clear around to the other side of the small oasis—before we could find a way to drive in to camp.

Supper was ready for us and we for it, but it proved difficult to eat. Out in the open the wind was blowing; but here, in the shelter of the willows, it was still, and millions of gray, downy moths were fluttering around the lanterns. They had a natural affinity for coffee, and it was necessary to reverse the usual niceties and place the saucer over the cup. Between us sat the six-toed cat, purring like a contented tiger and snatching with sharp claws extended for each morsel that we ate. Nothing short of hurting the animal had any effect; so Mr. Bromley simply gave her a large saucerful of stew under the table instead of on it, and she remained out of sight for a while. They had been doing this all day, and we repeated it at breakfast. She wouldn't need to hunt for some time, I thought, looking at her rapidly swelling contours.

The men, knowing that we would never use it in the daytime, had thoughtfully put our tent out in the open. There were no bugs there and the cat absented herself to remain near the satisfying smell of stew. The east wind honed continuously over Black Rock Range, whetting its cutting edge with blown sand and giving a playful swoop at our tent as it passed over on its way to the Calico Hills. One of our two difficult projects was accomplished, thanks to several people whom we are now proud to call friends.

Tomorrow we would follow the wind.

CHAPTER XII

Hail to California!

WE made our first acquaintance with High Rock Canyon several years ago. We entered from its western exit, having driven to it from Cedarville in Modoc County, California, during a wartime summer and with the saved-up gasoline of three families. Our party included Dr. Neff, Mr. Bromley, and our son Bill, on leave in uniform. At Cedarville we succeeded in interesting a retired cattle rancher, Mr. Syd Street, who went along to keep us out of trouble. We have been over the road since, but the first trip is the one we most enjoy remembering.

We left our car with Mr. Street at the end of the canyon and walked in as far as time permitted. The sides of the canyon are far lower than the spectacular fluted columns of the eastern end, but they edge the narrow flattish bottom and effectively hold it within approximately the same bounds. Springs now and then provide abundant water, and grass grows among the brush.

In one of the springs Mr. Bromley found a petrified oyster shell, and we all picked up fragments of petrified wood as had Delano. Obsidian was plentiful, and the Indians had used it for arrowheads; we found several imperfect specimens that had been thrown away. Evidently this was a favorite working place—one more reason for their dislike of the white man whose wagons rumbled along the natural roadway day after day.

Bruff described the excrescences along the canyon walls. They are plentiful, looking rather horribly like misplaced sweetbreads. Just before reaching the meadow that forms a bulb on the western end, the canyon narrows into a rough two-mile stretch. Coroden spoke his mind about it: ". . . and a worse two miles of road God never let a wagon be hauled over, or if He did it was very wrong."

The bulblike meadow is well watered and still ankle deep in grass and forage of various sorts. Coyly hiding from the eye, were round white toadstools. I kicked one and it proved to be full of brown powder. A small log corral fenced in a relatively insignificant amount of the luxuriant pasturage, but its area was beyond doubt limited by the number of logs available; from what I could see, it seemed as if the total lumber supply of the county had been sacrificed to make it as big, even, as it was. Through the center of the pretty meadow ran a creek. Amazing High Rock Canyon was well supplied with everything needed by the emigrants from the start to its finish at this point.

On returning, we found the car sitting where we had left it, hub-deep in a patch of little dark-blue iris. The trail had a dangerously high center, so that we drove no faster than we could have walked, skirting glasslike hunks of obsidian with designs on our tires, and keeping one set of wheels in the middle of the road when possible. Slender reddish grass, bearing an ear like wheat, made the scrub sage of the sidehill look rusty; but, for contrast, there were little lemon-colored sunflowers and thickets of buck brush with small yellow blossoms.

"This is the best kind of deer forage," Mr. Street told us. "And there used to be lots of antelopes. In fact miles of this country is a game refuge, but the war is hard on animals."

"Well, for mercy's sake," I wanted to know, "what did the U.S. Army ever do to the antelopes?"

"Nothing," he said. "Nothing at all. It was like the emigrants and the Indians. The emigrants didn't intend to do a thing to the Diggers, but they kept coming; and the Indians were scared and ran. That's what happened to the antelopes when the army trucks and planes took over. I guess they're somewhere in the state of Nevada, but they aren't here any more."

For a while we made progress of a sort on two wheel tracks with a high center of grass, sage, and hidden rocks. It was the old trail itself; and we had the satisfaction of knowing that if we ripped out the transmission, it would be a historic misadventure—romantic, in fact.

Mr. Street went on talking. "That low hill to the right is Nut Mountain. The name is modern I think, and comes from most peculiar hard earth formations, like hundreds of nuts, that roll around loose. We go to the left of it on the trail, and there ahead you see Massacre Ranch House."

It is, in these days, not much to see. The house is new, perhaps only sixty years of age, and has nothing of glamour to offer; but it used to be headquarters for a horse ranch. A spring was near by; it had, of course, determined the site of the house, and from it flowed a rivulet which is a good example of what the emigrants called a "spring branch." The whole place looked abandoned and showed lack of continuous occupancy, but on the corral fence were sheep hides left to cure in the sun. Someone came there now and then.

We forded the "spring branch," which had produced an inordinate amount of mud for such a little water, and soon came within sight of Massacre Lakes.

We were on a high hillside and they were below us to the north, lying, three of them, silver colored and glinting at the bottom of a large basin. To the west, and on a line with the lakes, was Red or Painted Mountain, which Bruff sketched. It has quite a flat top, as if cut off about two-thirds of the way up. We had struck a small dirt road after leaving Massacre Ranch and were making satisfactory progress slightly downhill and in the direction of the lakes.

"No more danger of ripping a hole in our crank case," I remarked, "which is some compensation for leaving romance behind."

"No, I suppose we won't hit anything from here on," said Mr. Street; "but this section of the road to Denio is practically the trail, just worked over a bit and with the rocks dug out."

"It's still far from romantic," Mr. Bromley agreed from his vantage point at the left window. "Look what's coming."

I looked but I didn't believe it. It was one of the things your mind just doesn't credit. But my nose believed it and I said urgently, "We've got to stop and look at it I know, but for mercy's sake go past it and get to the windward!" And just then we got the only puncture of the summer, with a stack of a hundred or so skinned coyote carcasses stacked neatly, like cordwood, beside the road. The first official road sign we had seen towered above them on a post at least ten feet high, straining up through a stench that lay like something solid. That smell could have been powdered and used for fertilizer.

Well, the men were stuck with it, but I wasn't; beckoning to Mr. Street, I walked on down the road. "What's the reason?" I asked, flicking a thumb over my shoulder at the horrible mass of dried bones and partly rotted flesh—some of it months old and some quite fresh. "Well," he said, "I wouldn't know positively, but it looks to me as if we have a pretty effective government coyote hunter. I suppose he has to put them somewhere after he skins them, and they constitute good evidence that he's earning his money."

"I don't see why it has to be at the edge of the road," I objected. "Some of the bones are actually in the wheel tracks; but I suppose everyone likes a little appreciation for a job well done, and they are certainly neatly arranged, if one cares for such things. Why is everything around here called 'Massacre'?" I went on. "Not but what it seems like an appropriate name."

"The usual reason," he said; "there was an Indian fight and a lot of people killed up on that lava-capped hill to our right."

"Surely the trail was never up there."

"No, you see our road makes a turn there toward the north. Well, the trail didn't. It headed for a spring—they call it Emigrant Spring—over there to the left beyond that little knoll. We'll walk over there and look at it on the way back to the car. A whole company of emigrants were camped at the spring and were attacked by Indians. They retreated to the vantage point of the lava cap and were finally overpowered and killed there—all but one, they say. Apparently there was no massacre complete without its solitary survivor. Somebody had to be left to tell the story, I guess."

"Does the trail go on down to the lakes after leaving the spring?"

"No, they aren't very good water—slightly alkaline—and they're out of the course anyway. The trail hits straight for Red Mountain there ahead to the left and passes to the south of it."

A half-hour later we had followed his pointing finger and were in the old trail's huge and jagged sage, with Red Mountain, flat-topped and rusty, on our right. It had brightly marked outcroppings with colored strata in horizontal stripings. From between them the eroded soil cascaded down in drifts. A flat plain lay below to the west, nicely variegated of white alkali soil and bright green greasewood. About two-thirds of the way across, the dry bed of what Mr. Street called Forty-nine Lake appeared to the south. The travelers skirted it and made their way to the beautiful Twin Springs at the foot of the next range. Here they camped, or at least rested, and let the stock graze before starting up the steep and rocky gorge of Fortynine Hill.

Bruff, who had been our favored authority for the camp sites and procedure of the emigrants on any given stretch, here seemingly became confused; and we had to discard his account of the afternoon of September 28th and all of September 29th. The discrepancy probably occurred when he was elaborating his field notes taken on the spot. How well I know that it isn't safe to correct a single thing which you have written while looking at an object, because you later think you remember that it wasn't quite that way; but we certainly may excuse the poor man who had laboriously climbed through so many canyons since leaving the Humboldt River that by this time he must have felt like an ant trying to get across a corrugated iron roof. The alkali flat containing Forty-nine Lake was eleven miles across to the Twin Springs, but the emigrants sometimes counted in the hill slopes, which were almost equally dry and barren, making the distance in the so-called "flat" longer.

There was water in Forty-nine Lake when Delano passed it. ". . . before us we saw a pond of clear water," he wrote, "perhaps five miles in circumference, and we all hurried to the muddy beach to quench our thirst, and eagerly dipped up our cups full. 'Salt,' roared one—'Brine,' echoed another—'Pickle for pork,' said a third; and with thirsty throats, we resumed our toilsome march. Turning an angle of the salt lake. from northwest to north, we continued on; entering a gorge, we began to ascend over a ridge about two miles long, when, coming to good grazing and water, we encamped." This camp of Delano's is the meadow opposite a deserted building called Forty-nine House.

Checking Bruff's mileage, backward from the Warm Spring where he next camped, we find that he was describing correctly the ascent of Forty-nine Hill on the morning of October 1st, having mistaken it for the first outpost of the Sierra Nevada Range. Said he: "The trail ascended a steep sand drag, very crooked, around a huge block of rocks, another trail—much longer—went around the other side of it, and they met on top, and in a few yards descended into a pretty grassy vale, with a small brook in it." This also is a description of the Forty-nine House meadow. As for the "huge block of rocks," it is an unmistakable characteristic of the ascent. Forty-nine Hill is so disfigured with grayish-white protuberances that it looks like something unpleasant on a medical chart. Bruff may have meant that one of these outcroppings lay in the path of the trail, splitting it, as indeed some of them seem to do; but more likely he meant the two trails that went over Forty-nine Hill, the one to the north being short and very steep, the one starting near Twin Springs being longer and with a better slope. One may see the southern branch very well from the county road which goes from the vicinity of the ancient willows shading Twin Springs and (along with the trail) follows up Forty-nine Creek from its salty ending in Forty-nine Lake to its better beginnings in the hills ahead, beyond Forty-nine House.

The two forks come together at a cluster of beehive-like rocks near the top of the hill, and the united trail proceeds through the meadow. It stays to the left of the county road in the bottom of a washed gully. The sage along its course is very high. Four cowhands were bringing a herd of red cattle up the mountain, and the mammoth old Jonathan stopped and stared in the window at me, raising his absurd pink muzzle and exhaling a long sweet breath which smelled of hay.

I often deprecate the lack of imagination, tendency to stay with the familiar, or whatever the quality or lack of quality may have been that caused our well meaning ancestors to run an otherwise suitable name so far into the ground that a steam shovel couldn't excavate it—and, as far as I'm concerned, it wouldn't be worth the expense. At any rate, Forty-nine House only served to usher in Forty-nine Canyon, at the far end of which a segment of the main chain of the Sierra Nevada was visible in the blue distance.

Down the western slope from Forty-nine Canyon, then across an insignificant sandy and sagy stretch, and the creaking, groaning wagons came to Tater Hill—gratefully I introduce this pleasant variation in names—so called because of a fancied resemblance to a winter potato hill. However, it is merely a nubbin on the eastern side of Surprise Valley; and now the trail is in California, on the extreme edge of Modoc County.

Surprise Valley is amazingly personable. Perhaps that is the reason for the name. Three shallow lakes stretch north and south for miles up its center. They are called logically Upper, Middle, and Lower. Sometimes they contain water, and then they give the impression that the glassy blue sky has broken and dropped fragments here and there. Water is water, whether it be an inch in depth or a hundred feet. That it is sometimes only an inch was unfortunately forced upon our attention by a fat mud hen standing ankle deep in the center of the lake, miles from shore. An inch of water doesn't last long in a dry year. The next time we came, a mud flat had replaced the shining mirror surface;

but we were glad to see it, as it showed plainly how the emigrants had been able to cut across the bed of the lake when they happened to find it dry.

The immediate objective of the emigrants, heading down past Tater Hill, was a group of warm springs in the basin of Middle Lake. To get there they skirted the south side of the hill, crossed little Sand Creek (which, for a distance, runs parallel with the lake shore), and headed for the springs. Usually they camped there in the midst of marshy ground covered sparsely with coarse grass. From this camp, so Bruff wrote, "Lassin's Pass bears N.W. dist. about 15 ms." They had come to the point where they could see and estimate the mileage to the dreaded crossing of the Sierra chain, now known as Fandango Pass in Warner's Range.

The next day was easy. Unless there was obscuring smoke from grass fires, it all lay within view. From the time the oxen settled into the yokes and pulled the wagons through the rough ground near the warm springs until they had chosen a camp site from among the many lovely places at the foot of the Sierra Nevada, they could see all that lay before them.

In the morning they headed north along the edge of the lake until they came to the higher ground between Middle and Upper Lakes. They then traversed this dividing neck of land at whatever angle the current size of the ever changing bodies of water dictated and entered the bed of Upper Lake.

When there is water, the little mud hens, waddling as they wade, leave plainly perceptible tracks under it for as far as they care to continue their constitutional. When there is no water, there isn't a tree, a shrub, or a cocklebur bush to be seen. The lake bed is four to five miles across. One can count the pines on the timbered slopes of the mountains to the west where the travelers might, if they wished, spend the next night in comparative luxury.

*   *   *

Our headquarters were temporarily at the Golden Hotel in Cedarville. On the day following our trip out to High Rock, we planned to see old Lassen Pass, now Fandango Pass; but the group seemed impossible to collect. Bill had gone down the street to telephone; Dr. Neff and my husband were comfortable on nail kegs in front of the CooCoo Club, talking to a bunch of the cronies who collect in such favorite places. Mr. Bromley was invisible.

I just sat and waited in the car. There weren't nail kegs enough, and they didn't want me anyway.

Mr. Bromley broke the impasse by arriving with an encouragingly large box of eatables which he shoved into the trunk. "I told them last night not to count on our being light eaters," he said. "I guess they took me at my word." He slid behind the wheel and gave five sharp honks for "rear flagman come in," which collected the men without a protest.

Leaving Cedarville, we drove a few miles northward along the west shore of Middle Lake and then connected with the trail as it emerged at any place the water permitted along the shore of Upper Lake.

The Forty-niners now had not only luxury, but a choice of luxuries. On the far-western edge of the basin were many hot springs—perhaps a hundred, said Delano. Grass was plentiful on the green-sheeted flats. They might camp near the woven witchery of the rush-bordered lake or go farther, as many did, to sleep under a pine six feet in girth, which at that point in their journeying they considered enormous. Or they might pitch their tents by a clear, clattering mountain rivulet, as musical as ice clinking in a glass and almost as cold. Delano was overpowered by the height of the mountains they were to climb on the morrow. "The Sierra Nevada," he exclaimed, "—the snowy mountain so long wished for, and yet so long dreaded! We were at its base, soon to commence its ascent. In a day or two we were to leave the barren sands of the desert for a region of mountains and hills, where perhaps the means of sustaining life might not be found; where our wagons might be dashed to atoms by falling from precipices. A thousand vague and undefined difficulties were present to our imaginations; yet all felt strong for the work, feeling that it was our last."

McCoy, who traveled about midway between Delano and Bruff, had a more favored position as one who was late enough to be positive of a practical road in front of him and yet was well ahead of the possibility of being caught by an early winter. He and his company were charmed with what he termed "a spell of indescribable beauty," and new animation appeared in camp.

Bruff came late. It was October 1st when, traveling at night, he crossed from the warm spring to the base of the Sierra. Things had been happening and, as was his way, he put them all down in his journal. Today his company was frightened (as well they might be, in the light of what happened to them later) by notices found at the last camp warning them of the distance still ahead of them before reaching the settlements. The emigrants in general "had much scurvy, little girl bad in mouth—1 man camp fever." It doesn't take much time to inscribe, but, oh, the hours and hours of patient nursing necessary for a little girl with scurvy "bad in mouth," and so little hope for improvement with the food supply what it was. "Man kill'd friend with Bowie Knife, on this ground," wrote Mr. Bruff, who was apparently camped on X marks the spot. "Said Murderer had also stolen a calf." Why, we wonder, did the man henceforth to be known as the murderer steal a calf and then use a Bowie knife on his friend? Maybe it had something to do with the food supply; we'll never know. "Ladies singing last night." Well, that's better! God bless the ladies, say I, as Mr. Bruff conspicuously did not. If they had what it took to sing, let them by all means. In the night eleven mules decamped and a man died of a fit. We hope that it had nothing to do with the singing, but, again, we'll never know.

The traffic emerged from the lake bed where it pleased and camped just as independently, but it finally wove itself into one line of traffic going north along the base of the Sierra. From the spot where the wagons first struck the mountains to the place where they ceased to go north and turned up toward the pass was variously estimated as five or six miles.

The first steep slope is quite bare. The upgrade is two miles, I am told, and part way is a spring that served in trail days as an emergency camp for those who came to grief on the up-pull. It is on a sort of rounded shelf and may have an acre or so of flat footing for the camps. Rich growth covers the ground and looks like a deep-napped grayish-green broadloom carpet. Shade is furnished by cushiony junipers. The oval basin of the spring is as big as many a swimming pool, but with scarcely any forage for the animals. Just above it, in a hollow, is the grave of John A. Dawson of St. Louis, who died from eating a poisonous root at the spring. Evidently in trying to find some cure for the scurvy that was slowly killing him, John succeeded only in speeding up his fate. I know the grave is there because Bruff said so, but we found no sign of it.

It was part way up the two-mile ascent that Alonzo Delano outdistanced his friends and stood alone at the foot of a precipitous cliff to admire its height. Fortunately, after having stood quietly for a moment, he suddenly changed position, and a whizzing arrow clipped the front of his coat. Two naked Indians, having unexpectedly failed to incapacitate their victim, leaped frantically for safety behind the rock, but not before he had sent a shot to speed them along. The rifle report, reverberating and rolling like thunder among the rocks, brought his companions running. Cautiously they investigated and found bloodstains but no Indians. The incident rates just one paragraph a trifle longer, perhaps, than the one Mr. Delano devotes to a description of the "species of nectarine, growing on dwarf bushes," and the "abundance of wild, black cherries—not very good" that grew on the mountain slope.

Above the spring the emigrants stopped and doubled teams; for three-quarters of a mile the trail is so steep that we, at first, refused to credit it and spent several hours looking for a more likely location. Henry Minton wrote late in life of his 1849 crossing of Lassen Pass: "—we struck the main chain of Sierra Nevada Mountains. We came to a spring and camped that night. Then we started next morning and had to double team to get up the mountain which was something over a half mile and which you might call straight up and down. It took five or six yoke of cattle to pull a wagon up. We got up and started down, we had barely room on top for the wagons to stand to start down, the mountains being so steep the cattle could hardly step a'tall but just had to shove their feet along."

The last two hundred yards of this pitch up to the summit is one of the most elemental phases of the whole trail. Here is no playing of favorites, no privacy, no comfort for the sick, no time to die. An old man on a jaded horse, mattress and coverlet under him and a blanket over, lies flat and clings around the neck of the climbing, lunging beast; little boys lead extra animals; tired women scramble behind the wagons in the flying dirt, chucking the wheels with rocks and stumps of wood. A man walking in the blinding, choking dust to urge his team along is seen in fragmentary glimpses to have a tiny baby in his arms. A fever-and-ague victim, shaking violently in the saddle, rides a faithful old mule; both are almost obscured by a blue blanket. A chain breaks and a great wagon comes crashing back down the mountain, dragging the wheel oxen. A favorite ox drops on his knees to die across the very path of the wagons; he is un-hooked, and the owner throws his own coat over the back of the willing beast to show that he is owned and is not yet dead; but he himself, with the rest of his team, must perforce keep climbing. To no avail. The ascending line of struggling, gasping animals and lurch-ing wagons cannot turn aside. When the owner returns, his ox is dead indeed, and the migration is proceeding west over his quiet body.

Heartsick, he turns again to climb the swarming hill and, looking up, sees Old Glory flying at the top as some discerning soul envisions that its gaining is indeed a victory and sets the colors whipping in the clear clean breeze to encourage those below.

CHAPTER XIII

The Evils of the Pit

EARLY on a warm morning—it was July 1—we came to the bird-haunted eastern shore of Goose Lake. We had seen it before, from the top of Lassen Pass, its pale, widespread waters gleaming faintly about ten miles away.

They were ten exciting miles for the pioneers, although, as far as physical well-being was concerned, they were shady, well watered, and comfortable. The wagons creaked and groaned along the bumpy south edge of a long grassy valley through which Willow Creek flows west; past Massacre Spring, whose name does not belie it; through a series of low rocky rises densely forested; and then, breaking free from the trees into open country, crawled down a steep bluff, with the great brackish lake covered with water fowl stretched before them.

We had opened and closed decrepit and stubborn gates, walked to lighten the car over ancient bridges, passed deserted Upper Fandango Mill, and propped up a fence that fell down when I leaned against it. I was a little fed up with nature, once improved and then left to rot. The fair road and the open lake looked good to me.

It was a relief, also, to the women of the migration in October, 1849, to find themselves clear of the confining forests and rocks that had encompassed them since starting up the pass, for Indians were everywhere. At night, signal fires blazed warningly on the peaks, and a crawling uneasiness pervaded the caravans. Each new camp was visited at once by some man whose wagons were placed and whose stock already was grazing. Mysteriously, he and the man or men in charge disappeared from the women's sight while he whispered the shattering information that the Indians had commenced a far more effective warfare than the raids so far experienced and had turned their small but vicious dogs of war against the overpowering largeness of a more or less benign civilization.

They had, it was said, ambushed and attacked a government party

under the command of Captain W. H. Warner. The emigrants didn't
know just where it had happened (which made it worse, if anything),
but knew that it was near Goose Lake. Captain Warner, it seemed,
had been riding in the lead with his guide, and the two had received
the bulk of the arrows. The guide remained mounted for a time, so
rumor pronounced, while Warner, pincushioned with darts, had been
carried part way up a gulch by his frantic horse and there thrown to
the ground—dead, it was hoped. Two others were wounded but not
unhorsed, though savoring the taste of their own blood, and were
able to ride to safety with the remainder of the party, who owed
their lives to the vainglorious desire of each Indian to kill the "chief."
Captain Warner's body had received enough arrows to have wiped
out the whole detachment. Rumor also stated (and this later proved
true) that the attack had occurred east and north of the Lassen Pass,
in which case the offending natives *might* have been the Pah-Utes, a
relatively peaceful race; but the whispering men feared that the speed
and decision of the attack indicated the obdurate and intractable
Modocs from the north, whose hunting grounds were in the mountains bordering Goose Lake. Time was not to solve this question,
as the offenders were never taken. Meanwhile, sporadic attacks continued.

In the hectic migration of 1849, there were but few Oregon-bound
travelers, and they must have felt a great weight of apprehension
settle down as they journeyed southward along the edge of Goose
Lake; for, as soon as the southern water line was reached, they were
to leave their gold-seeking friends, turn west across the dried mud
of the lake bed, and, on the far side, turn north again toward
Oregon. They would then be very much alone. The plodding caravans
skirted the water's edge as closely as they dared. It was a dry summer
in the Sierra in 1849, and the lake had greatly receded. The wheels
cut through the dried alkaline crust and pulled up a dark mud that
left a sort of tattoo mark, much as did the Donner wagons on the
Salt Desert. Then, as winter came, the waters covered it again. Of
late years it has not been uncovered often. Once in a long while, in
a dry year, the lake shrinks back and exposes the dark stain of the
Applegate Road. We are fortunate enough to own a fine photograph
that shows it plainly. The lake edge did not make an attractive camp.
The beach was white with saleratus and let the investigating men
sink to their knees in a pale gray muck. It was "a perfect quagmire."

The nauseous water was descended from various ancestries, predominantly salt and soda, and featured the worst characteristics of each.

I was riding with my head out of the window, looking ahead for a suitable elevation from which to take some pictures, and a particularly rough road threatened every moment to knock my teeth in on the window ledge; but I persisted, because it takes time, I have found, to have the car stopped. If I don't start to ask at least half a mile in advance, I have that far to walk back. Cars can't be stopped on curves, or on soft shoulders, or on narrow stretches, or on the upslope of a hill where some careless driver might come over the top too fast. In fact, cars can hardly be stopped at all unless it is to look for a likely riffle in a fishing stream. I saw a good place coming and, getting my teeth safely within the car, loudly demanded to get out.

For once I had estimated correctly. It took about a quarter of a mile, and we pulled to a groaning stop at exactly the right place.

The minute I emerged from the car, six or eight cows ambled out of the shrubbery and came over to help; but at least these were California milch cows, genteel and respectable, and not the half-wild stock of Nevada. Bill, knowing my noninterest in the near presence of cattle, got out and stood beside me while the sweet-breathed Jersey bossies shoved one another around in the effort to get both protruding soft brown eyes focused on us at once. One, braver than the rest, put out a long tongue tentatively toward the leather camera case, and Bill shooed her away. The rest of the men were on the far side of the road against a low bluff where Mr. Bromley, as pleased as a Scotchman with a piggy-bank, had evidently found a fascinating new type of mud. The lake proved to be high, and there was no sign of the old tattooed trail. Well, at least I had tried. When we got back to the car, we found the shooed cow retaliating by chewing the tightly fitting wristband of Dr. Neff's discarded leather jacket, which evidently contained enough salt to make it an entertaining substitute for her cud.

I found later, by talking to a Mr. Clark whom we met near by, that the wagons had proceeded down along the lake edge—not up on the high land where the county road now goes—and that the Applegate Trail turned off about where I took my picture, crossing the lake bed to strike the mouth of Mud Creek just beyond McGinty Point on the west side.

We passed through the town of Davis Creek, with its dignified old houses, and approached the south end of the lake, crossing, as we did so, several small streams. Almost all of the diarists of 1849 mention the cold, clear brooks which, together with the fresh-water springs along the edge of the lake, keep a quantity of fine grass growing beside its alkaline waters.

Captain Warner had been killed only a few days when Bruff arrived at Goose Lake and heard that one of the wounded men of Warner's party was a few miles ahead and in the charge of a noncommissioned officer. As soon as was possible, he hurried on in advance of his company, for Captain Warner had been a personal friend and he was eager for details. On one of the west-flowing creeks hurrying to drown themselves forever in the brackish basin of Goose Lake, he found a notice nailed to a tree. It had been drawn up by the company under Captain Warner's command and was signed by his lieutenant, R. S. Williamson. Its message was only for the California migration; therefore it had been posted beyond the split in the road. Hurried as Bruff undoubtedly was, he stopped to take a copy:

Lieut. Williamson's Top. Eng. Card.

	m.
From here, to where road leaves Pitt R.	78
To valley, with water & grass ½ m. beyond	
" where road crosses a brook	13
To Sp. of water, on right of road, grass in wood close to	12
" Valley with springs & grass 12 Oct.	14
" Lake, a mile to left of road	11
" Water & grass 1 m. east of road	13
" E. br. of Feather Riv. grass ½ m. up stream	6
" Next grass & water, very miry bad road (7)	6
" Where there is grass & water for	5
" Butte Creek (cut at end) grass	6
" Where there is grass & water, for	10
" Last water on the road	15
To Crossg of Deer Ck in Sacramento Valley	36
" Lassin's House	3
	‾‾‾
(24 ms. to cut grass, on Feather River)	225 (228
(6 m. lake & br. (brook?) Grass 2 m. down	
From Lassin's to nearest Diggings	40
From " " Sutter's Fort	115
" Sutter's Fort to Sacramento City	3
" Sacramento City to Sⁿ Francisco	100

When the road leaves Pitt Riv, it passes over the hills, and is very rough for 20 ms. Mr. Lassen recommends keeping to the left, & going around these hills, over a longer, but smoother road. With the above exception, the road is generally good, except for the last 40 ms. where it is very rough and hilly.

During this 40 miles, the road follows down a ridge, through a pine forest, & descends 5000 feet. Water may be found by going a mile or 2 down a steep hill on left of road; no grass. Recruit animals and cut grass, in the 10 m. valley. After striking Butte Creek (gone) (go on) this side. Beef at Lassen's is $50 a head, and Flour $50 pr hundred.

Plenty of provisions & clothing in Sacramento City, & cheap. Pork $35 pr. bbl. & flour $10 pr. hund^d Coffee 20¢. Sugar 15¢. In the mines provisions may be bought at prices the same, or higher than at Lassen's.

(signed)
R. S. WILLIAMSON
Lt. U.S. Army

Captain Warner's expedition had been a railroad survey. He was to find out if the lower crossing of the Sierra Nevada, which was the big drawing point of the Lassen Cutoff, would make a suitable railroad grade. Already the population of California was worrying about the possibility of railroad communication across the great chain of mountains that hedged them in on the east. It was exactly twenty years before their dream became a reality, and then the railroad followed the route of old Greenwood—up the Truckee River. The confused and angry emigrants were not Warner's business, but someone in the expedition had taken time to prepare this much needed information and leave it where it would do the most good.

Fifteen miles beyond the sign, or almost to the canyon of Upper Pit River, Bruff found the wounded man in camp. From him he learned that his friend Warner had been slain with eleven arrows through legs, body, thighs, and head—especially through the mouth and jaws. The accuracy of the Indians' aim was terrifying. As the company retreated, the savages had been seen wreaking their obscene vengeance upon the corpse, cutting and defiling the body. Bruff rejoined his company and, heartsick, moved on with them over low rocky spurs.

The Pit River Indians continued rapacious. In 1850 very few emigrants took the route along Pit River; but some, for reasons of their own, braved its many disadvantages. A quick sortie netted twenty-seven mules from one wagon train, and the emigrants were compelled to leave their wagons and possessions and proceed as best they could. "One gentleman told me," wrote Delano, "that he walked three days without a mouthful of food, leaving three companions, who fell exhausted in the road, one day's journey from Lawson's ranch. Supplies were sent back, and they were rescued. Another company of seven men were surrounded by a band of two hundred Indians, stripped of their clothing, and driven into the river, when they were assaulted by a murderous discharge of arrows. The whites had but a single gun, with which they dared not commence any defence, hoping after being robbed the Indians would spare their lives. Six of them were killed, and the seventh badly wounded, when providentially two men, who were hunting along the river, unconscious of the horrid butchery going on near them, discharged their pieces at some ducks. This alarmed the Indians, who thought a force was at hand, and they fled precipitately. The wounded man crawled out of the river, and being discovered, was taken to their train, and eventually recovered from his wounds."

We crossed another of the creeks (I have never counted them) and could see that we were approaching the rugged rimrocked canyon that conveys Upper Pit River to its junction with the South Pit. This is exceedingly broken country, sage covered and full of thistles. Here desert juniper meets the more rugged and picturesque mountain variety, which lives, they say, many hundred years and is one of the most picturesque of trees.

The travelers crossed, or skirted, the headwaters of the Upper Pit River and passed to the right of its canyon. Many of the wagons nooned at what is known as Emigrant Springs. (I can't help it—they *will* name things "Emigrant.") We found the springs on a rough lava-strewn plateau beyond Round Mountain. Great-trunked mountain junipers hovered henlike over small fat desert junipers; a few yellow daisies starred the sage. The springs were roughly oval and flowed together, flung any old how, like links of sausage, among the black, round lava rocks, which were perforated but heavy. Much of the water was a weird yellow-white and uninviting, with short reeds spearing through. It seeped slowly from one pool to another. The trail went squarely through them, crossing the rivulet from the last spring.

In the flat near Alturas, the main Pit River flows between cushiony banks where plump willows drag their hula skirts in the water. The trail strikes it approximately at the confluence of Rattlesnake Creek, and the wagons moved along with the river.

The Pit came by its name naturally, because of the habits of its first families, who lived in pits dug in the earth and covered with sod supported by crosspoles. P. B. Reading, who came through a portion of the Pit River country in 1843 with the Chiles Party, described the underground homes as having only one opening, which served as both door and chimney.

The pit dwellers seemed to be satisfied with their building program, but I can't help saying that they rather ran it into the ground. They also dug pits to facilitate the capture of big game, placing them fairly in the middle of the paths and animal runs. Reading called them about nine feet deep, undercut, and with small openings. A grizzly was far too dangerous under ordinary conditions to molest with arrows, but it became an easy prey at the bottom of such a trap.

The Reading-Chiles Party remained continually on the alert, for the openings were cleverly hidden under weeds and grass. Milton McGee, walking ahead of the pack train, suddenly dropped out of sight and had to be assisted from the pit in which he suddenly, and without the least warning, found himself. As I mentioned before, it has occurred to me that this man might be the "Magee" who, six years later, spearheaded the column of Forty-niners on the new road leading through this same country. This seems especially likely because Israel Hale wrote before leaving the Humboldt that some of the emigrants were taking the route (Lassen's Cutoff) *discovered by Mr. Childs* (Chiles), and that two mountaineers, Hudspeth and Myers, had also decided to take it. The latter fact was instrumental in deciding Hale's company to go that way.

In the "Valley of Pit River," near Alturas, many of the Forty-niners met the relief company from California. It was authorized by General Persifor Smith, willingly seconded by General Riley, and was sent at government expense. The officer in charge of supplies and *modus operandi* was Major Daniel H. Rucker. The man who was left in the mountains to rescue the almost pathetically helpless stragglers was John H. Peoples, and to him, personally, many owed their lives.

The expedition had pack mules loaded with flour and provisions and drove "meat oxen" to be butchered for the use of destitute emigrants. It was not adequate for the hundreds who needed help but, even so, it was of inestimable value and saved many. Not at the moment, perhaps—no one was reduced to starvation along the Pit— but later, when the storms caught them in the lower mountains, the assistance received ahead of the time of greatest necessity counted as a great boon. Some, sick and stranded without animals, would have died beside the road except for Peoples. And some, beyond assistance, died anyway.

From Alturas to Canby is more west than south, and the river is quite easy to reach at any time, the trail keeping mainly to the southeast bank. The river was forded if and when the company captains thought best—usually twice. Below Canby the Pit enters a canyon, and the trail betakes itself to the northwest side. The main ford was near the present Canby bridge. Bruff writes, in his abbreviated style, "Then S. To base of mounts where, at a bend of stream —to the N.W. we crossed." This is plain on any map, something that cannot be said for very many diarists' descriptions.

It was evident that, to see the trail, we should keep with the river; but away it went into a canyon, and there we sat, with 120 horsepower ready and willing to go if we would provide some sort of a road.

Much driving back and forth along the highway only elicited the information that the bridge over the Pit on the Stone Coal Valley road was out. Apparently, had it been in working order, it would have taken us across the Pit about midway of the canyon in which we were interested, and which extends roughly from Canby to Lookout. There was nothing to do but to tackle the proposition from the south end, which we immediately did.

At Lookout we crossed the Pit uneventfully on a proper bridge and went to the main store to see Mr. Loomis. He was a boon to us, knowing his river for miles in each direction—and with reason, for his father, who came to California by sea in 1846, had died fairly young and left his mother running a station for freighters in the vicinity. The men who ate at her table had driven the great wagons and trailers to Alturas and to Klamath, and common conversation concerned the state of the river and the road. He was brought up on it. According to Mr. Loomis, we would find the nearest emigrant ford a few miles up from the south end of Pit Canyon in a narrow spot called, in all seriousness, Gouger's Neck. There we were to ask anyone we happened to see for Munroe Shaw, who, Mr. Loomis was sure, would take over from there.

We found the farm. It was a lovely place with long fields sloping to the river and every uncultivated spot thick with wild roses in full bloom and short wild sunflowers; but there was no house. After we had located the family—Mr. Shaw with his son in the field and Mrs. Shaw with Jane getting lunch in a sort of camp—we found that their home had burned the week before. On their return from laying in supplies at Lookout, it was gone. Short of sickness and death, I can hardly imagine a more devastating experience; but they were entirely cheerful and, after explaining the reason for house-keeping in a cabin and under the trees, said no more about it.

Both Rebeccah and Munroe Shaw are too young to have any personal knowledge of trail lore, but he has lived on the trail many years and she is a teacher interested, as it happens, in things historical near at home. They immediately took an intense and personal partisanship in our struggle against adverse circumstances to get up the canyon.

"You'll have an early lunch with us, because I have to give Mr. Shaw and Bob something to eat before I can leave, and then we'll take the pick-up truck. You can't get your car very far beyond our ranch." Thus Mrs. Shaw as she competently put on the teakettle.

We worked together without waste effort, pooling our lunches and eating under the trees on a camp table while the men found out from Mr. Shaw the salient characteristics of the canyon and I wrote them down in my notebook, which is spotted to this day with a buttery thumbprint and a small blotch of coffee. Then we gassed and watered the little truck, left Pepper in our car, and started out with Mrs. Shaw at the wheel and three of the men standing with Jane in the rear. Mrs. Shaw was used to the truck and to the road and had no intention of letting either of these two inanimate and unimportant things defeat her purpose. We rocked like an empty scow in a gale; everything I reached for evaded me; and I could hear the men laughing and cheering her as they hung on behind the cab. Nothing pleases me so much as to arrive, preferably intact, at a desired spot which I have been told is unattainable. This was almost too good to be true.

In an hour we came to the condemned bridge which would take us eastward across the river into Stone Coal Valley. As that was our farthest point upstream, I will begin there to connect with the trail, which was, at the moment, up in the hills to the west. The canyon had widened into a broad bottom sloping up to gentle mountains and forested with yellow pines of medium size, while the center had some grass and a good deal of velvety sage. The flat-banked river was easily accessible for stock, but the rushing little torrent was clotted with great boulders, and, immediately under the bridge, it was narrow and swift.

"You are sure that the trail is along the right-hand side of the river here?" I asked Mrs. Shaw as we all got out to have a look.

"Yes, you can still see it in spots."

"Some very well informed authorities have said that it went through Stone Coal Valley," I told her. "Probably Lassen brought the first wagons that way and it wasn't used afterward."

"I have never heard of anything like that, but we can go over into the valley and ask the Shearer family, who have lived there for three generations. They ought to know."

A sign at the far end of the planking said: BRIDGE UNSAFE—LIGHT VEHICLES ONLY. "This is a light truck," she remarked. "Here we go."

The old bed of the bridge was broken and uneven, and none of us cared to look underneath; but it considerately maintained its integrity and we arrived on the east side, where a well used roadbed indicated that the farmers of Stone Coal Valley paid no attention to its supposed state of decrepitude. We went to the Ralph Shearer place for information.

"No," said Ralph Shearer's son Robert, "the trail goes west of the river."

"Can it be proved?"

"Yes, I should think so. Of course, with us, it's a case of always knowing it was over there. We wouldn't think of trying to prove it."

Mrs. Shaw came to the rescue. "But there are marks over there. I know there are some above the overhanging rock."

"Yes, the wagons were coming down the right bank and came to a place on the Big Bend where a rock jutted out and compressed the river. Sometimes, in low water, they went right down in the current until they got past the bad place; but mainly they had to pull out to the right—a tough pull, too—and go up and over the hills. You can see the scars where the animals dug in, hauling the heavy wagons."

Yes, indeed, in my mind's eye I could. We had seen such places before—above Red Lake on the Placerville Road, for instance. This would not be quite so deadly, because the elevation was lower and the pull shorter. It had been 4,400 feet at Lookout, and I didn't think it could be over 5,000 here. The men were momentarily talking crops, and I snatched a minute to look at my compilation of notes from journals.

Apparently it was every man for himself in the canyon of Pit River. Each wagon master crossed where he thought it best. Delano wrote: "We crossed and recrossed the river at least a dozen times," but he was more interested in the Indian signal fires which kept them on the alert all night, firing their guns and keeping bright fires burning around their cattle. A mile below them and just above the overhanging rock, "the Davis County train" was camped. The sentinels stood guard faithfully during the night, but as the last one turned wearily toward camp after full daylight, an Indian rose from the bushes and shot an ox. He had bided his time for hours, perhaps. Instantly the call went out, and the men, their weariness forgotten, took up the chase. The Indian also was tired from his vigil, and they began to overtake him, at least to come within gunshot. Through the trees and over the rocks went the wild race. The red man threw away two hatchets, a pair of bullet molds, and finally a quiver of arrows and his beloved bow, and they didn't catch him. The wounded ox was killed and divided among the near-by trains.

Sedgley crossed the river seven times within the canyon. McCoy forded seven times also, I noticed; perhaps seven was the regulation number. A man in McCoy's company let his gun slip. It fell below him, struck a rock, and shot him through the body. They camped and, on the next day, he died from his wounds. "Prepare me, Lord," wrote McCoy in his journal, "for whatever awaits me." He had had plenty of time to think of the future, bivouacked as he was in the canyon bottom, with the misery-hardened migrations swarming around and over him, waiting for the man to die.

Bruff went straight down the bed of the river. Yes, that would be right. He was late in the season. October 7th, it was. He wrote: ". . . we reached a point where the road was very narrow, and descended on left rugged and steep; on right a huge rock projected; considerable rocks also in the road.—The 2nd. wagon of my train ran foul of the big rock,—driving the fore wheel under the head, to the great peril of the axle-tree: however we soon extricated & rolled on. The others experienced no extraordinary difficulty."

The conversation had started up again about the Overhanging Rock, and the name brought me back to the present necessity of listening. "Absolutely," Mr. Shearer was saying, "the trail was across the river. The marks are there. I've seen them myself many times, and they're not many miles above the bridge."

"Maybe the low-water trail hit Stone Coal Valley," I suggested, "the one that came down the stream."

"Well, it stands to reason that if a wagon stayed right along the river bed and kept fording, they would be likely to travel along the bank somewhere in the valley; but," he added firmly, "I never heard of it."

"Where did the trail rejoin the river, then, after traveling up in the hills to get around the rock?" I asked.

"Behind Miller's house; it comes down a canyon."

"I can show that to them on the way home," Mrs. Shaw contributed.

And she did. Miller's proved to be a pretty white cottage with a stake and rider fence in front and a swale between the hills behind it, where the slopes were rosy with tasseled June grass bending silkily under the gentle hand of the wind.

"They make hay of it," I heard Jane tell Mr. Bromley as they hung on behind the cab. "It never gets much more than a foot high and it blossoms in June. It never stands up straight either; the heads are too heavy."

"Well, I think it's pretty. Your canyon is beautiful," he told her.

"Yes, Pit River is really quite nice," she agreed quietly, "when you know it."

"Here's Rose Canyon," said Mrs. Shaw after we had traveled a short distance. "This is the place where the pack trail came down from Oregon. From here to Big Valley the Lassen Trail stayed with it more or less—"

"Wait a minute," I begged, "I know I have something about that." As she obligingly stopped, I scanned hastily through my notes and found that Delano, goodness only knows how or why, had expected to pass this junction of the California and Oregon roads and had hoped to be able to buy provisions from teams who might be passing on the other branch. We sat and looked up the unspectacular little canyon sheeted with blue brodiaea, and I read aloud to the interested group: ". . . after passing over the point of a hill, the valley again expanded, and here we came to the junction of the Oregon and California road. From the appearance of the Oregon Fork, no teams had passed since spring, and all hope of further supplies was at once cut off; but we now felt sure that we were within two or three days' travel of the valley of the Sacramento. So strong was this opinion among the emigrants, that after we had encamped in a fine place on the river, a man came along on horseback, and on being invited to stop, he replied, that 'we were within ten miles of the diggings,' and (with an oath) said 'he would not get off his horse till he got to them.' I do not know whether he stuck to his horse all the while, but he did not reach the diggings in ten days."

"Was this the regular Oregon Road," Bill asked Mrs. Shaw, "or just a branch to it from the Lassen Cutoff?"

"It was the regular north and south pack road," she told him. "I'm sure that it had been used for several years by the time the Forty-niners came along."

The little truck rattled on until presently Mrs. Shaw stopped to make herself heard by the men in the back. "I just wanted to show you this rock work banking the lower side of the road. It was done at the order of General Crook, improving the section of the Lassen Cutoff that was used as a military road between Fort Crook and Fort Bidwell. Fort Crook was built in the late fifties in the upper end of Fall River Valley. Fort Bidwell, as you know, is just north of Lassen Pass on the east side of Warner Range. This used to be the Ostrum place, but it belongs to us now." Competently she got under way again and, in a very short distance, we passed Mr. Shaw, still in the same field.

Finding it impossible to get through to the next ford of the Pit, we decided to circle in from the far end, which was in a narrower part of the canyon. Mrs. Shaw turned the truck toward the river on an abandoned logging road and, as she stopped it, we found ourselves in natural rye grass higher than our heads. The river was narrow and glassy, reflecting the massed willow bushes that line the banks; but there was one spot where a few rocks showed beneath the current and a sparkle or two indicated that the smooth flow of deep water was broken. This, for most of the travelers, was the last ford of the Pit. The wagons took the water opposite the upper end of a ragged lava escarpment that hems in the western side of the bottoms. Mrs. Shaw said that they would be able to ford there later in the season with the truck.

The Pit is a peculiar river, a mountain stream and flowing through well watered country; yet it doesn't seem to grow any larger, but is really only a creek when it enters Big Valley below the Shaw ranch.

"Delano gives a good working description of this ford," I commented. "He mentions the long grass and the traprock, and that they tore their clothes on the willow and plum bushes."

"There are several more interesting points," said my husband, who had read the quotation over my shoulder. "See, they met a mule train *returning* from California to Oregon. The train had come down and was going back. This *was* the regular Oregon road."

"Yes, I think we can grant that," agreed Mrs. Shaw.

"Then, see here—the word 'Lawson.' People who didn't see Lassen's name written, but only heard it pronounced, were apt to spell it that way. There isn't much doubt that he pronounced it as if the first *s* were a *w*."

"That's common knowledge up in this part of the country," she said as we climbed into the truck again, "but then he was one of our local celebrities, and anything about him interests us."

Back at the Shaws' temporary camp we had to make up with Pepper, who felt aggrieved at being left behind, and to promise the Shaws that we would come again and see their new house—a promise which we kept this year.

Pit River Canyon was one of the salient features of a road filled with odd and unforgettable characteristics. It was remembered as a hodge-podge of unrelated incidents—happenings and crises in the lives of unrelated people whom fate had poured together through the funnel of the river bottom—a composite picture: Here a rider samples, with a wry face, a root to help his scurvy; there a woman milks a seemingly indestructible cow who is her main dependence for her babies. Here is a comfortable camp (or would be if they had a sufficient diet) placed by the side of the pretty little stream. The animals are grazing under guard, for to one side are the remains of a small fire not built by white men, with the shells of roasted mussels and part of "a wicker scoop" with which they were obtained; the carcass of a dead wolf lies close by. Here a heavy train heaves and groans out of the river bottom, struggling to surmount the rise that lies just ahead. Several dead oxen cut loose from harness lie here and there— the worried men have counted ten of them, and now a mule is down in the water and "near perishing." Here men take time from their own affairs to rebury a body. It has been dug up by patient wolves who make stealthy forays and work when and how they can between the passing of companies, making the dirt fly like dogs after gophers and leaving burrows down into the poor shallow grave. Large scraps of colored cloth have been exhumed to float off gaily with the breeze. Here a man bends over moccasin prints made when the frightened native fled through the brush at the coming of the first wagons. There a man takes the saddle from his exhausted mule, thrusts his rifle through a strap, and shoulders the combined load; he hopes possibly to buy a mount from someone who is abandoning a wagon. At a low-banked spot the animals are drinking, and the men exchange the will-o'-the-wisp gossip of the trail that comes from God knows where and runs up and down the length of the weary procession like wildfire. A Digger village is near, says rumor, with several hundred fighting men—mounted too, on animals stolen from the emigrants. It would be ahead, near the mouth of the canyon and to the left of the road; the danger is yet to be faced. But the harassed men are not too anxious nor too tired to cast a few side glances at a passing family wagon beautified with the presence of some attractive young females.

Between the Shaw Ranch and Lookout the canyon opened into the wide and cultivated miles of Big Valley, the trail meandering along the river for five miles while the cattle scattered to enjoy the splendid grass—always under heavy guard, of course. The emigrants were still along the river at the site of modern Bieber, the main settlement of the valley.

We drove up to the hotel late in the afternoon and bespoke two "suites" of rooms. This luxury opened off a porch where the most terrific clatter was going on. I opened the connecting door and stuck my head out.

An energetic little woman, whom we later found to be the proprietor's wife, was taking a piano to pieces. I have never seen anything more completely disemboweled. She had left the wires, but the felts were scattered with a reckless hand and ivory keys were all over the place.

"No use having a piano if it won't work," she announced, digging vigorously into its vital organs. "See, here's a mouse nest. That didn't do it any good."

We gathered that they had recently acquired the place and that this was House Cleaning with capitals.

"No, I don't suppose it did," I told her, "but you're a better man than I be. Do you think you can get it together again?"

"I hope so," was her restrained reply, and we left her with a hammer and a cold chisel, looking fixedly at the next object selected for removal.

"That's going to be an unmusical instrument when she gets through," Bill commented as we started down the sidewalk. "What'll you bet she has some keys left over?"

"No takers," said Dr. Neff, who is a realist.

But Mr. Bromley is a large and kindly man. "She looked like a determined little lady," said he. "I think maybe I'll bet the cigars on her." The noise of enthusiastic pounding followed us as we went to find the old ford just below the bridge.

On the way back we were shown an interesting sort of landmark by the proprietor of the hotel. I have never seen anything just like it. On the side wall of the post-office building, away from the street and passers-by, is a vague and shadowy sign: CHALK FORD.

"That was the original name of the settlement," Mr. Keene told us. "The ford you just saw is where the wagons crossed the Pit on a chalk ledge. It wasn't so soft nor so muddy as other places. It got the name Bieber later from a man who ran a trading post at the crossing."

"The sign on the post office dates from before his time?" I asked rather stupidly. It was self-evident.

"Yes, and this side of the building was out in the open then. You can see that the letters aren't formed with paint, for the house is painted uniformly all over."

"They look just a little bit raised," said Bill, stepping close to the wall to catch the side light. "They don't seem to be carved, but they're in relief."

"You're right. That's just what they are," he agreed. "For years and years that sign was kept painted on the side of the unpainted building. The paint preserved the lettering, but the rest of the building was weatherworn until the boards actually lost maybe a sixteenth of an inch of their surface. The only way to get the old name off that post office is to take it off with a plane."

"Which I sincerely hope they'd never do," my husband said quickly. "Too many things like that are disappearing year by year. You tell the people here in Bieber to hang onto that sign."

Back at the hotel the clatter on the porch continued. Quite a monumental noise it was, and I opened the connecting door again. Here was our ambitious little proprietress complete with hammer and glue, still hovering over the piano. It looked all right. The keys were in—something I would never have believed if my own eyes hadn't seen it—and it seemed in working order except for the pedal. Bill, always interested where pianos were concerned, investigated until he found the trouble. "Something is lost out of here," he announced.

Dr. Neff joined him under the piano, shoving to one side the hairpins, election cards, pieces of dry cake, and other foreign bodies that had been removed from its torso.

"Just a block, that's all it needs," he diagnosed. "We can make one of wood and glue it on." Which the two of them proceeded to do.

"Any woman," said the doctor, "who can take a piano apart and put it together again should have a little help when she needs it."

He bought the cigars, too.

Beyond the town, we drove the length of Big Valley, very much as did the prairie schooners. Never, never have I seen so many split-rail fences as there are in Big Valley and its environs. In the center of the valley is a mill with a log pond and the attendant lumber piles, although no timber was to be seen except on the surrounding hills. In the pond the logs lay straightly, side by side, a giant xylophone, hammered upon by little men who hopped nimbly from one to another. Much closer to us, on a platform under an umbrellalike roof, was a woman apparently filling the duties of a sawyer.

For about eight miles we drove down the valley. As the river swung to the right, the wagons had saved time by leaving it and cutting across, only touching it a couple of times in twenty miles. On the edge of both the river and the trail, in the midst of the flatland, was the grave of Samuel McFarlin, aged forty-four years; and beneath his name some embittered friend or relative had inscribed: "May he rest peaceably in this savage unknown country."

At the foot of Big Valley, Pit River enters another rocky canyon—impassable this time—and within the canyon makes an elbowlike curve back on its tracks and flows north. To some of the emigrants this elbow was reminiscent of the bend of Bear River near Soda Springs in what is now Idaho.

At the entrance to the canyon, on the Thompson Ranch, the trail split. The fork that goes up into the hills is well known. The right-hand fork that fords Pit River just above the railroad bridge and leads into the rocky land within the elbow of the river has been forgotten. We acquired our slight knowledge of it by reading the diaries of the men who took it; and also by reading the comments on its departure from, and return to, the regular hill trail in the journals of men who did not take it. Jewett and Foster were two who forded the river.

Mr. Thompson was glad to tell us about the one that took to the hills and was a shorter, but a much steeper, road. "Come out in front of the house and I'll show you," he directed.

A hill like a crouching dog's back left the river just before that meandering stream entered the canyon. The emigrants, true to their penchant for remaining on top of any convenient geographical protrusion to avoid Indian ambush and unnecessary creek crossing, had proceeded right up the backbone of this low hill.

"It extends too far east for them," I made a guess. "Where did they leave it?"

"If we were looking at a line of wagons," Mr. Thompson pointed, "pulling up that sloping hogback, they would turn to the right and duck out of sight down the other side of the hill just opposite that gulch that runs up between the house and the river—the one with the windmill in it."

"Bruff went that way, then," I interpreted from my notes, "and Delano and McCoy too. Bruff will tell us all about it. You can depend on him."

Later I looked it up: "We reached the end of Pit valley here," said Bruff, "the hills enclose it in gorges and canons now for some distance, and we have our choice of ascending a very steep hill close by, or crossing the stream, pass through a short narrow vale, and turn left—joining the other road, to proceed along through the mountains." Then, the next morning, he wrote: "I submitted the roads to the Company, pointing out the hill-road as the most rugged, and the shortest, while the ford road was the longest and smoothest; probably a couple of miles difference. They desired to take the former one, so on we went for it."

"I imagine the trail that forded the river must have gone right across the elbow," said Mr. Bromley, "and forded the stream again as it flows north. That would have brought them out somewhere south of Pittville, wouldn't it?"

"It seems to make sense," Dr. Neff admitted. And that's what we later found that it did.

And so, at the foot of Big Valley, we had to face that disquieting and recurrent crisis of the trail—a choice of unknown roads—just as every captain of every emigrant train had had to do since the first adventurous wagon wandered from the accepted trail to leave wheel tracks on an alternate route.

———

CHAPTER XIV

Devious Ways

THE country is forested and rough between the elbow of the Pit and Black Mountain. The lines of prairie schooners left but little impression upon it, and if one were uninformed in regard to the alternate trail, the whole thing would be most confusing.

On second thought, the whole thing is most confusing anyway.

However, we do have a few facts to guide us. Let us take first the hill, or short road, starting from the Thompson Ranch. It was traveled by Delano, McCoy, Howell, Hale, Bruff, and others, and from their journals we can gather a few morsels of information. Its travelers stormed the mountains at once and, having gained the high ground, more or less paralleled the Pit River as it flows toward the elbow where it turns north again. At the summit of the first mountain an inspiring view rewarded those who took time to wonder and admire. Bruff stood on the elevation and caught his first glimpse of Mount Shasta and Mount Lassen, which he termed Tschastes and Snow Butte. Both were white against a bright autumn sky and filled his troubled spirit with enthusiasm.

From part way down the next slope he could look to his right and see the vertical, rugged walls of Pit River Canyon cut from lava formation, and the forbidding, rock-strewn tableland that rises within the angle of its abrupt turn and ends in a snub-nosed, precipitous bluff at the elbow.

Much of the country here is so rocky that postholes cannot be dug properly, and the small telephone poles have to be held more or less upright by stones piled into triangular wooden frameworks around the bases. There are dingy canyons, dirty sage flats, hillsides draped with soiled aprons of juniper and then a transition stage of small yellow pine leading down to a rolling flat of scrub oak and lava rocks.

The wagons watered at Bloody Spring at the lower end of Spring Gulch.

Tradition has it that a whole wagon train was massacred here with the inevitable exception of the sole survivor, who escaped into the precipitous Pit River Canyon and made his way to Fort Crook. The elated Indians had no time to look him up. The wagon train was rich and the loot was interesting.

The wealth of the company is said to have been in $20 gold pieces, probably sewn in money belts. The Indians garnered the gold pieces carefully and took them to the canyon edge. They were a real find, and the strong men of the tribe got ready for competition. Never before had they had missiles of exactly the same size and shape. They lined up carefully to see which man could throw them across the Pit River gorge. When all the money was either in the river or in the almost inaccessible rocks, the warriors collected at the junipers on Horse Creek and had a sociable little war dance. Here they were found by the soldiers from Fort Crook and (in correct Western parlance) "eighty redskins bit the dust."

From Bloody Spring the hill trail passed through Clark's Valley and then, after three and a half miles more, to Little Dixie Valley— now called simply Little Valley and occupied by Bognuda's mill. The wagons came down the hill and with difficulty crossed Horse Creek where the mill now stands.

Some of these data, including that of the Bloody Spring Massacre, we obtained from Mr. Bognuda himself, who ushered us into his private bar in order to converse more pleasantly. "Private bar" in this case doesn't mean a small counter with two chromium-legged stools in the rumpus room. It was a full-sized building, adjoining and opening into the Bognuda Club, which was itself a busy bar, running at full speed and full of thirsty loggers. Our private accommodation was innocent of any furniture but the bar itself and, on a large sign outside the building, it was appropriately labeled "The Empty Holster." Under the lonely bar was Mr. Bognuda's excellent stock of liquor, and the ice was brought in from the club in a large wooden chopping bowl.

We asked him about the alternate trail which forded the Pit at the Thompson Ranch. It was, he observed thoughtfully, quite possible that part of the emigrants forded, but they would have had to traverse the tongue of land within the elbow almost due west (or straight across). The canyon, he said, becomes too rough, precipitous, and deep for fording as it nears the point.

No matter which way the emigrants chose, they regretted it, but actually the hill road was the more difficult, the steep, stony pitch down into Horse Creek being the hardest on vehicles.

We found Bognuda's sawmill right at the old ford of Horse Creek. A busy community hummed in its vicinity: store, lumbermen's club, dining room. We were permitted to eat lunch with the millhands and all sat, family style, at a big table. My place was opposite the superintendent and, between the lot of us, we threshed out some puzzling questions. The portly chef, who looked as if he enjoyed his own cooking, had produced a splendid meal: shaved raw potatoes fried and browned in a huge pancake, pork slices hidden in steaming gravy, potato salad with pickles carved into fantastic shapes garnishing the top, big deep-dishes of hot vegetables, and spiced pudding with a sauce to pour.

"Which way will you go from here?" asked one of the millhands.

"South," said Bill, between mouthfuls of crisp potato, "about six miles down to Schroder Lake."

"We're trying to find where the two trails that separated on the Thompson Ranch come together again," my husband told him and explained in some detail to those near enough to listen.

"Don't know anything about two roads," said the same man, "but one trail went through here, and we know that one went right by the Willow Spring just south of the Eldridge Ranch." And he pointed over his shoulder with a pickle.

"Maybe that's why they never seemed to have any connection," said another, effectually blocking any more conversation with an extremely large spoonful of pudding.

"There's a road that the old-timers say used to be part of the emigrant trail," volunteered a man farther down the table, "and it certainly doesn't seem to hitch with the trail through here; but I don't know whether it's passable for a car. Jake," he called to a man who was quietly cleaning up his plate, "do you know whether the little dirt road from Willow Springs to Eldridge can be traveled?"

Jake didn't know. Nobody knew.

As soon as we were out of sight, we pulled the car off the narrow, dusty road and parked under the shade of an oak to study diaries and other data. One old map, which was made while the trail still existed, showed it extending in broken snatches from Bognuda's south to Schroder Lake. This left the section passing Willow Springs without beginning or end as far as the left-hand, or hill, road from Thompson's Ranch was concerned. But (and it seemed to us an important "but") it connected beautifully with the alternate road which had forded Pit River, crossed the tongue of land in the elbow, and forded for the second time as the river flowed north.

This day's field work, combined with several years' library research in maps and diaries and two subsequent trips over the terrain have practically settled in our minds that the two branches of the trail follow these courses: The hill road left Bognuda's and (quoting Bruff) maintained a southerly course, whence the old map takes it to Schroder Lake and on to Patterson Flat. The right-hand, or ford, road from Thompson's Ranch (which was supposed to be longer but easier) crossed the tongue of land within the elbow, fording Pit River again after a horrible journey where "the rocks lay so thick that the cattle could not get their feet to the ground." After leaving the river, it crossed Beaver Creek and within six miles brought its travelers to good water, probably Willow Springs. Thence it used the forerunner of the little forest road, both rocky and dusty, that leads to Eldridge (not the Eldridge Ranch). Less than a mile north of Eldridge, some of the wagons turned east. A tiny dirt road follows their course. They were headed for Schroder Lake. Whether or not they went the entire distance depended upon whether they were ready to camp or needed water. Schroder Lake was slightly off their road. If they did not need water, they turned south about a mile and a half before reaching the lake and went to the water in Patterson Flat. They met the wagons from the hill road (which had come by way of Bognuda's) where they turned south near the lake, and all went on together, rounding the east side of Black Mountain before coming to Patterson Flat.

I hate to mention this, because it would be much easier if we could keep things simple, but some of the emigrants, not caring at all how confused their course would seem a hundred years later, did not turn east near Eldridge. Apparently many continued south, through what is now Jelly Camp and Hall's Flat, touching Poison Lake, keeping west of Black Mountain and meeting the other road in Bogard's Flat. The large-scale map of Lassen National Forest, issued in 1938 by the U.S. Department of Agriculture, shows parts of the almost obliterated old road that they may have used.

Both Jewett and Bruff made notations to the effect that the two roads had come together again.

Students of the old trails of 1849 are grateful to these two intelligent travelers who wrote daily in their journals all the way from "the States" to "the diggings." If they ever had been too tired to make the usual entries in their diaries, I believe that by this time I should be mentally incapacitated trying to figure out the conflicting data about this little-known segment of the Lassen Cutoff. I even introduce Mr. Jewett and Mr. Bruff with misgiving, deprecating both their (and my) slight knowledge in comparison with that of those who live in the neighborhood and have spent their lives riding over the hills of the Pit River Elbow country. But the two pioneers had one inestimable advantage. They knew exactly what the emigrants were doing each day along the trail and they wrote down some small fraction of their knowledge each night before they had time to forget. We cannot question data written on the spot, at the time. And my husband and I also have one advantage. We can study and compare old maps with new. We can study and compare the journals of the men who came as far as the Thompson Ranch, chose which fork of the trail to take, traveled the one of their choice, and then told about it in their diaries.

More journals surely will come to light; more information no doubt will keep rolling in—some, I hope, by reason of this publication. The beliefs which we have formulated are good. We think that they are facts; but they are tentative and are dependent upon any enlightenment which the future may bring.

*   *   *

It was probably near the crossing of Horse Creek on the Bognuda Ranch that the camps began. Everyone who had taken the hill road stopped somewhere in this valley or the next one south.

Delano arrived quite early in the season, and it was then September 5th. He had been told by a party of packers headed for Oregon that only friendly Indians were found on this stretch of road, but apparently the tribe had changed its collective mind or preferred to pick its friends, for the first thing that greeted his eyes upon arriving at the pretty little camping spot was the remains of five oxen, killed and partly butchered. The Indians had been interrupted beyond doubt, for there was no limit to their appetites and they exercised no nicety of selection. What they ate, they ate thoroughly, to the last scrid. Any portion that could be chewed and swallowed went through that necessary process. Fish were eaten head and all, without cleaning; so was the discarded offal from stock butchered by the emigrants, and cows that had died in calving. Birds, uncleaned and with the feathers still on, were consumed to the last chewable bite; and what couldn't be chewed, such as bones, feathers, and sinews, was pushed aside or spat out. If the consumers had time, they cooked the mess slightly; but they were not overly fussy about it. Delano and his company figured that if anything edible was left, the Indians were not far off; so a strict guard was kept, and no one but the unheeding livestock enjoyed the excellent camp.

Howell came a week later, when, on September 13th, in this same valley, he met the two who have given their names to so many items of topography in the neighborhood, Captain Warner and Peter Lassen. Howell spelled the name "Lawson," indicating the correct pronunciation; but our modern version, with the *a* pronounced as in "apple," probably never will be changed. Captain Warner was in charge of a "corps of U.S. Topographical engineers." Lassen was their guide. At that time Warner—young and vital—had fourteen days to live; Lassen, ten years. Both fell victims to the arrows of the vicious little Indians of the mountains. "From them," wrote Howell, "we have correct information of our whereabouts. The distance we have yet between us and the Sacramento Valley 148 miles and that it is a hard road to travel."

Hale was also in the neighborhood on September 13th, when the Warner Party arrived. "They had among them," Hale wrote, "several invalids, and I sold them one ounce of quinine for twenty dollars." In the official report of the Warner Party it was recorded that, as soon as they struck the mountains, every single man became ill. Apparently some of them had not recovered, and Warner was trying to get recruits from among the emigrants, paying $300 for man and horse per month. Somewhere along the line he was successful, for it was a young emigrant from Missouri who was wounded at the time that Warner was killed.

Many of the emigrants were very bitter toward Lassen and felt that he had willfully misrepresented distances on his new route in order to get the migration to pass his ranch, where he might trade with them at a profit to himself.

Major Haun and his party, who traveled near Bruff for much of the journey west, were of this adverse opinion. Mrs. Catherine Margaret Haun, in her reminiscences written many years later, was still bitter. "On the Humboldt Sink," she wrote, "we were met by agents who had been sent out by Lassen to induce us to go North to his place. Part of our company did so, to our sorrow, as it took us a month longer to reach Sacramento. This was a scheme to sell us provisions and fresh stock, and in this way, it is said, he made a good deal of money."

Bruff, too, made many slurring remarks about Lassen. It is noticeable that the companies who were straggling behind (and so were in distress about the lack of grass and the fact that winter storms were approaching) were the most enraged.

Certainly Howell, upon their pleasant meeting at what is now the Bognuda Ranch, said nothing to indicate that he shared their indignation.

The fact remains that a large percentage of the migration had thought the journey over the mountains to the Sacramento Valley would be a great deal shorter; finding 150 miles of some of the most mountainous country in the United States just where they didn't expect it and where they least wanted it was something of a blow. Israel Hale wrote, "I noticed, some days since, that this was an unknown route to any person on it, and the reports that we hear annoy us greatly. At one time we hear the distance to the mines is not more than twenty miles and perhaps in an hour we will hear it is between two and three hundred. The one will encourage, while the latter will greatly discourage and not a day passes but what we hear similar reports to the above."

I believe that Miss Read and Miss Gaines, in their Critical Notes concerning Bruff's journal, have at least partly solved the mystery. By a series of painstaking comparisons and deductions they have, almost beyond doubt, established that the low estimates of distance can be traced back to a trail guide of the Applegate Road printed in the *Oregon Spectator* of April 6, 1848, under the title "Way Bill from Fort Hall to Willamette Valley." It was signed by Jesse Applegate and was useful enough for the purpose for which it was intended—guiding travelers to Oregon; but at Goose Lake, where the

Lassen Road broke away, was the statement: "Sacramento river (long drive), 20 miles." This was turned loose on a public much given to wishful thinking, and they immediately figured that Goose Lake was twenty miles from the river in the Sacramento Valley which they so greatly wanted to reach.

The statement was not a falsehood. Pit River is still called the Upper Sacramento at times. It was just a painful misapprehension.

And Peter Lassen, who truly *did* advocate the use of his cutoff, was blamed for all the exploded beliefs; but, personally, I do not think that he deliberately falsified distances. The opening of his new route was to him an important individual achievement. It was his contribution to society. He stood back of that road with all his heart.

It just didn't occur to him that the emigrants, not being as travel-wise as he, would suffer and die on its mountainous miles. He couldn't possibly foresee how many of them would come.

Lassen was equally certain that his road would make a wonderful route for a railroad. He talked Warner into taking his expedition that way and went along to guide them. Lieutenant Williamson, who wrote up the report of the survey after Warner's death, said that Warner and his men had made a casual stop at the Lassen Ranch, with no idea of breasting the mountains at that point, but that Lassen had talked so eloquently that they had listened and had gone along with him. By the time that they found the route unpractical, it was too late in the season to try any other way. "The impression produced by Mr. Lassen," wrote Williamson, "as to the character of the road, was decidedly incorrect."

Peter Lassen, Danish-born blacksmith and rancher, and Lansford W. Hastings, brilliant young lawyer, were vastly different in education and background. One used English indifferently; the other was a polished speaker. One was nearly fifty and without social graces; the other, young and popular. But they were strangely alike in their power to persuade and in their failure to anticipate the suffering that came to the inexperienced emigrants as the direct result of following their unasked advice.

Both characters are important to the West. They were wrong on many issues, but it is impossible to ignore them when the history of their portion of the country is being discussed.

So here, near Little Valley, on September 13, 1849, were Lassen, Warner, and an assorted collection of emigrants. Being there was a mistake for all concerned, but as yet a mistake unrecognized, with its roots in the immediate past and its bitter fruits to be borne in the immediate future.

Almost a month went by and along came Bruff. His companions crossed Horse Creek with the usual struggle and property damage and then, turning to the left in about a mile, camped in a bottom with a mountain brook running through it and a quantity of marshy knolls erupting from the flat. The company was still operating as such and a meeting was called here to inflict penalties for neglect of guard duty. It was then October 10th: "Drizzly, with spits of snow." It behooved Mr. Bruff and company to hurry.

*   *   *

Six miles, calculating roughly, took the travelers of the hill road from the camp at Bognuda's to Schroder Lake, and six more placed them at what is now the well in the center of the game refuge at Black Mountain Experimental Forest. The second six had taken them past Black Mountain, which had been the most prominent landmark ahead of them ever since leaving Pit River.

I may be wrong, but I base my belief on my incorrigible habit of crawling into trail journals and insinuating myself between the lines in the pertinent (or impertinent) search for the last scrap of information they contain. In the course of this process I make a chart of camp sites and note similarities.

So, then, to my best judgment it was in the center of the game refuge, some twelve miles from Bognuda's, that Howell overtook the Hudspeth and Myers company. Our old friend Hudspeth again! It's amazing how the mountain men keep turning up here and there in the pages of history; but, as they spent exceedingly energetic lives moving about on more or less beaten paths between the Missouri and the Pacific, the people who traveled those paths were bound to encounter them. They were now on the last lap of their significant journey across the plains in which they had pioneered a new and successful road leading from Soda Springs to Raft River, Idaho (which was known as Hudspeth's or, less frequently, Myers's Cut-off) and had guided one of the first companies on the Lassen Trail.

"Myers, the pilot of Hudspeth's train," wrote Hale, "is the only man that has been in this part of the country before. But this road was not made at that time, consequently he knows nothing of the route of the road." Howell guessed that Myers and Hedspeth (as he spelled it) had been with Frémont on his trip south from Oregon, but neither name appears in Frémont's list of his company. The name John Myers, as before mentioned, appears in the roster of the Chiles Party which came down Pit River from the Oregon country in 1843. The presence of these "two old mountaineers" gave support and encouragement to the travelers near them.

A month later Bruff and other interested travelers saw in this vicinity one of the monstrosities of the trail. It was a peculiar home-made wagon with projections bulging above the wheels and a stove-pipe sticking through the forward part of the top. It was the home on wheels of the Alford family. At this moment the pipe was belching black and sooty pitch-pine smoke; and the migration, with its uncanny aptitude for nicknames, dubbed it the "Steamboat." Two small precise cows and the six oxen which drew it in the daytime were grazing happily; and the company, which included three ladies, was resting. In this homelike arrangement might be heard the cries of a tiny infant; for a boy baby had been born since turning on the cutoff, and he was but a month old.

We do not find many records of births on the Lassen Road. It was used mainly in 1849, when most men traveled alone in their hasty rush for the gold diggings and the women stayed at home; but in ordinary years a birth along the Overland Trail caused little commotion. Large families were the rule, the journey took several months, and babies were as apt to arrive en route as anywhere else, and usually did very well.

Besides the thin cries of the child, the camp was disturbed by a mule. It fell over a large rock and landed on its back between two other rocks, where it wedged, feet uppermost, and had to be extricated at the cost of great exertion by the tired and disgusted owners. The long-eared "Missouri canaries" had a laudable habit of remaining alive, probably from sheer stubbornness, through hardships where the oxen died like flies. In fact a Missouri mule had no intention of dying like a fly or in any other manner, if it could be avoided. In many of the losses of mules, which Bruff, for one, recounts almost every night through the reaches of the cutoff, it is noted that the animal was abandoned, not dead. But, short of the ultimate, there seemed to be no irritating exigency of the trail that did not happen to a mule.

The last-named gentleman awoke one morning to face a loss of two mules to the ever watchful Indians. It was growing colder each night, and the autumn-edged wind had driven the guards in to warm themselves by the luxury of the great fire, where, as Bruff told them forcefully later, they made splendid targets for the death-tipped arrows of the natives if those usually unforbearing individuals had cared to use them. But a plenty of wood was still an unaccustomed luxury to men who had left forests behind them on the Missouri frontier. They had burned dried grass and sagebrush and green willows for most of the two thousand miles before striking the great pines at Lassen's Pass, and a log fire was an irresistible magnet.

From the water in the center of the game refuge, the trail turned southeast for four or five miles to what is now Aspen Wells and then on, a mile more, to Dixie Springs. The rangers told us that several oxshoes had been retrieved from this segment recently. Now and then Bruff passed the remains of some fellow-traveler's wagon disintegrating beside the road. Black-tailed deer fled from the hunters, soaring over fallen logs on invisible wings of speed and connecting with the earth again with soap-bubble lightness. They gave a strange effect of weightlessness in spite of their size. Blackbirds rose in clouds before the oxen and caused the staid animals to sidestep and snort. This was a pleasant portion of the journey.

Suddenly, a short distance from the road, Bruff and his companions saw a hateful sight. At first glance it seemed to be a grave, opened and rifled by Indians; but a second look comprehended that it was not so commonplace as that. Some man, upon abandoning his wagon, had made a cache resembling a grave and into it put his possessions, miscellaneous papers, and the inevitable medicine kit, without which no careful company traveled. No doubt he had marked it as a grave so that he might find it again some day, for that was a common practice along the crowded emigrant trail. It would not protect the contents for a moment against the Indians, who would open a grave for the clothes of the occupant with greedy interest if they happened to think about it; but it was a good hiding place against the unscrupulous of the migration. In this case the ruse had failed. Someone had seen it in preparation, and it was rifled of its valuables, with the pathetic remainder—bottles, pills, and powders—scattered uselessly near by.

There was hardly a campground without its graves, of which Bruff faithfully copied the epitaphs. The one near Dixie Springs had four, grouped together for company. One night, in this vicinity, the needful rest of the camp was broken by a raid in which the Indians netted sixteen oxen, and by the much noisier posse which at once set out in pursuit, hastily mounted and equipped. They were close enough to track the natives some distance from the trail, where they discovered a great quantity of dried meat hanging in the trees. The acquired taste for beef which the Indians had formed was proving expensive to the emigrant trains as the red men laid in supplies for the winter.

The emigrants could gather no authentic information about the tribe which harried them night after night. There seem to be no records of friendly individuals who came into the camps for food or to trade. Apparently no Indian woman would have dealings with the white men. All the way across the plains the lower type of squaws had known that trinkets and food could be obtained from the rougher men of the migration in return for favors bestowed; among the friendly tribes, they constituted something of a nuisance. Every Indian village among the plains tribes had its upper and lower strata, just as any white village might have; it had its head men, whose dignity never faltered, with their self-respecting wives; and it had its tattered riffraff with no self-respect at all. But the Pit River tribe had been solidly belligerent.

* * *

This seems a good place to include two paragraphs of trail geography for those who are interested.

From Dixie Springs the trail proceeds slightly southwest through crowding forests to strike a Western Pacific branch line in Bogard Flat, a short distance northwest of Lodgepole Station, where a small dirt road may be seen. The road appears again on the other side of the tracks and for a way runs parallel to them, following the trail exactly. Near Bogard Pine the small road takes itself off, but the trail stays with the railroad until it crosses the highway, where the course of the old wagons is the same as that of the modern automobile for about a mile.

After a mile of highway travel (and about a mile and a quarter before the highway reaches Feather Lake) the trail seeker must turn to the right, southeast, on a tiny dirt road which approximates the course of the Lassen Trail, touches the southwest end of Feather Lake, and, in less than a mile, crosses the railroad. Here the fickle trail goes with the railroad again for about a mile, where, for some reason known only to our pioneer ancestors and inexplicable to anyone else, it makes a sharp detour to the east around Anna Lake and strikes it at its southeastern end, where it again joins the railroad and remains with it into Norvell Flat.

*   *   *

In Bogard Flat we could see that the wagons had emerged from the thick pushing pines and struck boldly into the sunny miles that lay between them and Norvell Flat. Bogard Flat itself is large and open, with the Western Pacific branch line, the highway, and the trail running through it from northwest to southeast.

The elevation here is close to six thousand feet, and the trees and meadows have the mark of the high mountains upon them. Wild geese rest here on their blue journey from north to south and, during the summer, may be seen in flocks of several dozen around the marshy places.

The trail through this section is worn deeply into the soil. We could hardly credit the evidence of our eyes until, with the help of the Forest Service Headquarters at Susanville, we matched up new maps with old and made an interesting discovery. From Poison Lake to the place where the trail strikes the railroad in Bogard Flat, and all the way to Norvell Flat, the Lassen Trail and the Noble Road run coincidentally for perhaps twenty miles. It is no wonder that the trail shows signs of heavy usage right here; it got it.

A few facts about the Noble Road must be included in any history of the Lassen Trail. I will give them briefly.

In 1851 a man named Noble, heading a prospecting party, found a splendid pass through the mountains leading from Old Shasta to Honey Lake (naming the latter for the honeydew found on the foliage about it), and was impressed with the importance of the new route. The Lassen Trail fell into disrepute in 1849, as well it might, and there was no adequate road to the mines near Old Shasta. He told of his discovery, and the town hired him to find and outline the course that should replace the long, difficult, and dangerous Lassen Trail. A number of citizens went with him, and by the end of June, 1852, they returned well satisfied.

The route was the same as the Lassen Road from the Humboldt River as far west as Black Rock, but had been slightly improved. New wells were dug at Rabbit Hole Springs and all the available water was collected in reservoirs. From Black Rock the Noble Pass Road proper began and crossed the Black Rock Desert to the west, instead of going north as had the Lassen Road; it passed between Gerlach and the point of the Granite Range, struck the Susan River about three miles from Honey Lake, followed it to Susanville, then out past what is now Hog Flat Reservoir to Norvell Flat, where it coincided with the Lassen Road as I said before. The notable difference was that the emigrants coming to California on the Noble Road were going in the opposite direction along this segment from those who had used it as part of the Lassen Cutoff—northwest in place of southeast.

In order that I may not leave such a useful thoroughfare dangling in the mountains with no given termination, let me add that from Bogard Flat the Noble Road proceeded northwest to the west side of Poison Lake, thence to the northern side of Mount Lassen; crossed through Noble's Pass and down to Fort Reading and Old Shasta. It was a good and useful road, but it was too late for the gold rush and can never hold the special place in the history of California occupied by the roundabout and execrated route piloted by Peter Lassen and traveled by hundreds of angry Forty-niners—Lassen's Cutoff, often called the Greenhorn's Cutoff, or sometimes, in reference to its needless miles, the Cape Horn Route.

CHAPTER XV

Mountain Meadows

It WAS not popular with my husband.

Most wives, at one time or another, have been unpopular with their husbands.

He wanted to go home. He was due at the office, so he said; although it could not be denied that we still had a week of vacation comfortably in front of us.

Here we were at Susanville, where we had come to "make up Rotary." There was still plenty of trail to see between us and home; there were still plenty of months before the proposed completion of our field work. Suppose we *had* skipped a few miles and a few unimportant lakes along the old Overland Road; we could always come back and pick up the stitches in our knitting. So said my husband in no uncertain terms as we sat at breakfast in the hotel coffee shop.

Dr. Neff and Mr. Bromley ate largely and said nothing. Both had offices of their own; but they did not seem to feel that things were on the edge of dissolution because of their personal absence, and consumed ham and eggs happily.

"But I need to know what is in that twelve miles," I insisted emotionally. I put my elbow on a misplaced piece of cold toast and held my head.

"Oh, come on; let's do it," said Mr. Bromley, coming to my rescue. "It'll only take half a day—if we have luck," he added sotto voce.

Bill was not along on this particular trip, and Dr. Neff, as was his habit, said nothing. So I had my way, removed my elbow from the toast and myself from the coffee shop, and we went by particularly irritating and dusty little wood roads to Feather Lake.

It took longer than we expected and the roads were bad. Finally we struck the trail as it approached Feather Lake from the northwest, and turned into it.

The way of the wagons! Bump by bump we drove it, rock by excruciating rock.

This was not my husband's day to enjoy trail geography. He stopped the car, regarded his surroundings with disfavor, and announced that he would sit right there while the rest of us hiked down to see the lake. Looking back, guiltily, I noticed that he was not too disgruntled to drive a few hundred yards into the shade of a tree.

Feather Lake is tiny, and by August there is not much left of it unless the season is exceptionally wet. We judged that we saw the little body of water just about as the pioneers found it. The part nearest to us was dry. We walked down to the shore past a salt log where the cattle ran frantically into the timber and we could hear them crashing long after they were out of sight. Evidently few people come into their territory.

After taking a picture or two and drawing a crude map we returned and collected my gradually softening husband, who had just tuned in a crawling contralto on the radio and had the supreme satisfaction of tuning her out again. Life has some compensations. Then we moved on with the trail. Great armor-plated yellow pines rose magnificently above us. They had never been timbered, for there were fallen giants but no stumps. Our road brought us to the west side of Anna Lake, high on a bluff above the receding water. The trail was out of sight, circling the lake to the east, possibly because of the difficulty of pulling the wagons over the hill on which we stood. Anna Lake was partly dry also. The south end is deeper and retains a pond after the rest is drained. Probably that is why the trail struck the south end only, instead of skirting the full length of the east side. The dry portion of the bed was absolutely flat, grassy, and polka-dotted with cattle.

The next point of interest, Norvell Flat, has been invaded by a logging road but is still beautiful. The trail comes into it from the north past a thick grove of white-trunked aspens. They stand so crowded together that a horse could scarcely make his way between them, but they keep within clean-cut boundaries and the meadow floor is clear, grassy, and bright with tiny magenta flowers. Encircling the aspens and the meadow are dark, spirelike tamaracks.

By this time everything was running smoothly in the accustomed groove, so I stopped being ebullient (which is hard to maintain on the trail) and became normally peevish over details. We did our best in the time we had left, hit the most accessible sections of the old road from there to Mason Junction, and came back, just at noon, into the highway we had left five hours before.

For those who may care to undergo some discomfort in order to see where their ancestors traveled, here is another paragraph of trail geography: Go south from Norvell Flat, through McCoy Flat for five and a quarter miles to a point just east of Jennie Mountain. Then (judging only by the contour of the country, as there is no trace left and nothing given on any map that we have seen), swing about three miles south-southwest along a tiny dirt road that more or less follows Robbers' Creek; follow about two miles more to a point a mile west of Mason Junction; thence about two miles more to where the little road crosses Dry Creek. From there one can only go by contours to where the old maps again show traces of the trail a quarter of a mile east of Rock Creek and one and a half miles below its confluence with Jennie Creek; it has made a sharp swing to the west and there is no dirt road left that approximates its course. From this point it makes a short sharp arc to the west and back and strikes a curving dirt road leading from a spot on the Westwood-Chester Highway, nearly five miles west of Westwood, to Big Springs Camp on the north shore of Lake Almanor.

Almanor is a made lake. It was, within the memory of many of us, called Big Meadows, a lovely expanse of spongy turf through which the main fork of Feather River lazily took its way. The trail struck the meadow near Big Springs and skirted just above the moist flatland, moving west until it struck the high land that is now a peninsula on which it turned south, keeping on the eastern slope almost to the end. Here the wagons climbed over the gradually lowering high land of the peninsula and moved southeast into the meadow where Feather River provided water for camp sites.

Howell wrote: "We descended a gentle hill into a beautiful looking valley; but in fact generally a very deep bog covered with good grass and fine springs breaking out at the foot of the hills everywhere. We camped near one large spring containing great numbers of fish 3 to 6 inches long."

The ground was treacherous on the approach to the Valley of Feather River and loose cattle were apt to bog down, even within sight of camp, but the luxuriant grass was worth any amount of trouble. We have so many pen pictures of this trail paradise that we can visualize it as if it were before us. It is like another existence for the weary emigrants. The travelers bathe and wash their clothes, pick flowers, and wander through the camps, noting old acquaintances of the trail and making new ones.

Bizarre sights greet them on all sides: An Irishman and his wife, camped alone, speak with a heavy brogue and are solicitously conveying a coop of chickens to California. At each stop along the way the fowls have been let out for necessary exercise. Strangely enough, the chickens are not too stupid to learn that they must not be left behind, and they rush, cackling, for their coop on the rear of the wagon when it shows signs of moving on.

In another camp a small girl carefully feeds a toothless ox, a skinflint trade into which her father has been forced by the death of his good team some weeks ago. In the ordinary course of events the beast soon would have become too weak to travel, but she has so faithfully chosen his food and fed it to him bit by bit that he is still in good flesh and will probably, barring accident, pull them through to the valley.

A dignified traveler, passing a recently deserted camp, salvages a slice of bread from the dirt where some child has dropped it, sits down, and eats it gravely.

A company of men who have been angrily following the bloody footprints of a child along the dusty trail trace them to the camp of a slipshod sullen family and threaten to horsewhip the man if he doesn't take better care of his little daughter. A grim, unpleasant little drama!

In attractive contrast, an eight-year-old girl is the only woman creature in a large company of men and is always busy at the campfire with her father. Her special duty is to see that the coffeepot and frying pan, balanced on burning twigs, do not upset. Her naïve air of responsibility over this truly important function pleases and amuses the surrounding womanless camps.

At the overflow from one of the springs a sad-faced woman is rinsing innumerable small shirts. She has buried her husband in the sands of the Platte River Valley and is taking their eight children on to an unknown future.

In another direction a careless cook has let his fire spark into the dry grass. Close by lie three dead oxen and one dying. The fire runs in among their bodies, and neighboring men, who have not quite attained the cook's magnificent callousness, hurry over and stamp it out so that the ox may finish the tedious business of dying as comfortably as possible.

Among the camps in the meadows, about the middle of October, the "Steamboat" may be seen belching smoke from its cocky little smokestack as the Alford family prepare their meals.

In an oxcart pulled under a tree is the young Missourian with a leg injury who was wounded in the Indian attack which cost Captain Warner his life; he is thus far on his slow journey back to civilization. The obsidian-tipped arrow caused a wound which will not stop bleeding and he is quite sick, but eager to talk. He tells his interested visitors that he was riding just behind Captain Warner and the guide when the shower of arrows pincushioned the two men. In the confusion that ensued, an Indian rose up from behind his ambush and, apparently with some solemnity, made a speech. A pistol shot discouraged him and he went away. No one followed him, as the odds were about fifty Indians against eight survivors.

One of the contributing causes of comfort at this camp was the proximity of the headquarters of the government-sponsored expedition for emigrant relief. The expedition had outfitted in Sacramento in the middle of September and had relieved distress as much as possible throughout the mountains. In October, Major Rucker, who was in command, had left a supply depot here in charge of a certain Mr. Rogers and had gone on to the assistance of those who might be stranded farther along.

Captain Warner's Railroad Survey Expedition reported that when they entered the mountains on August 24th, they met the advance emigrants (probably pack men) in a starving condition. When afterward the expedition met the first of the wagon trains, it was discovered that they were better supplied and still had food of a meager sort. It seems likely that the advent of the hungry pack trains into the valley gave an impetus to the sending of relief. The people of California remembered all too plainly the Donner disaster, and the charitable gesture saved many lives and measureless suffering.

The report of the Warner expedition also suggests that there might have been between ten thousand and twenty thousand people on the Lassen Road in 1849 and that many needed every teaspoonful of cornmeal before they struck the valley and succor. The relief headquarters added to their meager supplies; and later, when suffering could not be prevented, were able to mitigate it somewhat.

Feather River Meadow was the place where the wise ones cut hay to carry along. The need was not apparent, for grass enough for the animals' immediate use could be found beside the way for a day or two. But the long dry foothills were ahead, and on every road into the Sacramento Valley the animals had to eat oak leaves or starve for the last fifty or sixty miles. The meadow was also the larder of the journey. Deer and water fowl innumerable were there for the hunting; and the grizzlies, which formed the subject of many of the tall campfire stories, were considered good eating by those who were starved for fats. Roast bear meat was something like coarse pork. Fish were plentiful in the river, and even the springs had their quota of small fry.

This was as beautiful and as satisfactory a haven as could be found anywhere on any of the Overland trails.

The wagons forded the Feather River with some trouble. It was a hundred yards wide and only a few inches deep, but it was full of unexpected holes in which the overladen animals floundered and had to be rescued by the exasperated and profane drivers. When undisturbed, the transparent, winking brown water was shot with silver as the darting trout formed streaks of light; but during fording hours they were frightened and kept away.

Near the river was a grave elaborately marked: "Sacred to the Memory of W. Brown, of the Rough and Ready Company of Platte Co., Mo. Died with Skervy, Sep. 19th '49, Age 35 years."

Died of scurvy in the midst of plenty!

On the ocean or in the desert it would have been understandable, but here were thousands of square miles of greenery. He should have copied the Indians and eaten the tops from the clover that perfumed the air; but the value of greens was not as yet well understood by the average man. He probably carried sour pickles or vinegar, potatoes, and onions and ate them every little while as long as they lasted. Some emigrants claimed that they only recognized Sunday on the plains because on every seventh day they all ate pickles. When these homely deterrents were gone, it was recognized that scurvy came prowling along shortly. Brown's death would have caused no surprise. It was just one of those sad things that happened.

* * *

In deference to summer fire hazards, we chose a government camp in which to set up our tents. A dove-gray sky blended softly into saffron at the horizon, and a slim moon bowed graciously to the assembling stars. We had to spend the night somewhere.

The day had been full and it was late—eight-thirty.

California has some queer people of its own and, through the war years, has imported more. Both kinds were in sight, and our moving headlights picked up various tents and trailers and their camp fixings (scattered or neat) here and there under the pines. I got out of the car, leaving Bill to park it, and commenced to pile my own possessions under a tree, not making even a mental effort to be left out of the inclusive description "queer."

Bill was sawing the car skillfully into the narrow space between the huge trees when, hearing an odd groaning noise, I looked around and was just in time to remove a boy baby from behind the moving car. I put him safely to one side and went back to my suitcase for an apron when I heard Bill call, "Hey, Mom," and, looking for the cause, saw him point his thumb ahead. I removed the baby from in front of the car and a quarter of a minute later removed him from behind it again. As this was the final seesaw, I dismissed him from my mind after watching him go down through the camps, trundling a big toy wheelbarrow from whose greaseless wheel the groaning noise proceeded. No one had appeared to be interested in him. It was quite dark in fact, and I doubted if anyone could see.

I cooked a late supper and we all sat down to read by the light of our lanterns when, presently, I heard the wheelbarrow coming our way again. It stopped beside me, and there was my small acquaintance plus a fresh coating of cake crumbs that seemed to indicate a slight collation since last we met.

Bill was disgusted. "That baby should have been in bed hours ago," he said. "It's ten o'clock."

My husband looked up and made tentative advances. A cracker was accepted silently, but otherwise progress was at a standstill.

And, incidentally, so was the wheelbarrow.

The other two laid down their books and came around the table to look at him. He *was* a sight. Under his dirt he was rather a handsome little fellow about two and a half or three years old, but his towhead was in a birds'-nest state that argued nonpossession of a comb. His clothes were not ragged, but his little pants were too tight and in a condition of unbuttonedness approaching the legal limit. A coat flaring like a bell had been put on him and fastened rather peculiarly with a big safety pin under his chin. He was warm enough and, although an unsmiling child, appeared comfortable.

He had been with us about five minutes and had not uttered a sound—we never did hear him say anything—when his mother arrived in a dirty shirt and overalls and an all-embracing smile.

"Is Willyum bothering you?" she inquired politely.

"Not at all. How did you know he was here?"

"Oh, I listen for the wheelbarrow," she replied, beaming on her solemn baby with real affection; "and when I realize I'm not hearing it, I go out to take a look. I thought he went off in this direction."

"Don't you worry about him? After all, these are real forests; there's nothing make-believe about these miles of trees."

"Oh, not a bit. He'd never leave his wheelbarrow, no matter what. My friend ties little bells on her kid's shoelaces, but you can hear this farther."

And she picked Willyum up horizontally under one strong arm, took the wheelbarrow in the other hand, and bade us a pleasant good night. When she got back to her tent, she dropped Willyum straight into bed.

I know this because early the next morning, when we were pulling out of camp, he arrived; and the peculiar safety pin had not budged one hair's breadth from its permanent position. He had slept under the singing pines in his coat and, for all I know, his shoes too; and now, still encased in yesterday's dirt and fully equipped with his wheelbarrow, went trundling off noisily through the bright forest.

Who knows? Willyum may be President some day. That's what makes America great.

*   *   *

Seven miles from Feather River Meadows the wagons came to Butt Creek on the Baccala Ranch, and then to Soldier Meadows, where some of the Forty-niners wrote of finding troops encamped. Eight miles farther brought them to the meadows surrounding Deer Creek.

The company in which W. J. Pleasants traveled was plague-ridden with mountain fever. He himself—just a lad—contracted it and was very ill when they arrived at Deer Creek Meadows. One of the other sick men, David Myers, Sr., died here and was buried. Pleasants' father became frightened and sent a messenger to a train ten miles ahead to get the service of a doctor. The doctor came and expressed no hope; but, because of the father's pleading, he stayed with their train and managed to save the boy. They remained in the meadow long enough for young Pleasants to convalesce, which made them dangerously late in tackling the ridge.

Doctors and others called to prescribe for the sick were not always so successful. Listen to this, written by a Forty-niner: "Last evening at about dark I was sent for to see a sick physician who belonged to a waggon train from Missouri. I found him in a dying state having no pulse at the wrist, he had been sick of fever for 3 weeks. He died about midnight. I was glad they happened to send for me for I had not been to supper and there I found a plenty of provisions and I never enjoyed a meal better, they had an abundance of flour bread and warm biscuit, corn bread, bacon, *apple sauce* and coffee, having been on short allowance of bread with plenty of beef and coffee, it was a great treat."

The dying man was evidently nothing to him, whereas the meal truly meant a great deal.

At Deer Creek Meadows they gazed fondly upon the last green grass. Throughout the season the valley was continually filled with camps scattered here and there on its widespread and verdant bottom. It was also the last comfortable camp before reaching the valley, and they made the most of it.

When they left the meadows, Deer Creek had to be forded twice in about a hundred yards. By October 20th, when Bruff made the crossings, the beautiful little stream had lost all semblance of its former loveliness and was a shambles. The banks had been churned into bogs; trees were scored to allow room for the projecting hubs of the lurching wagons; brush was torn loose to throw beneath the wheels. Oxen, straining in the yokes, had fallen and died in the mud where they continued to serve the hastening migration by holding up the wheels. Over them, then, went the wagons. The leg of an ox was safe and solid; the neck was not so good, but it had to serve, being more resistant than the ooze through which they must pick their way.

Ahead rose a rocky hill. They started up. But many of the animals had reached their limit and could not pull another foot. If others were available, they were used; if not, a wagon was left. It caused little comment at this stage in the journey.

And so began the ascent of the last ridge.

CHAPTER XVI

The Big Hogback

A т Deer Creek Meadows, near the confluence of the North Fork, the Lassen Road starts up to the right of the highway. A new lumber road, which is practically the Lassen Road straightened out, has been put in by the Collins Pine Company. Sometimes the old ruts are obliterated beneath the heavy dust made by the logging trucks; sometimes the curves of the trail can be seen coiling this way and that from the main stem of the logging road like a snake around a stick.

This interesting thoroughfare is wide, graded, and so new that it looks raw. It leads into the heaviest kind of timber and, through it, to the tail bone of the hogback along which the migration moved about sixty miles toward the Sacramento Valley. For years we have wanted to ride that ridge, which is not a mere rise, but as long, as high, and as bulky as a mountain range, and differs only in that it does not divide into mountains but remains a unit.

It is no place for horses, for it is stony to an extremity difficult to describe. For twenty-mile stretches water is unobtainable except by climbing in and out of the deep canyons. The ridge is lonely beyond anything I have ever experienced, save only the crossing of the Rockies near South Pass. We gave up the idea of horses.

A jeep was the answer, and the only one. The Lassen Trail along the ridge was one place, the forest rangers told us, that a pick-up truck could not go.

And so Wesley J. Brokenshire, Mineral District Ranger, public spirited and interested in the history of the old trail, allotted us a jeep. He took the edge off our sense of importance, rather, by saying to Ralph Cioffi, who was in the office, "Has anyone been down the ridge this year?" and, on receiving a negative answer: "It should be kept open in case of fire. Why don't you drive down tomorrow and take them with you?"

So it happened that, early the next morning, we collected at the ranger station at Mineral and watched them lead in the jeep—prancing.

Mr. Cioffi is only there in the summer months and consequently had not taken this particular trip for a good many years. He knew it would be a workout, but he was looking forward to it as something of interest not done every day.

This was to be our last field work of the year; everything I should have worn was disintegrating and had been discarded. My outfit was scrupulously incorrect for a vehicle which I now observed to lack top, doors, and almost everything else detachable.

Let the people who have to look at me worry about it, I thought, and climbed on. From necessity, Dr. Neff and Mr. Bromley were staying at camp; there was not room for more than the three of us. I occupied the other front seat, separated from the driver's by a six- or eight-inch gap; my husband was accommodated with a third seat placed back of mine. There was a certain economy of springs and upholstering noticeable when I bounced, but the space allotted to him was so unsumptuous that for days he winced at the sight of a chair.

I was, I flattered myself, becoming a connoisseur of jeeps. This one had no roof off which to volley, no doors to return one to one's seat. There was nothing but the grace of God to prevent one from being unjeeped at any given moment.

We waved good-by and were struck into motion as you strike fire from a match. I felt like a hen balanced on an apple box in a cyclone. That wave was the last thing I attempted to do. It took me all the way to Deer Creek Meadows to get the feel of my transportaion. I may interpolate that it took me all the rest of the week to get rid of it.

At Deer Creek Meadows we stopped to admire the grassy flat which has been familiar to us for years, for this is where the trail comes slanting in from Soldier Meadows and crosses the highway.

"The first part is easy," said Mr. Cioffi. "The Collins Pine Company's road will take us to the end of the timber. That may be about eighteen miles from here. After that we'll have to put up with what we find."

We turned into the newly slashed-out road and started bravely up the hill. I grew more courageous with necessity and began to take field notes in a blank book. My pencil was attached to it with a long string, so that when I dropped everything, as became advisable now and then, it remained among those present. I am a decidedly deciduous individual and go through life strewing my valuables on all sides. For that reason my family has arranged to attach them to my person. My camera swings from my shoulder on a strap. My light-meter in a leather case hangs around my neck on what looks like a shoestring. My notebook, from which I am never separated while doing field work, tucks under one arm complete with the pencil on a long piece of twine. At the best, things are not simple. When they get complicated, a buzzing bluebottle in a cobweb is less involved. As long as I remained seated, my impedimenta rested pleasantly in my lap; but I couldn't seem to remain seated.

Mr. Cioffi continued a homily on the beauties of the forest through which we were making our way—the car so small and the trees so big that it seemed a subject of enchantment.

"It is one of the finest stands left," he finished. "Some of it was absolutely virgin timber until a few months ago. This company operates on a sustained-yield basis, so that a stand as large as this one should furnish lumber indefinitely."

"I don't suppose they care to have the public use this road," my husband hazarded.

"No, they don't. They spent a lot of money to get a private road so that they won't have to look out for traffic; but we aren't the public. The Forest Service patrols this section. They're used to the jeep."

Over the snapping, popping noise we were making rolled a thundering roar, blotting out and beating down our ineffectual efforts to be heard. Closer and closer. A curve hid the monster, but I knew that the first of the logging trucks was almost on us. We gave a quick jerk to the outside of the curve (which happened to be the left) and perched on the filled-in edge—a soft shoulder, if ever there was one. Our tiny conveyance offered no protection, and we just sat by the side of the road, as if on kitchen chairs, while the mighty load raced by on the downhill stretch.

I looked up at the tremendous logs, dismembered now into clean brown cylinders. For a few seconds they remained high above my head. Dear God, I thought, don't let the chain break now! Then they passed, to be succeeded by a blinding cloud of dust.

Mr. Cioffi peered over the edge of the seat at the wheels. They were almost hub deep in loose dirt. Here's trouble, I thought, and got ready to disembark.

"Four-wheel drive," "compounded low!" They must be magic words like "open sesame" or "abracadabra." We oozed out of that equivocal position without a moment's hesitation.

This small but exciting drama was repeated many times in the next hour. Sometimes the monsters came singly, dragons from the enchanted forest breathing dust instead of smoke; sometimes they came in pairs. They came fast and hell-for-leather. After all, it's their road. Logs scattered royally along the way showed that sometimes chains do break.

Our first stop of interest was Round Valley.

We had no speedometer, but the map seems to make it six miles from Deer Creek Meadows. The little open flat is surrounded by thick dark timber and furnished with a still darker pond of water by Round Valley Creek. It nestles at the western foot of Butt Mountain and is, in good weather, a comfortable spot, shaded by large cedars.

At this point in the journey, Delano was walking ahead of his company as an advance courier to the valley. He was to try to acquire supplies and become informed as to the best diggings, so that his companions would not, when they arrived, have to waste time.

Howell stopped at Round Valley and barbecued some venison. Bruff nooned and filled the water kegs, commented on the fact that ox yokes and chains were scattered numerously, and was astonished at the eighteen-inch cones of the sugar pine.

Bachelder and Kimball Webster nooned here and camped for the night on the summit.

"How can we tell whether or not the old Lassen Road is the same as the logging road?" I asked Mr. Cioffi. "When it wriggles off to one side, I can see it go; but if it's under me, I don't know it."

"You can't always tell," he said; "but the Lassen Trail was marked quite thickly with old game-refuge signs. When you see one of those, you know you're on the trail."

"That sounds rather incongruous," my husband said.

"Yes, I suppose it does," he replied; "but it was used for years as a fire road—the only road up here, in fact; so any signs that the Forest Service needed to put up, were put along the Lassen Trail."

It was close on eleven o'clock and about eight miles beyond Round

Valley when we reached the summit of Barclay Ridge, as the first slope is called. We were 5,471 feet above sea level and in one of the most impressive stands of yellow pine, white fir, and cedar that I have ever seen. So far we had been submerged in great trees, safely wedged in on the top of the ridge, and had not thought much about how high we were or how very narrow it happened to be. Now we suddenly shot out to the Deer Creek, or south, side of the top and looked off over a great blue canyon roofed in crystal.

"Glory be, what a view!" I breathed and shrank a little smaller. Sitting on top of that jeep was the most exposed position I had ever occupied.

More log trucks passed, almost strangling us with dust. The cloud that enveloped us was a solid thing. We couldn't see the front of the jeep, which was about four feet in front of my toes. When they had disappeared and the dirt had finally settled, it was discovered that much of it had settled on us. We were sunk in wind-erosion deposits.

"I suppose it isn't smart to use any of the water we're carrying?" I said with a distinct question in my voice.

"There's no use." Mr. Cioffi spoke but the obvious truth. "And we might happen to need it. You never can tell." So I remained sunk.

"There's Mill Creek Canyon." My husband distracted my attention to better and more uplifting things. We had, by moving to the right a hundred yards or so, come out on the northern brink of the ridge. "This mountain isn't very wide, is it?"

From there we went straight down to Lost Camp.

A man was filling his canteens at a spring. He was Stanley Thompson, who patrols this section, and we asked him if he thought the spring had been there in 1849. Quite likely not, he thought. It probably had been developed. Could he tell us anything about the country ahead? Yes, he could and did. Did he know where the place called Bruff's Camp was? No, that wasn't a name he was familiar with, and he couldn't say.

"I imagine," my husband remarked, "that it had been completely forgotten until Miss Read and Miss Gaines came out here to get material to edit Bruff's journals, just before the war. They published them, you know, under the title *Gold Rush*."

"The place actually is marked, though," said Mr. Cioffi. "The Forest Service had it done; but it's off the road, and I'm not sure that I know where to look for it."

"They gave me some general instructions at the Susanville head-quarters," my husband answered my anxious look, "and I guess we'll manage to find the sign."

"Unless the bear have chewed it up," said Mr. Thompson.

"What *do* you mean by that?" I wanted to know.

"Well, the bear like wooden signs," he explained patiently. "They stand on their hind legs and chew the tops right off. I wouldn't be surprised if we have to replace them all with metal ones some day."

"But why, of all unlikely things?"

"I haven't an earthly idea," he replied, "but I've often seen the bark ripped completely from small trees where they have reared up and sharpened their claws. They rip the signs with their teeth; maybe they're just putting an edge on them, too."

So far I hadn't noticed any signposts, but, shortly after leaving Lost Camp, we came to the road leading north to McCarthy Point Fire Lookout. It was marked with what I should have considered a uselessly thick and massive sign. And, even so, it was minus the top quarter and bore the marks of great teeth.

Of all the landmarks mentioned by the Forty-niners who traveled the Lassen Road, my curiosity had been most intrigued by their descriptions of "the Narrows"—probably because I had never talked to anyone who had seen it.

We found it startling, to say the least. As we started across the razorback, I opened my mouth for a request to be allowed to get out and photograph the jeep as it reached the middle; but I caught the words just back of my teeth and disposed of them noiselessly. If I got out, I would later be accused of nervousness. I rode across. What went on in my mind was my own business.

We did stop on the other side, and I tried to find a spot from which the camera would give some idea of the thrilling narrowness of the mountaintop; but nothing of the sort is possible. An aerial photograph is necessary.

It must have been a rather hair-raising place in trail days, but the modern traveler need have no qualms about crossing. The Collins Pine Company has lately scraped off the top until it is wide enough for two of their tremendous log trucks to pass if necessary, although I am willing to bet that they never do.

When well beyond the junction of Ponderosa Road, we began to watch for the Barclay drift fence. The ridge is named for the old

family, and the Barclay cabin, made in two parts and boasting a
puncheon floor, used to extend hospitality on the mountain. Their
drift fence now appeared rather indefinitely on our right. After some
hesitation caused by the difficulty of sighting a gate in a section of
fence which happens to have fallen down, we found our marker
opposite it among the trees and parked the jeep in the flat where
Bruff arrived on October 21st, 1849, and stayed until December 31st.
Amid the frantic scramble of the trail, he was a permanent fixture.

The government relief men passing back and forth to the valley knew
and spoke of the spot as Bruff's Camp.

Upon his arrival he found another more or less permanent camp.
Its occupants were not travelers, but men hired by Peter Lassen to get
out shingles from the giant cedars on the ridge top. Lassen had great
plans for the development of the northern Sacramento Valley.
Bachelder wrote, on October 13th, that Lassen had men employed in
splitting stakes and rails for the purpose of starting a new settlement;
we can only guess that these shingles also were meant to be used in
the construction of his dream town, Benton City, just across Deer
Creek from his adobe ranch buildings. The callousness of the shingle

splitters to the sufferings of the migration aroused Bruff's anger at once. They had almost ceased work, said he, in their excitement over gathering up the property and animals that were being abandoned on all sides. Every stray was carefully driven "by these mountains pirates —gleaners on the misfortunes of their brother emigrants," to a meadow in a deep gorge and there recruited so far from the trail that they could be of no further use to the footsore migration. They had two piles of shingles and would, so he said, occasionally hammer away at the job; but mainly they watched for plunder. They had formed abandoned wagons into a corral laced in and out among the trees, and every day they added to it.

Water was not to be found in Bruff's Camp. The shingle makers had dug a spring about a quarter of a mile away, on the north side of the ridge, and a broad path was soon beaten to it. Its supply was easily exhausted, but it replenished itself in a few hours.

The wagons and property of the company were getting to be an unbearable burden, endangering their chances of a safe arrival in the valley. A consultation was held and Bruff volunteered to stay in the sheltered flat, standing guard over the wagons, until help could be sent from the settlements. He had been a conscientious company captain and apparently thought that, in a debacle such as was upon them, the rule of a sinking ship should apply. He planned to remain with his responsibility.

There were many signs of deer and bear; the ravines, a couple of miles down on either side of his hilltop camp, were full of wild grapes. He would be comfortable enough, he said, and they would come for him in a few days. The company seemed grateful. They divided with him what they had left: two square ship biscuits, a handful of rice, half of one man's fortune, amounting to one dollar; some pipe tobacco, a cake of cold bread, some parched coffee, and a couple of pounds of meat.

Every day emigrants passed, many of them known to Bruff from former encounters along the trail and delayed by some accident. They became increasingly tired, decrepit, and ill equipped; they were the weak and exhausted of the migration, the tailenders. Bruff wrote of them in his journal and became almost unwittingly the trail chronicler.

Once a sufferer from scurvy passed by, riding a mule and carrying a pair of crutches across the saddle. A woman invaded his camp, leading a pale and emaciated child. It had been sick, she said, and not knowing what else to do, she had given it calomel, which salivated it. She asked for beans, for the child craved some. Bruff had none and she went on. A Prussian passed who was in the habit, Bruff said, of maltreating his wife. They had a pony heavily overloaded with dry goods for speculation, a cow packed with sundries, and a skinny steer rattling with frying pans, kettles, and various camp kit. There was also a handsome boy of twelve with a baby on his back, papoose style; and the rear was brought up by the wife (whose face was so heavily bruised that she had required the services of a passing doctor), carrying a pack.

Weeks went by and no one returned for Bruff. By this time most of the oaks in the grove were cut down and the tops lopped off as food for the passing animals. Then it began to rain; the wind blew from the southeast with concentrated venom; the sky thickened and became an enveloping gray blanket. The companions on the mountaintop made everything as compact as possible. Wagons and tents were huddled into the shelter of trees, and those who could find room slept in them.

Bruff, and probably all the camp as well, was awakened in the night by a voice calling desperately for help amid the wailing of the gale. A great tree had fallen on a tent near the "Steamboat" and the Alford family, as such, was no more. Father and one son were dead. Another son and a young man who traveled with them were crushed so badly that it was beyond the ability of anyone to assist them. A great limb had to be cut away before the main trunk could be removed from the men caught in the wreckage.

The swollen storm, a huge saturated sponge, sogged down upon them. It rained and rained; it hailed; it snowed. Bruff loaned his tent to keep the dead and dying dry. At nightfall the second son died, and at daybreak the young man, Cameron.

They dug the grave with hail sluicing down on their heads and, because the ground was so very hard, they undercut it to accommodate all four bodies.

They are there, in Bruff's Camp: Mr. Ormand Alford, aged fifty-four years, on the right; Willard M. Alford and Lorenzo D. Alford, nineteen and fifteen respectively, in the center; and John W. Cameron, aged about twenty-two, on the left. The men put in a ridgepole and a roof of slats above them, then covered in and banked up the grave. A cross, formed of rifle barrels, marked the place.

Mrs. Alford had another son in the settlements, and so the miscellaneous company gave her provisions from their scanty stock and a young man volunteered to drive. Everything was left behind that could not go in the one wagon. The last Bruff saw of them was the chimney of the "Steamboat" moving slowly along the trail.

In reading the *Recollections* of N. E. Hanson, it comes to light that he (then eighteen years old) was the youth who drove their wagon until other assistance was forthcoming. He did not write his recollections until he had reached the age of eighty; he remembered that the place where the accident occurred was called Bruff's Camp and thought that Bruff must be the name of the afflicted family. His memories are interesting because they seem to prove that the place was called Bruff's Camp by the passing emigrants even then.

Meanwhile the relief expedition was not wasting time. John Peoples, Major Rucker's chief assistant, accomplished wonders single-handed. On November 4th he evacuated Feather River Meadows, taking all the women, children, and the helpless. He was caught by a snowstorm in the night a mile west of "Bute Creek," and the next day every man walked and pushed at the wagons. At 4:00 A.M. on the morning of November 6th, he saddled all the mules that still could stand and put such women and children as could ride upon them. Eleven women and about six children started with him; but the storm was so violent and the snow became so deep that he left all but six women in some abandoned tents and wagons, giving them such provisions as he had and killing a large beef for food. Ten miles farther along it rained with such fury that he could no longer see the road. He and the six women had to camp without food of any kind. The next day, November 7th, it rained only intermittently, and they all passed Bruff's Camp safely.

At about this time Peoples sent some supplies to Bruff from the settlement, but the mule on which they were packed became bogged down in mud at the bottom of Steep Hollow (ahead on the trail) and was lost. In fact several mules, packs and all, were left just as they sank. By December, Bruff was out of provisions and alone, save for a young man named Poile and a little boy deserted at the camp by his father. They also had a little dog, called Nevada, and her they supported on the feet and boiled hide of deer. Finally they found and excavated from the snow two dead oxen. By December 29th they had lived forty-seven days on bad beef and venison. Fortunately, they had had enough coffee and salt.

Finally, thoroughly frightened for themselves and for the boy, the two men traveled a half-day's trip to the log cabin of the Roberts family. Apparently these were emigrants who had decided to winter on the ridge rather than to lose all their possessions and they had built themselves a warm house. The humane women treated them kindly and gave them provisions, including some raised bread, and suggested that they go back and move their camp to a point near their house. A healthy middle-aged man who was with the Robertses went back with them to help. He had come along as an ox driver and was bound to them by no family ties, but he at once felt a great compassion for the honorable, eccentric Bruff, who had undertaken so much more than his slight physique could endure. His name was Clough.

They placed the boy and a few necessities on a quickly made hand sled; Bruff saved his priceless notebooks (else we, a century later, would know little about that terrible episode of the gold rush), and they moved. Then Poile and Clough started at midnight for the settlements, assuring Bruff of succor in a few days. As they shook hands in parting, Poile gave to Bruff his share of the bread.

That night those at the Roberts cabin and at Bruff's newly set up camp became ill—horribly ill. They took what was left in the way of medicine. Bruff had camphor. Roberts and his sons took opiates. Bruff and the women worked with the child as best they could. Upon investigation it came to light that Mrs. Roberts had raised her bread with caustic soda instead of saleratus. In the morning the little boy died. It was New Year's Day—here as well as elsewhere in a happier world. They buried him when their strength had somewhat returned. The grave was at the door of Bruff's tent. The heat of the fire had made it possible to dig there, and anyway, it seemed less lonely. His epitaph read: "WILLIAM, Infant son of LAMBKIN—an Unnatural Father, Died Jan. 1, 1850."

We wish we knew exactly where the Roberts cabin stood, but because it was well within the high timber zone, as shown by one of Bruff's sketches, and must have had a water supply, it was probably at Obe Fields's flat.

*   *   *

We stood in Bruff's Camp and looked around. It only lacked a year of being a century since Bruff had made sketches under these same trees. They are reproduced in *Gold Rush* and show that Bruff's lodge was on the far side—the north, in other words. The grave of the Alfords appears on a little rise at the south side of the trail as it enters the flat. The fallen oak, instrument of the Alford tragedy, lies on the south edge of the trail in the middle of the picture. Wagons and tents stand here and there, wheels, ox yokes, chains, boots, hats, deer horns, and broken guns. Ravens are hovering over a dead mule; which was fortunate for Bruff, as later they were sometimes the only living thing he saw, and he was glad enough to eat them when he could.

While here, my husband made an interesting find—not a relic, for we saw none, but a blaze upon a pine tree. Mr. Cioffi said that the tree must be more than two centuries old; and the blaze was old, also, with the bark rolled up in ridges around it. In the center of the blaze, and perfectly recognizable, was carved the Masonic square and compass. Bruff wrote that he carved the square and compass, with his name and Poile's, at the Roberts cabin. We have never found it anywhere else along the reaches of the Overland Road. We like to think that this neat symbol of the organization, carved at his first camp, was also his handiwork.

The next small open flat beyond Bruff's Camp has a name, Sheep Pelt, that dates back to the seventies or eighties, when sheep were pastured far and wide upon the ridge. It recalls the time when the slaughtering and skinning camp occupied the flat and hides were cured here.

The quaint name of the next flat, Four Lantern, isn't so obvious, in its meaning, but it is derived from the lights hung nightly on the corners of the sheepfold to discourage wolves and coyotes.

One more open flat brought us to the last of the large conifers, where we planned to eat our lunch in the heavy shade. This place is called Obe Fields's, and it is necessary to add the apostrophe at least mentally; for Fields was a settler who once had a cabin on the spot, and the name is not an indication of any spreading territory. Such level land as may be found in the flat is covered thickly with the dusty green of horehound. There must be a spring somewhere, but I forgot to inquire for it (to my shame) in the excitement of passing sandwiches and thermos bottles of coffee strong enough to push out the corks. We had decided that washing would be a useless formality and, in my case, definitely hard on the skin, which was now thoroughly protected from sun and wind. Consequently I do not know where the Roberts family obtained their water, but Bruff dipped his easily from a "snow-rill" in front of his tent. Somewhere near by, there must have been a living spring all through the season for the thirsty emigrants. Somewhere, also, is the grave of little William Lambkin. From here, on March 25th, Clough went off to hunt and never returned. From here, on April 4th, Bruff and his pup started for the settlements. Both of them were weak and starved, but the pup continued alert and warned him of the approach of the many bear and wolves which threatened him and which he was too weak to shoot for fear of enraging without killing them.

Beginning at Obe Fields's, the trail looked (and felt) much as it did in 1849. The main trend is west, along the top of the stupendous mountain. It had to be on the top because the center of gravity in the prairie schooners was so high that they had either to proceed on a level or go straight up or straight down. A sidling place was rare on the trail and productive of grinding labor in holding the wagons upright with ropes; it was equally productive of accidents. Once on top of a ridge, the emigrants stayed there until they had no further use for it.

We left the timber immediately and came out into thick buckbrush.

Many of the emigrants called the whole ridge "the desert of the mountains," because of the shortage of forage for the animals. The name had seemed inapplicable as we traveled through heavy timber with sufficient water, but from here on I did not quarrel with their term.

Delano walked along here, meeting bear occasionally and passing by them unmolested. He wrote: "The road continues along this ridge nearly twenty miles, though there are occasional indentations which make hard, rocky and sidling hills for wagons to pass."

The first, and surely the grandfather, of all the "indentations" is a tremendous ravine which was named Steep Hollow in trail days and still goes by the title. Bruff had heard of it. "Late in the forenoon I reached 'Steep Hollow,' 7 miles from the cabin, and was astonished when I found that I had so miraculously travelled thus far. I had never been here before, but knew it by the description of travellers. There was a trail led to the right around a narrow curved ridge,— a good path, but I had forgotten that, and descended the long, steep stony and rugged road, falling several times, and with great difficulty rising each time, and at length reached the deep seated narrow bottom, and sank exhausted, on the ground."

Our jeep could negotiate the old pathway that Bruff missed. It has been widened slightly through the years, but it is a pretty crisp proposition for all that. The top of the ridge here is far too narrow and too bristling with rocks to support a wagon. The path is just below the top on the south side. Far beneath us the old wagon road dipped to the bottom of the hollow, which is brush filled from rim to rim. Down in its depths Bruff rested beside the rotting carcass of the mule which had died in the effort to bring him supplies for the winter. No doubt it had been looted of its load long since, as had all the other pack animals and wagons which failed to make the grade out.

Steep Hollow is still a sarcophagus of broken bones and wagons. However, it was too far away to visit; and it would not have been a walk, but rather a struggle through solid buckbrush. To go down might take all afternoon, and it was still a tossup whether we would win through to the valley or have to retrace our course. Even I knew that seeing the wreckage in Steep Hollow was out of the question, and I did not raise the issue.

Ahead of us swung the highly suicidal arc of trailway hanging on the gaunt gray mountain at the head of Steep Hollow. The little car tackled it and zoomed up, ricocheting from one impediment to another. I bounced up and down, but I wrote always on the downbeat. Sometimes it required the descents from half a dozen rocks to complete one letter. Meanwhile I wedged the edges of my shoe soles under some convenient projection (I never did look to see what it was) and remained in the car.

"There are the canyons," my husband shouted over the racketing of the jeep, which sounded like a guinea hen with hiccups,—"both of 'em. You can see into both of them at once," he insisted.

But I was concentrating furiously on the final syllable of Steep Hollow. "I can't bother with the canyons now," I shouted back; "they'll have to get along as best they can."

My husband recognized sheer frustration. "Maybe we'd better stop," he suggested kindly, "and give her a chance to catch up."

Mr. Cioffi executed an example of the plain and fancy driving for which he is justly noted, spun the wheel with accuracy, and we dropped from the current boulder with a thud.

I slid over in the seat, casting a surreptitious glance behind me
to see if I had lost any vertebrae. Mr. Cioffi disentangled my pencil
string; my husband unhooked a trailing strap and stood holding it
from further misadventure while I eased off the edge like a dirigible
with a ground crew.

To the north was the canyon of Mill Creek; its waters gleamed
phosphorescently in patches.

On the other hand Deer Creek Canyon swept magnificently southward to let the rugged watershed of Dry Creek intervene between it
and the ridge. This was a monochrome gulf into which we looked—
blue depths, blue mountain slopes, blue timber, blue sky.

*   *   *

For the rest of the day's travel I had much the sensation that must
come to a bug crawling along a very knotty ridgepole of a large
campmeeting tent. I have never, in a reasonably large experience
of rocks, seen anything like the trail over which we squirmed and
bumped: mile after mile of mountaintop, thousands and thousands
of rocks. Now the trail thrust itself up a steep slide of small black
stones that slipped with us; now we drove over a sweep of naked
lava solidified, where in some far-gone day it had poured in a broad
sheet over the earth.

I could not manage to write. For that matter, neither, a century
ago, could the faithful keepers of journals, but filled in from memory
when they were camped in the valley.

All but Bruff, whose notebooks and poor little skeleton of a dog
were his salvation during his solitary ambulation over the rocks. He
was two and a half days completing the seven miles west of Steep
Hollow. For food he ate a candle with salt and pepper, and gave the
pup the wick. Carcasses there were in plenty, but the thaw had come
long since and the wolves had left nothing, not even for the dog. It
was April 5th when he found a camp site where, sometime in the fall,
seeds had been spilled. They had sprouted and, down on his knees,
he gathered them—little cabbages, lettuce, and radishes—none over
two inches long. He shot and ate a bluebird, also, giving the dog her
share. Spring had come to the mountain.

The next morning, just before daybreak, his pup barked furiously;
and dawn showed that a moccasined Indian had passed. The hope of

shooting and eating that Indian urged the partially demented man over the brow of the mountain, and by noon he found that he had reached the edge of Dry Creek, at the base of the hills. He had traveled eight miles.

Our afternoon drew toward its close, and now we could not take time to stop for pictures. I tried to snap them as we bumped frantically up and down and broke a spring somewhere in my camera. I dragged out the extra that I always carry and went on trying with it. Down a solidified lava flow we reeled and staggered to a safe stop at Clough's Goat Camp. I suppose there is no possible chance that the Cloughs who kept goats here many years ago have any connection with the sturdy, kindly soul who companioned Bruff, hunted for him, and doubtless lost his life to the prowess of a grizzly or an Indian near by. There is no connection, but I felt a sense of satisfaction, just the same, that his name should be perpetuated on the ridge.

Occasionally we had glimpses of the Sacramento Valley, from which the summer had long since scorched out all green. It was toward evening when we reached the beginning of the downgrade. We were now on a hunters' road, but here and there the trail could be seen dimly, snaking its way through the scrub-filled downlands.

The day had been custom made for our convenience—not hot, not windy; either of which conditions could put one out of commission on the ridge. Nothing had gone wrong so far. The sky was coloring for the day's end, and part way down we took time to stop. The far hills looked flat, like polished cross sections of semiprecious stones inlaid upon mother of pearl—tourmaline-pink, amethyst, garnet, and deepening into lapis lazuli.

It behooved me to dwell as long as possible upon the beauties of nature, for the moment would soon be upon me when I must try to make myself presentable enough to meet civilized America. We were leaving the Lassen Trail. Fences and fields intervened, but, in the old days, it had proceeded across Dry Creek to strike the swift current of Deer Creek about three miles above the ranch of Peter J. Davis. Two miles below, and on the opposite side of the stream, was Lassen's Rancho—the Mecca of the hundreds whose gnawing misery ended there.

Along a smooth ranch road toward the highway we sailed evenly at forty miles an hour. It seemed preposterously fast. The thick dirt commenced to erode from the hood and fenders, but the floorboards gritted beneath my feet and I could have collected several spoonfuls of dirt from my lap. What my moist hot face looked like I could guess by looking at my moist hot hands.

We swung smoothly into the Chico and Red Bluff Highway twenty-six miles north of Chico and stopped at the first gas station for repairs. I turned for the first time in miles to consider my husband. His face and hands were exactly the same color as his clothes; the coating of thick dirt encompassed them all equally. Mr. Cioffi looked

better. The broad brim of his ranger's hat had intercepted much of the falling dust and he added a definite tone to the group. I hesitated before sliding out. "Washing won't do me much good," I told them. "What I need is a bath."

"A broom and dustpan would take off the worst," my husband suggested helpfully.

Either seemed impossible to arrange at the moment, so I went in and met, in a full-length mirror, something remotely in my own likeness. I was in an absolutely transcendent state of dirt, and my clothes would never have been allowed in a self-respecting rag bag. Fortunately, I didn't know until bedtime that I had worn five holes the size of quarters in the seat of my heavy wool skirt.

I started scrubbing the visible portions of my anatomy and afterward gazed on my face with pale pride. True, I was used to a higher standard of cleanliness, but it would do. My hair defeated me. It was so thickly covered with powdered dust that the part didn't show at all. So I tied it up, peasant style, and emerged.

No matter what happened from here in to camp; no matter what I looked like to the astonished tourists gassing up at the pumps; no matter for the broken camera. I had traveled the Lassen Trail, and nothing can ever take that fact away from me.

CHAPTER XVII

The Valley of the Sacramento

THE Valley of the Sacramento was something such as the travelers from the East had never seen before: a grazing country whose rich grasses were vividly green through April and platinum blond in the fall; whose straight pure watercourses were lined with noble trees as soon as they emerged from the foothills; where antelope, elk, and wild cattle pastured by the thousand and the small but hardy wild horses roamed in nervous bands. It was easy to believe in nature's lavishness, because it lay spread out before them and nothing interfered with their vision. For ten, fifty, a hundred miles the valley walked away from them to the south; their tired eyes lagged and gave up in the effort to follow. At the north, Mount Shasta hemmed them; to the west, the recumbent Coast Range sprawled its broad back toward them but bent its knees farther away as their journey took them toward Sutter's Fort. The Sierra Nevada was immediately at their left, two to five miles from them.

Deer Creek is a large stream, showing, even in the fall when the water is low, of what it is capable in time of flood. As it leaves the shallow-soiled foothills and commences to ditch its way across the fertile alluvial loam of the valley proper, it is striped on either side by heavy undergrowth and a wide line of sycamores, oaks, and alders. In their welcome shade, a short distance from its junction with the Sacramento, Peter Lassen built his ranch house on the south bank. Across from it, and close to where the highway now cuts Deer Creek, he founded his short-lived settlement, Benton City, named for Senator Thomas H. Benton, the father-in-law of John C. Frémont. It was for the Masonic lodge of this embryo town that Lassen brought a charter overland in 1848, while opening the Lassen Road for the wagon train he was guiding. The Western Star Lodge of Benton City thus became the first in California to have an official charter. Because of the natural delay in the transmission of news, and probably also the fact that San Francisco had a large Masonic membership eager for the honor of founding the first lodge, that city received and retained the honor of having lodge No. 1; but no one now questions the fact that Benton City, which received the second number, already had been organized. When Lassen's settlement terminated its existence, Western Star Lodge No. 2 was removed to Shasta City, where it now is. Benton City, called home by a few families who were induced to build houses there, lasted on into the 1860's and gradually faded out.

Those Forty-niners who bested the difficult trail and arrived early in the season no doubt enjoyed the beauty of what was to be their future state. The suffering souls who struggled down the ridge in the late fall wanted only to reach food, warmth, and help.

Bruff came down the stony yet muddy trail across the foothills and met an Indian with a small black dog. His pup was frantic with joy to see one of her kind, but Bruff thought only of food. The Indian had nothing; he showed his empty hands, indicating that he was going hunting, and turned away. Bruff, almost delirious, thought seriously of killing and eating the Indian but gave it up because the man's back was toward him. He staggered on and came to the giant oak timber of the Deer Creek bottoms where he again was forced to rest. In the branches of a fallen oak he found a place more comfortable than the shriveled ox carcasses which had been his only chairs for miles. He leaned back and passed into a lethargy from which he might never have roused had it lasted longer; but he was awakened by the excited barking of his little dog and opened his eyes to see his friend Poile standing over him.

Poile had food; he was, in fact, on his way up the ridge to help Bruff. He gave him a hard ship biscuit which it was impossible to devour too fast and supported him to the house, only three hundred yards away but out of sight in the timber. Bruff wrote, "Poile assisted me, I arose and went on, and in 15 minutes was at Davis' rancho, greeted cordially, by him." That night he and his little dog slept safely before the fire.

Amazingly enough, after months of long-distance dislike and repudiation, Bruff had no sooner recovered some of his strength than he went to work for Lassen, surveying, of all unlikely things, the very town that the shinglers at Bruff's Camp were supplying with building materials—Benton City. The emigrants of 1849 seemed to make no distinction between the rancho and the town. They called everything here "Lassen's Ranch" and, although they had looked forward to their arrival at food and shelter as the greatest boon that could happen to them, they had but little praise for the establishment.

Here, on Lassen's Rancho, which extended on both sides of Deer Creek as far as the Sacramento River, the emigrants again crossed the path of Jedediah Smith. Maurice S. Sullivan, who edited Smith's journal, states that the watercourse which Smith called Black Sand Creek, and where he was camped on April 5, 1828, is, of a surety, Deer Creek. Many naked Indians who carried bunches of green leaves visited his camp. "They were under the impression," wrote Smith, "that the horses could understand them and when they were passing they talked to them and made signs as to the men."

On the next day a bear sprang for Smith's horse and seized it by the tail. "The horse being strong and much frightened exerted himself so powerfully that he gave the Bear no opportunity to close uppon him and actually drew him 40 or 50 yards before he relinquished his hold."

A few days after this, Smith turned northwest toward the coast for his historic path-breaking trip to the Columbia.

The Lassen Cutoff as pioneered by Peter Lassen ended at his ranch. The road down the valley to Sutter's Fort was called Lassen's Road because, from 1844 on, his ranch was the outstanding northern landmark and travelers were apt to be bound for his house. If one includes the horde of gold seekers who angled in from the Truckee Pass at modern Nicolaus, this road carried the greater proportion of the Overland Forty-niners who came by the northern, or Humboldt, route.

From the Rancho the trail down the Sacramento River continued south a few miles to a fork where the right-hand road branched southwest to cross the Sacramento and to continue down its westerly bank. The left fork, used by most of the travelers, went slightly east of south, paralleling the river on the east side but staying close to the foothills of the Sierra, where, of course, their main interest was the gold diggings. It would be more than twenty-five miles, however, before any but an occasional straggler turned from the main trail toward the mountains, where distant white-topped Mount Lassen dominates the landscape.

In addition to the rickety, creaking, dirt-encrusted emigrant wagons of the Forty-niners, a variety of traffic passed up and down the east side of the valley, for this was a portion of the main north and south road to Oregon which the Lassen Cutoff had intersected on Pit River. It was also the means of communication between the scattered ranches. All through the year the hard-used trail carried riders and pack trains. A house called Potter's appeared below Lassen's on maps of the era, but the first well known place to the south was Rancho Chico, headquarters of John Bidwell, some twenty miles away. The Forty-niners speak with gratitude of the road signs (nailed to a tree and signed "Bidwell") which showed distances and directions to the mines, but, as far as I know, only one Forty-niner mentioned seeing a cabin.

John Bidwell, known in later years as the Prince of Pioneers, acquired his money by mining in 1849 and, from then on, lived in almost feudal state. A rancheria of harmless Indians provided workers who considered themselves paid if fed, it having been the sole occupation of their former lives to collect food. There is no doubt they were all quite happy. Californians look back on Bidwell as one of their great men. He came in the first overland emigration, that of 1841. He established himself at Fort Sutter as a valued friend and assistant of John Augustus Sutter, so much so, that, while digging around in the Sutter manuscripts contained at the State Library in Sacramento, my husband found a letter from Bidwell to his valued friend Sutter in which the former refused the latter's daughter Eliza in marriage. The letter is a marvel of diplomacy, but the refusal is absolute. Probably the daughter, who came from Europe with her mother and brothers in 1850, never knew of the proposition. It was to be an old-country arranged marriage.

In the course of years, John Bidwell became an authority on all sorts of agricultural pursuits. He studied types and varieties of grains, trees, vines, and poultry and established an experimental farm that still functions a few miles below the present city of Chico. Each department of the great ranch had its own superintendent and, some years ago, we had the privilege of interviewing Mr. George M. Gray, nephew of the famous Asa Gray, botanist. He had been superintendent of the orchards. "General Bidwell was kindness itself," he said, "but there was one thing he didn't readily forgive, and that was failure to come to the weekly breakfast on Sunday morning. We met then and talked over the affairs of the ranch. The general liked company and had a great deal. One Sunday morning there were several guests from the East and they particularly enjoyed the fried cakes which the Indian cook browned like hot cakes on top of the stove and served in stacks. Replenishments came in once or twice and, when the last disappeared, the general asked for more without result. So he sent for the cook, a fat glum-looking squaw. She filled the doorframe as she stood stolid and resentful. 'Fix some more cakes, now,' he told her; 'we can eat more.' Her black eyes stared straight ahead at the wall as she issued her ultimatum. 'No. No more grasshopper meal. No more cakes.' "

John Bidwell served in the state legislature in 1850 and was a member of a committee, headed by General Mariano Guadalupe Vallejo, which had for its purpose the dividing of California into counties and naming them. It is said that most of the names of Spanish origin were given by Vallejo and almost all the others by Bidwell. Later he served in Congress and was appointed brigadier general of the state militia by Governor Stanford. In the last years of his life his chief interest was the city of Chico, which grew up on his estate, and the Chico Normal School, forerunner of Chico State College, which now uses his turreted mansion as a campus building.

John Bidwell was a great citizen of his state. If someone else had chosen the titles, we might now have a county named for him, together with Lassen and Sutter.

To the east and south of Rancho Chico, the high, sudden ridges of foothills parallel one another in diagonals, running into the valley on a southwest slant. The path the emigrants traveled stayed with the flat bottom land as long as practical—why should they travel over the hummocky toes of the foothills?—but below the ranch the Sierra bends to the southeast and the trail turns also, heading for the well known landmark, Table Mountain, at whose southern end Oroville is built.

Butte Creek, when reached, presented fording problems. It was a deep-flowing watercourse, stealthy, silent, growing sluggish. Here was land belonging to Sam Neal, who had come to California with Frémont. Downstream from the crossing were two squalid rancherias. They were fortunately far enough away so that they did not offend, but the inhabitants, some two hundred extremely dirty Indians, were sometimes seen. They were almost without exception stark naked and, in spite of the abundance of food, always hungry.

A group of United States surveyors under Lieutenant George H. Derby were near the Butte Creek crossing of Lassen's route in October, 1849, and met their little dark brothers out gathering wild grapes. The tall sycamores and oaks were festooned with the beautiful vines, sometimes clear to the top and draped from one tree to another, in jungle fashion. The fruit could be had in great quantities and the ripe bunches were easy to pick; but it was the little dark sisters who carried the load, in big conical woven baskets, each holding as much as its owner could possibly lift. The men managed to struggle along under a bow and two or three arrows.

About ten miles beyond Butte Creek a branch road struck out for the Feather River mines. This was the first real turnoff. Young Hanson, reaching the junction, "hawed" at his ox team until he was hoarse; but the oxen had picked up their heavy hooves and laid them down like paving blocks behind that familiar string of wagons for so many weeks that they would not obey and continued to plug along in line. Drastic measures had to be taken, after which the Hansons finally turned toward Table Mountain and the upper crossing of the Feather River. The road was muddy, of course, and tedious. Herds of antelope drifted in the open plain, but the canny creatures kept sentries in all directions and there was not even a bush as a shelter for the hunter. A shot or two sent them pellmell toward the mountains.

When the Feather River was reached, the Forty-niners were in the mines at last. A German named Gerstaecker gave a good description of conditions. There was a camp at the ferry called Long's Store, probably at the spot upstream from Ophir (modern Oroville) named Long's Bar. The dwellings were nothing but tents and brush-covered huts, which were not as good as those the Indians made for themselves. Fires glittered all along the riverbanks, but the consensus of opinion (delivered in the rain) was that it was a miserable place. They should really have waited to see how beautiful their "miserable place" could be in April and May.

The ferry was a simple wagon bed capable of holding four people. They would be dry for the first half of the distance across the river, progressively becoming wet the rest of the way. It cost Gerstaecker's group $1.50 for the trip, leaving them with exactly a dollar. Anything to eat cost $2 a pound. They had no tools to make a shelter and their blankets were soaking wet. They existed for about ten days and then started back toward Sacramento to save their lives.

Meanwhile the regular Lassen Road went as directly as possible across the low rolling hills to the big bend of Feather River. The emigrants were traveling through what is now locally called the Red Hills, slightly billowing rust-colored knolls that, in a wet year, will raise grain and, in a dry one, grasshoppers. Nothing could have suited the naked Indians of the scattered rancherias any better than the latter. One of their community projects was the summer grasshopper drive, in which all the able-bodied members of any given village formed a great circle on the dry hot upland and walked toward the center, where a large hole had been dug. As they beat the grass, the grasshoppers scampered ahead and, falling in the hole, were settled for good and all with hot rocks. Nicely roasted, these were consumed as hors d'œuvres or were powdered to make the grass-hopper meal already mentioned. I do not speak from experience, but I should imagine that they would not look nor taste worse than shrimps.

Food garnering seemed always to be done by Indians in groups. Acorn gathering, fishing, grasshopper drives—the emigrants always saw a large party so engaged. Apparently, if there was food, the whole village ate; if not, it was time to go out and get some. There was no lack in California. It was a veritable cornucopia of plenty; but, strangely enough, the Indians preferred the fish, grasshoppers, berries, sweet heads of clover, and even earthworms to meat from the roaming herds of cattle, elk, antelope, and wild horses that flourished in such numbers as to blacken the valley floor. Spirits of a very uncertain character lived in the animals, so their superstition ran, and it was wise not to molest them. The fact that they were shy and canny (much more so than the buffalo on which the Indians of the plains subsisted) and that they posted sentinels so that it was hard to approach within arrow shot on the treeless grazing land may have had something to do with establishing the notion. But once a belief of that nature is rooted, a simple people will starve to death rather than violate it. We have only to remember the sacred cow of India to realize the fact.

The emigrants called all Indians, from Utah to the Pacific, "Diggers." They have been so called with such persistence that not one person in thousands has ever heard the true name of the tribe to which these Sacramento Valley Indians belonged, the Wintun.

The Red Hills are hot in summer. I have seen the thermometer stand at 120° in the shade, which, I may add, had to be artificially contrived. Shade is not one of the commodities provided by nature. Pity the poor horse and rider who traveled this stretch in September (as many did), when the curved earth gave back a fierce refraction to the noon. In ordinary years it is a matter for congratulation when the first rains of autumn dampen the cast-iron ground and bring the pricking spears of green through the mat of last year's dry grass. Probably there was never a time nor a condition of weather when the traveler did not look forward to his arrival at Feather River, either for shade or for shelter from storm and wind.

In early days it was bordered with a growth of stately trees, two miles wide in places, which in these modern times has been reduced by reclamation to several hundred yards in width. Dredging for gold has ruined the appearance of the river in many places.

We drove in our car from Chico, as directly as possible, to the bend of the Feather. It wasn't possible to be too direct, as it had just rained and the reddish soil was as slippery as soap. Just below the bend is a dam and, between the bend and the dam, new head gates were being constructed by the Sutter-Butte Canal Company. A good dirt road led in that direction and we took it, creeping tentatively up a high narrow fill between the waters of the canal and a gravel pit. We pulled slowly up the sharp pitch and nosed over the top. A particularly large truck was parked on the roadway, filling it almost from edge to edge. This was no place to attempt to out-maneuver trucks, so my husband shifted gears preparatory to backing and I took the opportunity to get out. "You do whatever you have to," I said. "We'll go over to the river and see what the curve looks like."

The "we," in this case, included Mrs. Lola Neff of Biggs, whom we had picked up an hour before in the hope that her thorough knowledge of the country might help us.

"An Indian rancheria was somewhere near here," she told me; "I asked Henry Hazlebusch. He owns the next ranch downstream."

"Would he know as much about it as anyone?" I wanted to know.

"Well, when I was a girl, we used to call the remains of the village 'Hazlebusch's Indians,' because quite a lot of them worked for him.

They were something like Bidwell's Indians, useful and more or less self-supporting as long as they had someone to tell them what to do."

We reached the water's edge and looked around. There were, of course, no Indians; there was, of course, no old road. There were no carvings on the rocks—all round and river washed. There were no tire-marked boulders in the ruts—Heavens above! No ruts! I turned and sent out an S.O.S. for my husband.

He arrived looking pleased; the driver of the truck had appeared, like the gentleman he was, and driven to a turnout. "No question at all about this place being on the trail," he enlightened us. "This was the first spot they could strike water. What is the little cemetery we just passed on the dirt road?" he asked Mrs. Neff.

"That is all that's left of Hamilton, an old settlement," she told him.

"Well, if we had any doubts, that would settle them. Hamilton House was the road station where the stages struck the Feather River."

A glimmer of understanding began to shine on a clouded subject. I looked at Mrs. Neff. "Some of the Forty-niners said that they passed near an Indian village, and some said they went right through the middle of it," I told her. "It is beginning to clear up in my mind. The village was on the rounded curve of the river, so that the trail could go right through it or could, by veering to the south just a little, hit the river lower down."

"Well, of course they could," my husband said casually; "just consider the topography."

"You consider it," I told him rudely. Topography, I admit when I have to, is completely out of my ken. It rattles around on the outside of my brain and bounces off. Whereas, in my husband's case (if I understand him correctly) topography is something that he took to bed with him in his infancy instead of a Teddy bear.

"The journals say that the river made a sharp curve to the east and back just below the bend," he went on patiently instructing me. "It took less than four miles."

"Oh, yes, of course," I agreed brightly; "that scallop in the river that the trail skipped across instead of following around."

"Well, cartographers don't call such curves 'scallops' as a rule."

"It's a scallop to me. Now all we have to do is to find where the trail next hits the river after it leaves it (right here where we're standing) and we'll have the famous ford of the Feather, because they crossed as soon as they struck the river again."

"I can tell you that," Mrs. Neff spoke up. "If the wagons forded the river in the neighborhood of four miles from here, they crossed at the riffles on the old Musholt place that was later the Rio Bonito Ranch. I was talking to Charlie Bayles about it, and he said that it used to be called 'the old ford' and that his father thought nothing of taking his harvesting machinery across it."

"I know myself that it is shallow there," I said. "I have seen salmon going up the river and wriggling among the rocks at those riffles, with their backs partly out of water."

"And I have waded it," my husband added to the weight of evidence. "It wasn't over my boot tops, anywhere."

"Well, you'll never see it again," she said with finality. "The river has been dredged and the Rio Bonito Ranch is just about hidden under heaps of gravel and rocks."

"That's too bad," my husband admitted, "but we'll go on down the river and find where the *scallop*"—he stressed it sarcastically—"begins and ends. First, though, while we're on the spot, what do you have about the rancheria? This was the first Indian village the Forty-niners actually went into after striking the valley."

"Gerstaecker described it," I said, finding the required notes. "He said that there were three villages just above the ford. One was directly on the trail and the other two were a short distance away. It seems likely that one was here or hereabouts and that the other two were on the river in such a position that the emigrants, cutting across the scallop, missed them. The first village consisted of permanent houses—about thirty of them, he thought. The Indians made them by digging four feet below the surface of the ground and then walling the pit until the structure extended six to eight feet above the ground and arched into a perfectly round earthen roof. In the exact center was a hole for the escape of smoke."

"How did they get in and out?" Mrs. Neff asked.

"There was another hole, large enough to crawl through, just above the ground; and Gerstaecker said that the roofs shed rain and the huts were dry and warm."

If so, I thought, they were better than some of the Nebraska sod houses, of which the women used to complain that after a three-day storm the roof dissolved onto the rag rugs in the likeness of porridge.

"Each hut seemed to have a storage place for provisions near it," I went on aloud. "Gerstaecker said there were 'cylindrical, plait-work erections, made out of cane, about ten feet high, and four feet in diameter.' The cane was probably tule."

"Yes, and the storage places held acorns," said my husband. "They harvested the crop in the fall, and any year that was bad for the acorns was bad for the Indians."

When Gerstaecker went through the rancheria, the women were sitting in the entrances of the clustered huts, cracking acorns with their teeth into pieces of cloth laid in their laps. They wore the ordinary costume of California-Indian women, two thick mats or aprons of reeds, a short one in front and a longer one behind; and, in deference to the cold afternoon, they had blankets around their shoulders. The men, of course, were doing nothing and had moved up on the roofs to be in the thin November sunshine. Some of them had on a few rags and tags; some were mother naked; while some had a garment or two of American clothing which looked about as suitable and necessary as fringe on a locomotive.

As the party of miners passed between the huts, the Indian men raised themselves to a sitting position and, hitching back to back, sat that way, thus providing against the necessity of having to stiffen their own spines.

"I've had a pretty good mental picture of that Indian village for a long time," I told Mrs. Neff as we walked back to the car. "It's nice to be able to add the scenery as it really is. Do you think we can get near enough to see the little curve downstream where the other two villages were?"

"I don't think there's a chance," she said discouragingly, "but we can always ask."

So, as best I could, I described to a nearby workman what we were looking for.

"Sorry, lady, to spoil your plan," the man told me politely, "but there is no such little curve. Of course I haven't walked all the way along the river for the next four miles, but the aerial maps that were taken before the river was dredged show that it is pretty straight, once it gets around the big bend here by the dam."

Our next stop, at the Henry Hazlebusch Ranch, was also disconcerting. Mr. Hazlebusch was informative about Indians, Hamilton House, the dam, the Sutter-Butte Canal, and a lot of things past and present, but he would not admit any scallop in the river back of his house. We went on and interviewed Mr. and Mrs. Williams, present proprietors of Rio Bonito. They were cooperative and produced the aerial map of the ranch and environs taken before the dredging started. The river was straight.

"This is a darned shame," I complained. "We can't prove locations if the curl has come out oi the Feather."

"That's the brightest thing you've said all day," my husband encouraged me. "I'll bet the river has changed."

"I know where we can find out," Mrs. Neff contributed. "The offices of the Sutter-Butte Canal Company will have every map of the county they could lay hands on. We'll go there."

So to Gridley we went and were kindly supplied with an imposing stack of maps. Almost the first one we looked at showed the river as quite straight for the four miles under discussion but, in dotted lines to indicate a former course of the river bed, there was a sharp curve to the east and back. My scallop had materialized, proving that the ford was certainly at the riffles on the old Musholt Ranch.

It was a simple crossing for the wagons—noisy, rushing, white-topped water and a hard, uneven bed of river-washed round rocks. The animals scarcely wet their knees as they ascended the left bank, and the wheels did not swell enough to set the tires.

This was the last time that the emigrants on the Lassen Road had to cross the Feather, and the river now stretched, an ever deepening and more difficult barrier, between them and the width of the Sacramento Valley.

And so the wagons rumbled along the eastern bank, and the many who had lost their animals and equipment walked. If hot or raining, it was a comfort to have the thick-leaved limbs of oak, willow, or sycamore interposed between their suffering heads and the weather. In the weeks of spring or fall, when each day was a crystal goblet filled with such heady wine that to experience it was almost to be drunk with sheer pleasure in living, it didn't matter where they walked or rode—it was all California.

The most conspicuous objects in the whole great valley of the Sacramento are the Sutter Buttes, an amassment of small peaks six miles long that rise startlingly from the flat valley floor, without preface or apology, to a height of 2,690 feet. The peaks are precipitous, gashed with gorges and pocked with living springs. They cut the sky west of the junction of the Feather and its lesser tributary, the Yuba, and cannot be forgotten nor ignored.

When opposite the main peak at the north end of the Buttes, a branch trail broke from the Lassen Road and ran southeast. It was in existence at least as early as 1849 and went straight to Johnson's Ranch, on Bear River just above modern Wheatland, where the trail from Truckee Pass struck the Sacramento Valley. At about one-third of the distance, the branch trail crossed the Yuba River at Rose's Rancho, where travelers noted few improvements but a small adobe house "redolent with the odor of whisky, and festooned with strings of jerked beef." This trail was the accepted turnoff for the Yuba mines and was a short cut to the mines on Bear River.

When the emigrants had moved down the main road as far as Honcut Creek, they were on the Cordua Ranch. This was true from 1842 until the spring of 1849.

From the fall of 1842 until 1844, Cordua was the only settler north of Bear River, with the exception of whatever employees of Sutter's might be at Hock Farm, eight miles down the Feather River. Beginning in 1844, the country was settled gradually: Lassen on Deer Creek, Charles Roether, Thomas Fallon and Edward Farwell on Honcut Creek, Charles Flügge and Nicolaus Altgeier below the Hock Farm on Feather River, George Peterson and Jack Smith at what is now the town of Linda. In 1847 Michael C. Nye, who, as well as Flügge, had come with the Bidwell-Bartleson Party in 1841, bought a piece of land west of Smith's from Sutter, with whom he entered into some sort of an agreement for the joint raising of cattle.

One of the interesting anecdotes attributed to the Cordua Ranch was the visit, in the fall of 1846, of young Jacob Wright Harlan, who had been sent hurrying over the Sierra by his father, captain of the Harlan-Young Party, to buy beef on the hoof and to drive it back to relieve the distress of the company. Tom Smith was his companion in this enterprise. On arrival, a man who was recruiting for Frémont's army persuaded Tom Smith to go with him. It was much easier, much more thrilling, much more patriotic to join the army than to travel across those stupendous mountains, whose canyons were even now filling with snow, to take twelve stubborn beeves to the hungry Harlan Party. The recruiting officer was probably William Fallon, who was engaged in that work during the fall of 1846. So Smith went off to fight for his country if he and the fighting could ever connect, and young Harlan was in a pretty fix. There would be no sleep for him. Cordua, wrote Harlan, solved the problem by sending along two *vaqueros*. The beef on the hoof arrived in time to solve their food problem, and the Harlan-Young Party came through safely to the valley.

After gold was discovered, all of Cordua's men, except the Indians, left for the mines; and so he took a partner, Charles Covillaud, a Frenchman with whom he did not always agree. Covillaud married at Christmas time in 1848. Almost at once Cordua sold his interest to some emigrants for $20,000 and left in February.

Charles Covillaud's wife was Mary Murphy of the Donner Party, who had previously been married to William Johnson of the famous Johnson Ranch on Bear River. Her sister, Mrs. Harriet Pike, also of the Donner Party, married Michael Nye. Family life was really beginning in the northern valley. So Mary was mistress in her time of two of the best known ranches of early days, and by 1849 a little town started up at the forks of the Feather and the Yuba that bore her name, Marysville, and its population soon outnumbered all other cities except San Francisco and Sacramento.

A few miles of easy traveling through Cordua's herds put everyone in good humor, although Spanish cattle were dangerous to pedestrians. There was no need to look wishfully at the good fat animals; anyone was welcome to butcher a beef anywhere in California and take all the meat; however, he must skin it carefully and hang the hide high in a tree out of reach of the coyotes. The herds were raised solely for their hides and tallow.

The first white visitor within the forks of the Feather and the Yuba, so far as is known, was Jedediah Smith. He was on his way toward Oregon with his trappers and camped in the angle of the rivers on March 16, 1828, naming the Feather and the Yuba respectively the "Ya-loo" and the "Hen-neet." Apparently they were never so called thereafter. The Yuba was eventually named for the Yuba tribe that lived on its banks. The Feather River is Anglicized from Rio de las Plumas, bestowed by Luis Arguello, exploring in 1820, because of the quantities of wild-fowl plumage found floating on its waters.

The town of Marysville had its beginnings immediately within the angle of the rivers, as this was practically the head of navigation on the Feather. For color and description of the budding settlement, we are indebted to Mrs. D. B. Bates.

Apparently neither Mrs. Bates nor her slightly reprehensible husband was ever so forgetful of what was socially correct as to use the other's first name; so as plain Mrs. Bates she will go down in history. They went here and there in California in 1851, renting and running hotels, which seems to have been too much for her strength, as she was ill a good deal. When she was too sick to run a hotel or even to leave her bed, he solved the difficulty by renting a cabin, locking her in it for safety, and going off; but whatever the situation, she bobbed up eventually with a ladylike and flowery version of her experience.

Mrs. Bates saw everything, heard everything, and told everything. From the time when, in 1851, she sat on her trunk in a dray, being taken to her husband's choice among the four "first class hotels" in Marysville, to the spring of 1854 when, greatly disillusioned, she went East again, she didn't miss a trick. She saw and wrote about many characteristic sights of the town: the Mexican-driven burro pack trains, heavily overloaded, that left town so reluctantly for the mines, and of how the burros hid behind buildings at every chance and sometimes managed to be left. She told of the superhuman horsemanship of the native Californians; about horse breaking through the city streets of Marysville, and the time that a horse charged across the piazza and through the door of the Tremont Hotel, stunning his rider against the doorframe and attacking the other horse he saw in the large mirror behind the bar, doing a thousand dollars' worth of damage, which was unquestioningly paid. She admired the animated Californian ladies who lacked the clear olive complexion of the Castilians but whose dark eyes flashed with equal intelligence and passion, and who danced with grace and used the cigarito so artfully that it rivaled the fan as an appliance of coquetry. She also admired, in their own environment, the Indians spearing salmon with unerring aim. She shuddered at terrible floods where people trapped in shacks climbed on tables and, when the tables floated high enough, knocked holes in the roof and climbed on the ridgepole, which, as like as not, they shared with a few blasé rats who had lived through floods before. Minor annoyances were "misquetoes" so thick and bloodthirsty that men worked in the fields wearing green veils over their hats and tied around their necks; coyotes who kept the untended cemeteries a scene of horror; strange Chinese who cut their hair like Americans, save for the cue coiled under their hats.

Such, with the whistle of steamboats reaching the head of navigation, the ceaseless noise of the gambling halls, and the rumble of emigrant wagons thrown in for good measure, was Marysville, third city of the state.

To get out of the angle of the two rivers and proceed southward, the emigrants forded the Yuba. The crossing was just a short distance above the confluence. The banks were steep, but the men shoveled them down to a practical slope; a large wooded island in midstream divided the current and thus simplified the problem. The Yuba is the smaller of the two rivers, but in the rainy season it is a tumultuous stream and capable of tremendous floods. The Forty-niners who came along in November had a bad time of it. Fortunately, most of the crossings were made earlier in the fall, at the period of lowest water.

The Lassen Road left its leafy shelter of trees at this point and struck straight across the flat plains, a little east of south, toward the spot where the Bear River joins the Feather. The travelers had only gone about three miles from Marysville when a branch trail broke away on a southwest slant, plunging right into the tempting greenery again to strike the Feather River eight miles below the town. Few people turned aside on this short road, for they had just left a settlement and had their faces newly turned toward Sacramento. The few who did so found themselves on the river's edge, looking across the broad, deep current of the Feather, at a swarming, noisy rancheria and the white buildings of Hock Farm.

Johann August Suter (Swiss by birth, Mexican by citizenship) had his subsidiary ranch here in the early 1840's. It played second fiddle to his headquarters at Sutter's Fort until after the discovery of gold. Then John Augustus Sutter, American, hoping for the governorship of the new state but destined to be disappointed, moved to Hock Farm to stay.

A good description of the place was written on October 15, 1849, by Lieutenant George Derby, in charge of a party of United States engineers who had just selected the site for Camp Far West (about a mile from the Johnson ranch house) and were returning. The Feather River at Hock Farm was six hundred yards across and heavily lined with white-trunked sycamores. The neat adobe house faced the river. It was the loveliest place to build a home that Derby's men had yet seen in California. They decided to stay for the night. Besides, there would be bread and wine—meat they always could have for the hunt-

ing—and a large rancheria just upstream promised diversion. Evidently
the men emptied their wagon and took the goods across on the mules;
the far bank looked pretty steep.

The far bank *was* pretty steep, steeper than they had expected; but
out from the rancheria buzzed the Indians. They never missed anything if they could help it. All of the three hundred who were physi-
cally able and could get close enough grabbed the wagon, the mules,
the tongue, the wheels, and hoisted it to the top of the steep embank-
ment. The sound effects throughout the affair were deafening, for
each Indian clacked to the mules, gabbled at the engineers, and
screamed at his fellows without once pausing for breath.

Their rancheria was close. Derby could have thrown a rock to its
nearest mud-bubble dwelling. There seemed to be about twenty of
them to a population of three hundred. It became a problem in
simple arithmetic—fifteen to a house. They had just begun the fall
harvesting under the big white oaks, and the high basketry bins
already contained some forty or fifty bushels of long pointed acorns.
The Diggers retreated noisily to their own domain, no doubt taking
some of the men with them for a closer look; almost every man
traveling the valley road made at least one foray for curiosity's sake,
and some never passed by a village without a visit.

Derby turned to the house. It was one of the picturesque whitened
adobe dwellings that seem to have been placed by nature instead of
by man, as germane to the scene as a flat white rock on the river
cliff. It was reminiscent of Fort Sutter: high walls surrounded the
outhouses, corrals, and sheds. About one hundred acres of wheat
were fenced away from the devastating raids of the wild herds. Grain
yielded amazingly and without care in soil so rich that it was practically fertilizer. Limitless pasture land of last year's grass—sleek
and silver gilt—spread shimmering to the far horizons. On it, singly
or in groves, but always placed with consummate dignity, stood the
kingly valley oaks on whose bounty the Indians lived from year to
year.

The surveying crew stayed overnight but they didn't enjoy the
village, whose emotions always seemed to be expressed in clamor of
one kind or another. It was the season for fever and a Digger had
died. As soon as the screaming of excitement and welcome had died
down, they went back to their houses, dug their heels in and commenced to howl in good earnest and (probably) in relays, as it was

expected to last all night. The whites were also suffering with fever. Derby gave them all quinine and, when the dawn broke, was glad to leave.

Hock Farm was of vital importance to the political leaders of the new state; it was even used for a time as headquarters by Frémont in the troubled days before the raising of the Bear Flag; but it was of no moment to the emigrants and is seldom mentioned in their journals. On the Garden Highway, south of Yuba City, its heavy iron gates have been set up beside the road as a landmark.

CHAPTER XVIII

With My Washbowl on My Knee

RUNNING placidly through the deep-loamed flatland came little Bear River to join the Feather. It was sometimes, in gold rush days, called Bear Creek or its Spanish equivalent, Rio Oso.

Here was the ranch of Nicolaus Altgeier. Everyone passed through his hospitable stronghold and it held a warm spot in the hearts of all alike. In 1849 Derby noted dutifully in his report that the large two-story house of adobe was truly a mansion for the time and place and that there was a fenced inclosure one quarter mile square. He estimated the "wretched Indians—playfully termed Christian" at about one hundred but the rivers boiled with salmon, the valley popped with grasshoppers, while the lusty oak trees showered their acorns down. It took little extra to keep them.

My husband and I have been through the settlement still called Nicolaus many times; but last month, as I needed this particular information, we decided to pay it another visit.

A few inquiries led us to the neat house of B. L. Drescher, quite elderly, who was born here. He lives alone and was just washing up for dinner, with great vigor, when we knocked; but as soon as he had eaten we took him along on what was for us an exploring expedition.

"I notice you pronounce 'Altgeier' with a long *i* and without sounding the *t*," my husband began tentatively.

"That's the way my father always said it," Mr. Drescher replied, "and he worked for Nicolaus a long time."

"I don't think Nicolaus could write very well," I hazarded. "There are some documents at Sutter's Fort—deeds or what not, in connection with his business—done in several handwritings; some of them use the spelling 'Altgeier,' but one, written by John Bidwell, is spelled with two *l*'s. He accented the first syllable. Probably that one is right."

By this time we had gone through the town, passing the white, green-trimmed Arens house that used to be the county seat, and were out in the country, headed for the site, a mile and a half downstream, where the old roadhouse had stood.

"Tell us about Nicolaus from the beginning," I urged the old gentleman.

"Well, the story goes that he came with one of the first trappers' parties. I don't know about that, but he got here very early. He'd been in the country a long time before Sutter came in 1839. He was living here with the Indians on a rancheria, so I guess they must have been on the grant that Sutter got from the Mexican government. I don't know whether Sutter just wanted a neighbor, or felt that there should be a sort of store and hotel out here to help the emigrant companies, or what his idea was. Anyway, he got in contact with Nicolaus and had him put up and run that sort of a tavern. It can't be much farther now to the place where he built it. Of course there's nothing left of it any more."

"Did Sutter give him the land?"

"Did he? Of course he did; acreage didn't mean a thing in those days. Sutter gave Nicolaus," he accented his words impressively, "a strip along the left bank of the Feather River approximately four and a half miles long. It ran from about a half mile above town to four miles below. Stop here," he added, giving a searching look at the terrain. "Here's where we want to get out."

"Do you see that low dike between us and the river, and the bigger levee behind it?" Mr. Drescher asked when we had gone through a gate. It was a purely rhetorical question; we couldn't see much of anything else at the moment. "Neither of them was here when the house was built, of course. The low one was put up in 1868 and the big one in 1911. They just happened to be thrown up each side of the place where the house stood."

We toiled up the sloping grassy side of the low dike and looked down into the depression between the two. The men stood talking and I unslung the expensive appliances with which my family has lately endowed me for the improvement of my photography. It is a beautiful camera. It is a fine exposure meter. They are both exquisitely small and covered with excruciatingly tiny figures which I cannot read without glasses. I used to take useful pictures out the car window that saved two pages of written description. Now, I see some interesting feature of the landscape and start operations, grab for my glasses, test the light, set the camera to all the necessary niceties of lens opening and light adjustment. As the desired picture is some half a mile behind by that time, I snatch my pencil and write what I can remember of what it looked like. Some day, they tell me, I will have learned the short cuts with the new equipment. Right now, nobody was hurrying me, but a depression between two levees simply doesn't lend itself. I haven't seen the finished picture yet, but I'll bet it won't be an artistic production either.

"How early did your father come here?" my husband asked as we were walking back to the gate.

"In 1849. He was a surveyor by profession and he chained Nicolaus's ranch for him. After that there wasn't anything more of that kind to do, so he took a job as chief cook and bartender at the new roadhouse. Of course Nicolaus had more land than money, so he paid him for the survey with 160 acres. The family has been here ever since."

Although the first house was of adobe, the one Mr. Drescher remembers was frame, built of timber brought up the river on a steamer. It was quite an imposing residence, he said.

We then went back to town; but, before our guide left us, he showed us two more interesting buildings. First, the old "Miners' Store," standing just above town in a field—if anything so dilapidated can be said to stand. Its blackened boards will not hold together many more years and it dates from the fifties. Then we returned through the town, crossed the bridge over Feather River, and proceeded three and one-tenth miles toward Marysville on the Garden Highway to see the house which Sam Brannon, famous Mormon pioneer of San Francisco, built on the west bank of the Feather just about opposite the confluence of the Bear. It was a beautiful site and of much the same order as the situation of Hock Farm, but without the giant sycamores. The house has been moved over to face the highway and looks so modern that the average passer-by would not give it a second glance.

At the present town of Nicolaus the road from Lassen's house forded the Bear quite easily, passed Nicolaus's roadhouse, and in another mile was joined by the emigrants from the Overland Road through Truckee Pass. Their columns came along a trail from the east, striking boldly across the open plain from the Johnson Ranch.

Immediately after the acquisition of the travelers from the Truckee route, the road from Lassen's Rancho split again. The travelers had a choice. They might continue straight on across the open plain, which was flat as a table and covered with nothing shadier than grass, dead, of course, in the fall, and a perfect reflector of the sun's rays on a hot afternoon; or they might follow the Feather in a curve toward the west, remaining under its belt of trees until it met and mingled with the waters of the Sacramento, when they would continue with the latter. Those who chose the open plain went faster, doubtless. There would not be much incentive to linger. There were one or two pools of standing water a few miles from the split in the road, then no more until they came to Dry Creek.

The pack trains, as usual, were the sufferers when water was scarce.

Little low hills encroach here into the wide valley, and the road kept as much as possible beyond their scope. They are barren and hardpan is just below the surface. Perhaps it would be more accurate to say it *was* just below it, for the whole area was patiently mined. Every bit of the surface dirt was scraped from the hardpan and run through the long toms, which in turn deposited the worthless tailings in small terminal moraines a foot or two high and perhaps six feet across. They are as thick as is possible for miles, and look as if the little hills had goose-pimpled during the chilly winter. Just north of Roseville they are especially interesting, but few people who see them day after day know what they are.

Those who took the river road fared better. It was more comfortable and more interesting. Below Nicolaus they came to Vernon, a ferry town. Carriger, who came in 1846, said that it was the first ferry he had seen since leaving the Missouri River. It antedated all the trail ferries of the overland trek from the Missouri west to California. About one hundred people lived there in those days. Lately there would seem to be fewer, but there is still a town. Its name is now Verona. Some post office in the south took the old name Vernon from it, having, no doubt, a much greater population. It certainly did not have seniority.

The confluence of the two great rivers is silent and majestic. The best view is from the west side of the Sacramento at the site of old Fremont, the companion town of Vernon and the opposite landing of the ferry. The crossing was made a few hundred yards downstream from the river junction and the old pilings may still be seen perhaps a quarter-mile below Vernon, near the crossing of the power line.

The great Sacramento was tidal even at this distance from the ocean, and the variation was said to be from six to fourteen inches. The trail paralleled its course, but beyond Vernon it stayed a respectful distance away because of the dangers of the dreaded tule. In the summertime the tule beds were passable, even rather good walking, for, when perfectly dry, they were elastic, springing up with the release of weight. When wet they became a "thick tenacious quagmire."

Lieutenant Derby and his men started across a tule land west of the Sacramento early one morning after a rainy night. They knew it to be impassable for six months out of the year, but this was the first big rain—the one on November 2, 1849—and they thought it would bear them up until it had time to get thoroughly soaked. So they set out with their mule-drawn wagon, keeping on the packed road and watching carefully for signs of a soft spot. The Indians would have known better.

They had to cross at least three miles of what amounted to a thickly wadded rush mat thrown over a lake of mud. The tangled mat lost its stiffness, began to bend, separate, and apparently to dissolve. They hurried, twisting the mules this way and that for better footing, but always keeping to the thread of road where the tules had been beaten flat to give a surface. It was impossible to see far in the forest of yellow-green rapiers that were as much as an inch through at the butt and towered ten to twelve feet high. So thick they grew that a man could not thrust his arm in the mass without pushing one or more aside. Even standing on the wagon seat Derby could not tell to a certainty whether they would soon come to the end. As it happened, they had only a half-mile left to travel when they met a strong current of water flowing down the road to meet them— storm-overflow water from the nearest creek. It was perceptibly growing deeper and stronger. They tried to turn the wagon to race back ahead of it, overran the fast softening roadway, and mired hopelessly. Recklessly snatching their most valuable instruments, they cut the mules loose and mounted them. Even then they were not sure that they would save the animals or, for that matter, themselves. The water, they afterward found, gained at the rate of four feet an hour. Soaked, floundering, running, tugging, they raced ahead of the lumbering, elephant-gray clouds and gained safety to the distant trumpeting of thunder.

At Dry Creek the river road and the plains road, which had separated just below Nicolaus's ranch, forded some three-quarters of a mile apart and angled together about a mile south of the creek. The name of this disappointing so-called "watercourse" did not belie it, and the thirsty animals had to be taken a mile up the "creek" for water from a hole. After the rains set in, though, it was a torrent. A small tule extended from near the fords almost to the Sacramento River and was probably the reason that the river road swung so far east to join the other. Five miles more brought them to the crossing of Rio de los Americanos, rumored to be so called from the fact that Jedediah Smith and his trappers visited it in the winter of 1826-1827, before Americans were common in California. By 1849 it was called simply the American River. At the ford where North Sacramento now stands was the little trail settlement of Boston. Three miles up the American was another ford at a mill; the banks were high, but it was possible to cross. Derby's report to the War Department says eight miles between the fords, but his map shows three and the terrain shows three. It seems likely that the longhand report was misread and the figure 3 mistaken for an 8.

At the Boston, or Lower, Ford the banks were thirty feet high, but the slope was gradual and easy. During the low water of October, an exposed sand bar was useful in midstream, the water being but one and one-half to two and one-half feet deep. Three days of rain in the mountains would be sufficient to raise it four to six feet. At such times prospective travelers to the north valley changed their minds and stayed at home.

The willows at the ford were cool and inviting; wild blackberries were plentiful and ripe. Heinrich Lienhard, who traveled with the Harlan-Young company, tells how the ford appeared in the fall of 1846: "As I rounded a sharp bend in the irregular road, I saw in the distance several cattle corrals; beyond them, not far from the trail, stood a plain, even primitive house where two attractive white women were leaning out of an open window, watching us approach. They spoke to us as we drew near, and said the property on which they were living belonged to a Mr. Sinclair, a Scotsman who was justice of the peace. One of the two women who talked to us was his wife. The building was delightfully situated near the bank of the American Fork at a point where the river was unusually smooth and broad.

"There was no ferry across the American Fork, so Thomen and I had to wade the crystal-clear but shallow stream with our bare feet. We reached the opposite bank without difficulty, where the trail meandered first through marshlands which were often entirely under water when the river overflowed, and then up and across high ground, where a solitary Indian hut stood on a dry knoll near a deep waterhole.

"As the road we were walking now curved again, suddenly a commodious adobe structure, whose walls contained large holes that held guns, loomed up near us; directly east of it stood two small corrals and a dry lake which was filled in the spring when the American Fork broke through its banks. This was where Sutter kept the flocks of sheep he hired me to take charge of two years later. Even a superficial glance showed that the soil on either side of the trail leading to the fort was too poor to raise crops on, but not far away was the lush, river-bottom land where the energetic Sutter had planted the grain that yielded such enormous harvests. His wonderful wheatfields were already famous all over California.

"A mile or more beyond the river, the trail crossed a small hill; from its crest the massive walls of Sutter's Fort, which its owner called New Helvetia, were now visible. It was one of the happiest moments of my life, as I stood there and gazed at my actual, my final destination."

For nearly five months he had strained his eyes, awaiting this moment. Sutter's Fort sat compactly on a knoll, comfortingly dry during floods which were practically annual; comfortingly non-inflammable as a swallow's nest during the sweeping grass fires; comfortingly walled and with heavy gates protected by cannon; comfortingly provisioned from its acres of wheat and great herds of cattle; and, more comforting than all, presided over by such a generous, humanity-loving host! He was sympathetic to the point of gullibility, so people said. He didn't seem to care. While his fort was the port of call for distressed Americans in California, big-hearted Sutter never refused aid to anyone.

Johann August Suter, or General John Augustus Sutter as he was later to be called, did not look dashing, brilliant, nor especially courageous with his plump face and mutton-chop whiskers topped by a broad-brimmed white hat; but his rise from obscurity to be the great man of the romantic West Coast is a compelling story. Picture to yourself the sheer nerve of it. Think of the winning personality he surely had. Arriving by boat in the Sandwich Islands, Sutter made friends of some Russians who were about to leave the country. He sailed away with them and, not caring for Sitka, returned to California on one of their small vessels. He had a distinct plan even then, for he had persuaded some native Hawaiians to come with him. Arrived on the coast, he began to treat with a third nation and, becoming a Mexican citizen, was given a grant of land. With unbelievable wisdom, considering how little anyone knew about the interior of California, he chose a section one hundred miles inland, where Sacramento now stands. It was well away from the ranches of the native Californians, which were mainly in the more temperate coastal valleys. It was arable land and on navigable water. Because he was of Swiss parentage, he called his new stronghold New Helvetia.

Once installed on his new grant, he must perforce make friends of the Indians. He did more. He made willing workers of them. One wonders about the language problem. To whom could he talk in those first busy months?

The situation of his refuge was strategic for subsequent events. How was he inspired to select a spot so remote from the settlements? How was he moved to choose a place so central for the travelers of the overland trails (not yet established), so much the hub of the northern valley that it became in later years a main railway center and the capital of the state? What impelled this man to become so much the good Samaritan in this raw new land that the thought of him, benevolent and open-handed, gave hesitating souls the courage to make the journey west? All greeted the sight of Sutter's Fort with joy beyond measure.

*   *   *

Sacramento! Journey's end! What a place! Dirty but not squalid; tough but not mean; drunk but not besotted! There was about it a frightening air of finality. What happened, happened. There were none of the agencies of civilization in 1849 to mitigate untoward events. A sick man lay in the attic of a saloon or in a tent in the sun and was given only such nursing care as it was possible or practical for a friend or stranger to give. Dependent upon chance, he got well or died. If he died, somebody would take time out and bury him. There were no hospitals, no police, no fire department, no flood control. And yet I suppose there was never a time in history when a heterogeneous crowd was so self-sufficient and equal to each emergency that presented itself.

And so Lassen's Route ended, as did all other northern Overland routes to California, at Sacramento. A bee swarm with a new queen, *gold,* had settled temporarily among the trees on the banks of the river.

Seemingly the mass was in confusion; but because of the intrinsic worth of the individuals of whom it was composed and because of their years of living under American institutions, the emergence of order was practically instinctive.

The draggled dirty parade of Forty-niners had good brains above their whiskers and good hearts beneath them.

Each settled into his own line of work. Forward-looking men took time to organize the remainder. In one year from the September when the Forty-niners first began to trickle over the foothills and down into the valley, Sacramento was a city and California was a state.

Order had come to the Pacific Coast. It does not have a so-called "glorious" heritage of many years of blood and war before its government was formed. There were no great battles, no great victories. Its people live in peace together. Its young Indians have every opportunity that is given to the descendants of the early settlers. The native Californian families, dark-eyed descendants of pioneers from Spain and Mexico, are of the socially elect. Their names are matters of pride, both to themselves and to the sons and daughters of the pioneers from the States.

They all work together for the betterment of state and nation; they are all important and integral parts of an American citizenry.

We can credit this happy circumstance to the fundamental democracy of the travel-worn Forty-niners to whose courage and stamina we look back with incredulous astonishment. And on no route were those qualities more in evidence than on Lassen's Cutoff. Peter Lassen's road had nothing to recommend it. Every pioneer who took it would have made better progress and suffered from fewer difficulties had he never heard of it; but it played a dramatic part in the history of California when thousands of our forebears came that way one hundred years ago.

BIBLIOGRAPHY

ALLEN, W. W., AND AVERY, R. B., *California Gold Book*. San Francisco and Chicago, 1893.

ALLSOPP, J. P. C., Leaves from My Log Book (description of a trip across the plains to Calif. in 1848). MS in the Bancroft Lib., Univ. of Calif.*

ALTA CALIFORNIA, "The Emigrants in Safety," Dec. 15, 1849.

ALTA CALIFORNIA DAILY, articles about Peter Lassen, May 24, 1854; Aug. 4, 1859.

APPLEGATE, LINDSAY, "The Applegate Route in the Year 1846," *Oregon Historical Society Quarterly*, Vol. 22, p. 12 (1921).

ARAM, EUGENE, sketch of the life of Capt. Joseph Aram, dated Sacramento, April 30, 1907. Typescript, Calif. State Lib., Sacramento.

ARAM, CAPT. JOSEPH, Across the Continent in a Caravan in 1846 (experiences compiled by Col. James Tompkins Watson, Clinton, N. Y.). Photostat at Calif. State Lib.

BACHELDER, DR. AMOS, journal of a trip overland in 1849, by way of Lassen's Cutoff. Typescript of unpublished original at Calif. Hist. Soc. Lib., San Francisco.

BALDRIDGE, WILLIAM, The Days of 1846 (written from the author's dictation by Lovisa Thompson for the Bancroft Lib., 1877). MS at Bancroft Lib.

BARNES, DEMAS, *From the Atlantic to the Pacific, Overland* (a series of letters written in 1865). New York, 1866.

BARTON, H. D., diary written while crossing the plains in 1865. MS in Calif. State Lib.

BATES, MRS. D. B., *Four Years on the Pacific Coast*. Boston, 1860 (privately printed).

BECKWITH, LIEUT. E. G. See digest of survey by Beckwith in *Reports of Explorations and Surveys to Ascertain the Most Practicable and Economical Route for a Railroad . . . to the Pacific Ocean, 1853–6*. Senate Exec. Doc. No. 78, 33rd Congress, 2nd Session. Washington, D. C., 1855.

BENNETT, WINSTON, "A Pioneer of 1843," *San Jose Pioneer*, May 22, June 2, 1877.

BIDWELL, JOHN, *A Journey to California* (diary written on the Overland Trail in 1841). Pamphlet printed at Weston or Liberty, Mo., 1842; only known copy in Bancroft Lib. Reprint ed. by Dr. H. I. Priestley. San Francisco, 1937.

———, Bidwell and Altgeier papers. MSS at Fort Sutter, Sacramento.

BIGLER, HENRY WILLIAM, diary of a Mormon in California and the discovery of gold, 1848. Rewritten by him from his journal in 1872. MS at Bancroft Lib.

BLACKBURN, ABNER, diary of journey with Mormon pioneers in 1847 and of several subsequent trips across the plains including one by way of Hastings' Cutoff. Photostat of unpublished MS in possession of Robert Allen, Carson City, Nev.

BLOOD, JAMES A., diary written on Overland Trail in 1850. Typescript at Calif. State Lib.

BLOOM, HENRY S., diary written on Overland Trail by way of Hastings' Cutoff in 1850. Typescript at Calif. State Lib.

* Hereafter given as Bancroft Lib.

BOARDMAN, JOHN, journal, "Kansas to Oregon in 1843." *Utah Historical Quarterly,* Vol. 2, No. 4 (Oct. 1929).

BOGGS, W. M., reminiscences of his father, Gov. Lilburn Boggs of Missouri, and of early days in Calif. MS in California Pioneer Scrap Book, Bancroft Lib.

BONNEY, B. F., *Across the Plains by Prairie Schooner.* A personal narrative of his journey to Calif. in 1846, compiled by Fred Lockley, Eugene, Ore., 1924 (?).

BOOTH, J. W., J. W. Booth's Scrap Book—Ophir, Feather River, Cal., April A.D. 1852. MS in possession of Mrs. H. S. Rassbach, Paso Robles, Calif. Typescript at Bancroft Lib.

BOURNE, EZRA, diary of an overland journey to Calif. in 1850. Typescript at Bancroft Lib.

BRADWAY, DR. JOSEPH R., diary written on Overland Trail in 1853. Longhand copy certified by notary. Calif. State Lib.

BROWN, JOSEPH, *A True Story of Pioneer Days* (recollections of crossing the plains in 1849 by way of Lassen's Cutoff). Marysville, Calif., 1916.

BRUFF, J. GOLDSBOROUGH, *Gold Rush: The Journals, Drawings and Other Papers of J. Goldsborough Bruff, April 2, 1849–July 20, 1851,* ed. by Georgia Willis Read and Ruth Gaines. New York, 1944.

BRYANT, EDWIN, *What I Saw in California: Being the Journal of a Tour, by the Emigrant Route* [by way of Hastings' Cutoff] . . . *and Through California in the Years 1846, 1847,* 2nd ed. New York, 1848.

CALIFORNIA, a compilation with the subtitle: "Its Past History—Its Present Position —Its Future Prospects." London, 1850.

CARRIGER, NICHOLAS, diary written on the Overland Trail in 1846. MS in Bancroft Lib.

———, short narrative of same trip, written in 1874. MS in *Calif. Pioneer Scrap Book,* Bancroft Lib.

CARSON, KIT, *Kit Carson's Own Story of His Life, As Dictated to Col. and Mrs. D. C. Peters About 1856–57,* ed. Blanche C. Grant. Taos, New Mexico, 1926.

CHALMERS, ROBERT, diary of a trip across the plains in 1849, by way of Hastings' Cutoff. MS in Calif. State Lib.

CHILES, COL. JOSEPH B., A Visit to California in Early Times, MS written in 1898, in Bancroft Lib.

CLAYTON, WILLIAM, a daily journal of the journey of the original company of "Mormon" pioneers from Nauvoo, Ill., to the Valley of the Great Salt Lake. Salt Lake City, 1921.

CLYMAN, JAMES, adventures of a trapper and covered-wagon emigrant who traveled Hastings' Cutoff, as told in his own reminiscences and diaries, ed. Chas. L. Camp. San Francisco, 1928.

CORDUA, THEODOR, "The Memoirs of Theodor Cordua," ed. and transl. by Erwin G. Gudde. *California Historical Society Quarterly,** Vol. 12, No. 4 (Dec. 1933).

CORODEN, J. S., diary written while crossing the plains in 1853. MS in possession of Mrs. Willis Compton, Pullman, Wash.

CROSBY, ELISHA OSCAR, *Memoirs: Reminiscences of California and Guatemala, 1849–1864.* Huntington Lib. Publication, 1945.

DARWIN, CHARLES BENJAMIN, diary of a journey overland, 1849–50. MS at Huntington Lib., San Marino, Calif.

DELANO, ALONZO, *Life on the Plains and Among the Diggings: Being Scenes and Adventures of an Overland Journey to California* (by way of Lassen's Cutoff). Auburn, New York, 1854.

* Hereafter given as *C. H. S. Q.*

DEMAREST, DAVID, diary written while crossing the plains by the southern route and while in the California mines, 1849-50. MS at Bancroft Lib.

DERBY, GEORGE H., Lieut. Top. Engrs., report to Maj. E. R. S. Canby about the founding of Fort Far West on Bear River in California, in P. T. Tyson's *Geology and Topography of California*, Report of Secretary of War, Senate Exec. Doc. No. 47, 31st Congress, 1st Session, Pt. II. Washington, D. C., 1850.

DE WOLF, CAPT. DAVID, diary written while crossing the plains in 1849; letters of 1849–50. Typescript at Huntington Lib., San Marino, Calif.

EBERSTADT, EDWARD, "The Journal of Riley Root," *C. H. S. Q.*, Vol. 10, No. 4 (1931), pp. 396–405.

FAIRFIELD, ASA MERRILL, *Fairfield's Pioneer History of Lassen County, California, to 1870*. San Francisco, 1916.

FERRIS, HIRAM GANO, letters from California, 1850–56. MSS in possession of Joel E. Ferris, Spokane, Wash. *C. H. S. Q.*, Vol. 26, No. 4 (Dec. 1947).

FISH, LAFAYETTE, diary written while crossing the plains in 1860. MS in possession of Mrs. Hazel Thode, Orland, Calif. Typescript at Bancroft Lib.

FLINT, DR. THOMAS, *California to Maine and Return in 1851–1855: A Diary Written on the Emigrant Trail*. Reprinted from the *Evening Free Lance*, Hollister, Calif. 2nd ed., 1924.

FOSTER, REV. ISAAC, diary written while crossing the plains in 1849 by way of Lassen's Cutoff, Roxana Foster's in *The Foster Family, California Pioneers of 1849*. San Jose, Calif. (?), 1889.

FOX, JARED, Jared Fox's Memorandum (kept from Wisconsin toward California and Oregon, 1852). Typescript at Bancroft Lib.

FRÉMONT, JOHN CHARLES, *Memoirs of My Life*. Chicago, 1887.

——, *Geographical Memoir upon Upper California in Illustration of His Map of Oregon and California*. Addressed to U.S. Senate, 30th Congress, 1st Session, Miscell. No. 148. Pub. by Wendell and Van Benthuysen, Printers, Washington, D. C., 1848.

GARNER, WILLIAM ROBERT, "Letters from California—1846, by W. G.," from the *Magazine of History*, Extra Number 103, reprinted by Wm. Abbott. Tarrytown, New York, 1924.

GERSTAECKER, F., *A Journey Around the World*. New York, 1854.

GORGAS, SOLOMON A., diary from Saint Joseph, Mo., to Placerville and return by way of Isthmus—1850–51. MS at Huntington Lib., San Marino, Calif.

GOULD, CHARLES, diary written while crossing the plains in 1849. Typescript in Bancroft Lib.

GRAVES, WILLIAM C., "Crossing the Plains in '46," *Russian River Flag*, Healdsburg, Calif., April 26, May 3, 10, 17, 1877; Dec. 30, 1875.

GRAY, GEORGE M., reminiscences concerning his long acquaintance with John Bidwell, printed in *Sandy Gulch News*, Sandy Gulch, Calif., beginning April 28, 1938, and continuing weekly for some months.

HALE, ISRAEL, diary written while crossing the plains in 1849 by way of Lassen's Cutoff. *C. H. S. Q.*, Vol. 11.

HALL, MARY, diary kept while crossing the plains; date doubtful, but since the Union Pacific was in operation at least part way across the plains, probably in the late 1860's. Typescript at Bancroft Lib.

HANSON, N. E., Recollections of the Days of '49 (of travel by way of Lassen's Cutoff). Typescript at Calif. State Lib.

HARGRAVE, WILLIAM, California in 1846 (related to Ivan Petroff for the Bancroft Lib. in 1878). MS in Bancroft Lib.

HARLAN, JACOB WRIGHT, *California, '46 to '88*. San Francisco, 1888.

————, Reminiscences. MS at Bancroft Lib.

HASTINGS, LANSFORD W., *The Emigrants' Guide to Oregon and California*. Cincinnati, O., 1845.

————, *A New Description of Oregon and California and the Various Routes over the Rocky Mountains*. Cincinnati, O., 1857.

HAUN, CATHERINE M., A Reminiscence of 1849 (of travel by way of Lassen's Cutoff). MS in Huntington Lib., San Marino, Calif.

HILL, JOHN BIRNEY, "Gold: A Story of the Plains in 1850, A Reminiscence." *Annals of Wyoming*, Vols. 7, 9.

HISTORY OF NAPA AND LAKE COUNTIES. California, 1881.

HOPPER, CHARLES, Narrative of a California Pioneer of 1841 (inscribed in 1871 by R. T. Montgomery). MS in Bancroft Lib.

HOPPER, SILAS J., diary kept while crossing the plains from Nebraska City to California in 1863. MS in Huntington Lib., San Marino, Calif.

HOWELL, ELIJAH P., diary written while crossing the plains in 1849 by way of Lassen's Cutoff. Typescript of unpublished original at Bancroft Lib.

HUTCHING'S CALIFORNIA MAGAZINE, articles on the life of Peter Lassen, Vol. 3, No. 8 (Feb. 1859); Vol. 3, No. 11 (May, 1859).

————, article on the death of Peter Lassen, Vol. 3, No. 12 (June, 1859).

IRVING, WASHINGTON, *The Adventures of Capt. Bonneville, U.S.A., in the Rocky Mountains and the Far West*. New York, 1869.

JEFFERSON, T. H., booklet accompanying a map of the emigrant road from Independence, Mo., to San Francisco, Calif., by way of Hastings' Cutoff. New York, 1849. Photostat at Bancroft Lib.

JEWETT, GEORGE E., diary written while crossing the plains in 1849 by way of Lassen's Cutoff. Typescript of unpublished original at Bancroft Lib.

JOSSELYN, AMOS P., diary written while crossing the plains in 1849 by way of Lassen's Cutoff. MS in Calif. State Lib.

KELLOGG, BENJAMIN FRANKLIN EPHRAIM, letter to Preston G. Gesford dated Platte Crossing, 15 miles from Fort John, July 5, 1846. Typescript at Bancroft Lib.

KELLY, CHARLES, *Salt Desert Trails*. Salt Lake City, 1930.

KELLY, WILLIAM, *An Excursion to California over the Prairie, Rocky Mountains and Great Sierra Nevada* (diary written on the emigrant trail in 1849). London, 1851.

KERN, EDWARD, report of the journey of that section of Frémont's exploring party of 1845 of which Kern was in charge, listed as Appendix Q to report of Capt. J. H. Simpson, *Explorations Across the Great Basin of the Territory of Utah in 1859*. Washington, D. C., 1876.

————, letter concerning his journey west with Frémont in 1845, written to Richard H. Kern, politeness of Commodore I. D. Sloat, dated U.S. Fort Sacramento, July 27 (or 29) 1846. In volume of MSS entitled Fort Sutter Papers, at Huntington Lib., San Marino, Calif.

KLEINHAUS, DANIEL W., Memoirs (reminiscences of travel by sea to California in 1849, in Sacramento, and in the mines). Typescript at Bancroft Lib.

LANE, S. A., diary written while crossing the plains in 1850. Photostat of MS at Bancroft Lib.

LEESE, JACOB P., letter to Gen. Mariano G. Vallejo, June 19, 1843, introducing Lansford Hastings. Typescript of translation in Bancroft Lib.

LIENHARD, HEINRICH, "Heinrich Lienhard in California—1846–1850" (including description of journey across the plains by way of Hastings' Cutoff), transl. by Reuben L. Spaeth, 1914. Univ. of Calif. thesis, typescript at Bancroft Lib.

LIENHARD, HEINRICH, *A Pioneer at Sutter's Fort,* transl. and ed. by Marguerite Eyer Wilbur. Los Angeles, 1941.

LOHSE, JOHN F., diary beginning in San Francisco on Sept. 18, 1849, and ending in the gold region June 30, 1850. MS in possession of Dr. John Louis Lohse, Oakland, Calif.

LOOMIS, LEONARD, letter dated Macaloney River, California, May 4, 1851. In possession of Mrs. Ella MacBeath, Elk Grove, Calif.

LORD, ROBERT WATERSTON, "Five Years in California in Its Early Days" (beginning in 1849), *New England Quarterly.* Society of Calif. Pioneers' Lib., San Francisco.

LOVELACE, THOMAS JAMES, diary written while crossing the plains in 1854. MS in possession of Mrs. Daisy Tiffany, Santa Cruz, Calif.

McCOY, SAMUEL F., *Pioneering on the Plains: Journey to Mexico in 1848—The Overland Trip to California* (the latter a diary, written in 1849, of travel by way of Lassen's Cutoff). Kaukauna, Wis., 1924.

McKINSTRY, GEORGE M., diary written while crossing the plains in 1846. MS in Bancroft Lib.

MILLER-REED DIARY, written while crossing the plains in 1846. From May 15 to July 2 the diary is in the handwriting of Hiram Miller, thenceforth to October in the handwriting of James Frazier Reed, the latter section being the only day-by-day account of any portion of the journey of the Donner Party. Contained in *Donner Miscellany: Forty-one Diaries and Documents,* ed. Carroll D. Hall. San Francisco, 1947.

MILLINGTON, ADA, diary written at age of 13, while crossing the plains in 1862, and elaborated 5 years later. Photostat at Bancroft Lib.

MINTON, HENRY, reminiscences of crossing the plains by way of Lassen's Cutoff in 1849. MS in possession of Dr. Henry W. Minton, Tacoma, Wash. Photostat at Bancroft Lib.

MINTURN, WILLIAM, *Travels West.* London and New York, 1878.

MITCHELL, LYMAN. diary written while crossing the plains in 1849. MS in possession of Mrs. Elon Mitchell, Vallejo, Calif.

MOORMAN, MADISON BERRYMAN, diary written while crossing the plains in 1850 by way of Hastings' Cutoff, ed. Irene D. Paden. San Francisco, 1948.

NEW HELVETIA DIARY, a record of events kept by John A. Sutter and his clerks at New Helvetia (Sutter's Fort), Calif., from Sept. 9, 1845, to May 25, 1848. San Francisco: The Grabhorn Press in arrangement with the Soc. of Calif. Pioneers, 1939.

NEWCOMB, SILAS, diary written while crossing the plains in 1850. MS in Huntington Lib. San Marino, Calif.

OLIVER, CATHERINE JANE, a description of her journey to California in 1861. Typescript in possession of Richard Oliver, San Francisco.

PALMER, JOEL, *Journal of Travels Over the Rocky Mountains.* Cincinnati, O., 1852.

PARKMAN, FRANCIS, *The Oregon Trail.* New York, about 1847.

PLEASANTS, W., *Twice Across the Plains, 1849–1856* (by way of Lassen's Cutoff in 1849). San Francisco, 1906. Microfilm prints at Bancroft Lib.

PRATT, ORSON, portions of diary written while crossing the plains in 1847, *Mormon Hist. Record,* No. 9, ed. Andrew Jensen. Salt Lake City, Utah.

RAMEY, EARL, *The Beginnings of Marysville.* San Francisco, 1936.

READING, PIERSON BARTON, "Journal of Pierson B. Reading Across the Rocky Mountains to California in 1843," *C. H. S. Q.,* Vol. 7 (1930). Diary of journey by way of Fort Boise and Pit River. MS, copied by himself in 1844 from his original MS, in Soc. of Calif. Pioneers Lib., San Francisco.

REED, SAMUEL B., "Report of Surveys and Explorations from Green River to Great Salt Lake City" (for Union Pacific R.R.), dated Joliet, Ill., 1864.

REVERE, JOSEPH WARREN, Lieut. U.S.N., *A Tour of Duty in California, Including a Description of the Gold Region,* ed. Joseph N. Balestier. New York and Boston, 1849.

RICHARDSON, ALPHEUS, diary written while crossing the plains in 1852. MS in possession of L. V. Richardson, Stockton, Calif.

ROBINSON, FAYETTE, *California and Its Gold Regions.* New York, 1849.

SACRAMENTO UNION, "The Death of Peter Lassen," May 10, 1859.

SEDGLEY, JOSEPH, *Overland to California in 1849* (by way of Lassen's Cutoff). Oakland, Calif., 1877.

SEYMOUR, E. SANFORD, *Emigrants' Guide to the Gold Mines.* Chicago, 1849.

SHERMAN, EDWIN A., *Fifty Years of Masonry in California.* San Francisco, 1898.

SHINN, JOHN R., journal as kept by him in crossing the plains to California in 1850 (by way of Hastings' Cutoff). Photostat of MS at Bancroft Lib.

SIMPSON, CAPT. J. H., *Explorations Across the Great Basin of the Territory of Utah in 1859.* Washington, D. C., 1876.

SMITH, JEDEDIAH, journal, in Maurice S. Sullivan's *The Travels of Jedediah Smith— a Documentary Outline, Including the Journal of the Great American Pathfinder.* Santa Ana, Calif., 1934.

STANSBURY, HOWARD (of U.S. Bureau of Topographical Engineers), *An Expedition to the Valley of the Great Salt Lake of Utah.* Philadelphia, 1852.

STEPTOE, E. J., Bvt. Col. U.S. Army, report of the march of his command from Ft. Leavenworth to Benicia, Calif., in 1854–55. Photostat of MS at Brancroft Lib.

SULLIVAN, MAURICE S., *Jedediah Smith: Trader and Trail Breaker.* New York, 1936.

SUTTER, JOHANN AUGUST, *Diary,* with introduction by Douglas S. Watson. San Francisco, 1932.

———, personal reminiscences. Photostat of MS at Bancroft Lib.

SWARTZLOW, RUBY JOHNSON, "Peter Lassen, Northern California's Trail-Blazer," *C. H. S. Q.,* Vol. 18, No. 4 (Dec., 1939).

TAYLOR, W. E., diary written while crossing the plains in 1846. MS at Sutter's Fort, Sacramento, Calif.

THORNTON, J. QUINN, *Oregon and California.* New York, 1849.

TOOMEY, NOXON, "Mountain Fever and Spotted Fever of the Rocky Mountains— Clinical Studies," *Annals of Internal Medicine,* Vol. 5, No. 5, p. 585 (Nov., 1931).

TRUBODY, WILLIAM ALEXANDER, "William Trubody and the Overland Pioneers of 1847," ed. Charles L. Camp and reprinted from *C. H. S. Q.,* Vol. 16, No. 2 (June, 1937).

UDELL, JOHN, *Incidents of Travel to California* (three diaries written on the Overland Trail in 1850, 1852, and 1854, one while traveling by way of Hastings' Cutoff). Jefferson, O., 1856.

WAGNER, WILL H., letter, dated Feb. 29, 1860, written in his capacity as engineer of Fort Kearney, South Pass and Honey Lake Wagon Road, to F. H. Lander, superintendent of fort, reporting an authorized exploring expedition. MS in Bancroft Lib.

WARD, MRS. HARRIET SHERRILL, diary written while crossing the plains in 1853. Typescript at Bancroft Lib.

WATSON, DOUGLAS SLOANE, *West Wind, Life of Joseph Reddeford Walker.* Los Angeles, 1934.

WEBSTER, KIMBALL, *The Gold Seekers of '49* (diary written while crossing the plains by way of Lassen's Cutoff). Manchester, N. H., 1917.

WEST, S. H., *The Life and Times of S. H. West.* Bloomington, Ill., 1908.

WILEY, FRANCIS A., "Jedediah Smith in the West." Univ. of Calif. thesis, June 10, 1941.

WILLIAMSON, R. S., Lieut. U.S. Top. Engrs., report (of railroad survey following the Lassen Cutoff) to Bvt. Lieut. Col. J. Hooker, Asst. Adj. Gen., Pacific Division, in P. T. Tyson's *Geology and Topography of California,* Report of Secretary of War, Senate Exec. Doc. No. 47, 31st Congress, 1st Session, Pt. II. Washington, D. C., 1850.

WOOD, JOHN, diary written while crossing the plains in 1850 by way of Hastings' Cutoff. *Motor Land,* Dec. 1928, April, 1929.

WORK, JOHN, *California Expedition, Fur Brigade to the Bonaventura, 1832–33,* ed. Alice Bay Maloney. San Francisco, 1945.

YOUNG, SAMUEL C., biographical obituary compiled from accounts by relatives and former conversations with Young. *San Jose Pioneer,* No. 9, 1878.

MAPS

BIDWELL, JOHN, "Land Surveyor," Map of the Valley of the Sacramento including the Gold Region: A correct tracing by Thos. O. Larkin Esq., late Consul of the United States for California, and by him stated to be the best for reference in California. Calif. State Lib. (?) date.

CROFUTT, GEORGE A., Crofutt's New Map of Salt Lake City, in *Great Transcontinental Pacific Railroad Tourist Guide.* New York, 1872.

EPLER AND PARKINSON, county surveyors. Map of Humboldt County, Nev., 1866.

FREDONYER, Map of north-eastern California and north-west Nevada. Compiled and drawn by him, 1865.

HORN, map to illustrate Horn's *Overland Guide to California and Oregon.* New York, 1852. Copy in possession of W. G. Paden, Alameda, Calif.

JACKSON, WILLIAM A., Map of the Mining District of California. New York, 1850. Copy in possession of W. G. Paden, Alameda, Calif.

JEFFERSON, T. H., Map of the Emigrant Road from Independence, Mo., to San Francisco, Calif. (by way of Hastings' Cutoff). New York, 1849. Copy in possession of W. G. Paden, Alameda, Calif.

MILLESON, M., AND R. ADAMS, A Complete Map of the Feather & Yuba Rivers with Towns, Ranches, Diggings, Roads, Distances. Compiled from the recent survey of M. Milleson & R. Adams, C. Engineers. Marysville, Calif., no date.

PREUSS, CHARLES, Map of Oregon and Upper California from the Surveys of John Charles Frémont and other authorities. Drawn by Charles Preuss under the order of the Senate of the U.S., Washington City, 1848, and inserted between pp. 944 and 945, House of Representatives Exec. Doc. No. 17, 31st Congress, 1st Session. Ordered to be printed Feb. 6, 1850.

Index